White Picket Monsters

A Story of Strength and Survival

Bev Moore Davis

White Picket Monsters

A Story of Strength and Survival

Copyright © 2020 Bev Moore Davis

For speaking inquiries or bulk order requests, please email bevmooredavis@gmail.com

Formatting by Rik – Wild Seas Formatting

ISBN
978-1-7774680-1-9 (Hardcover)
978-1-7774680-0-2 (Paperback)
978-1-7774680-2-6 (eBook)

www.bevmooredavis.com

Table of Contents

Dedication

For those who have had their innocence stolen. For those who grew up hearing and believing that they were not good enough, and for those who - as adults today – continue to struggle with these negative influences that have been cemented into our very foundation. I leave this thought with you: there is no greater evil than those who willingly hurt an innocent child, and I assure you, our voices will make a difference.

This was a difficult book to write. I have always been a private person, though I have stepped outside my comfort zone to tell my story; I hope it can help other survivors. As a child, you cannot take responsibility for the actions of an adult. If you are a survivor, please know you are not alone. And the abuse was not your fault.

I truly hope the book will inspire those responsible for the wellbeing of children, including parents, grandparents, aunts, uncles, neighbours, teachers, coaches, doctors...etc. As adults, we all share the responsibility of protecting children. No red flag should ever be ignored.

This book is dedicated to all survivors of child abuse.

Also dedicated to my nephew and niece:

Adam King
October 20, 1993 - August 12, 2020

Melinda Ryan
March 11, 1983 - September 23, 2015

"Your wings were ready; but our hearts were not."

May you both Rest in Peace.

Forward

I was incredibly honoured when Bev asked me to endorse her revealing book. It tells her story of living and surviving a pain-filled childhood. It may be a difficult read for some, but in describing her journey, her personal insights provide the "system" with an awareness that should not be ignored. Bev has worked tirelessly to raise awareness and truly educate the general public, but most especially service providers. She emphasizes that workers need to have a full understanding about what a young person is feeling and thinking while living in a dysfunctional environment. This is a paramount consideration for Bev as she knows that a true understanding of the dynamics is pivotal to real change.

I have known Bev for several years in my capacity as an anti-violence advocate and retired police officer of 30 years. This lady is the epitome of professionalism, integrity, and perseverance. For many who have survived traumatic events during childhood, their experiences take them on a dark journey, not Bev! She used her pain to assist others in coping with theirs - with her primary focus being the prevention of child abuse.

Despite my experience in documenting painful disclosures, I had never heard of blood cells in a person's body showing signs of trauma until I read Bev's story - it was jarring. This fact alone takes the pain and the damage to a whole new level. It should dramatically increase our awareness about the extent of child abuse, the urgent requirement for early interventions, and the need for a wider array of services to deal with the aftermath. Her poignant and touching summation on becoming a teenage mom - "I knew what NOT to do!" Ironically, Bev knew exactly what she HAD to do to ensure this didn't happen to other children.

In the spirit of doing more, Bev put her own pain aside. She focused on rising above and she availed of every opportunity to turn a negative into a positive. Her attributes, compassion, and empathy have uniquely combined to offer us a new perspective and a new mission. We should all be grateful that this fighter and survivor stayed in our province as communities have benefitted from her willingness to share the insights from the most severe type of traumatic experience.

Bev's impact in the community has been nothing short of phenomenal. Bev's quiet disposition and captivating story of real life, spoken hundreds of times, leaves her audiences with a much better understanding of the dynamics of abuse and the effects on those who have been victimized. Her credibility is enhanced exponentially as she speaks from experience and not a textbook or from second-hand knowledge. This feature sets her apart in the awareness sphere; as sadly, most victims suffer in silence. Her experience is riveting and powerful; it has often resulted in others feeling sufficiently empowered to speak of their own horrendous experiences, and she has heard many disclosures.

Some of Bev's community awareness initiatives include the Miles for Smiles Foundation, a local chapter of ASCA (Adult Survivors of Child Abuse) which offers a regular monthly support group, and Blue Shirt Day. Years ago, Bev began a province wide tour to ask municipal councils to officially proclaim April as an awareness month. Her efforts were well rewarded as most councils, after learning about her story, were anxious to get involved. Her idea to have the province also proclaim April as Child Abuse Awareness Month was ambitious and took time but her dedication to that one project did not go unnoticed. Government officials finally agreed to her persistent and repeated request in 2016. Since April of 2013, the annual walk in Bowring Park has become an informative, supportive, and therapeutic event. Additionally, Bev, despite physical pain, completed a cross-province bike tour to raise awareness. These are just some of her game-changing educative strategies; there are others.

To say she is a focused, determined, passionate change-agent would be a major understatement. Bev is making a real difference in people's lives and her quest to stop the abuse of children has been groundbreaking in our province. Our sad reality is there are still four new cases every day in NL, and shockingly we know that only 10% are ever reported. These statistics have not changed for decades. We need to question why. There is much more that must be done!

Connie Pike, B.A Police Studies
Police Inspector (ret'd)

2

Silent Screams

The room was pitch dark and silent. All I could hear was the sound of my breath. Suddenly, I realized I wasn't alone. My mouth opened wide as I desperately gasped, pulling air deep into my lungs. My diaphragm contracted, forcing the air out in a scream that should have been heard for miles - but there was no sound. Terror consumed me as I attempted another scream. Again, just silence. I could now hear my heart pounding as my body quivered and I suddenly felt the painful impact of a hammer striking the back of my skull. I fearfully sprung out of bed when a familiar voice reassured me.

"It's okay babe. You're okay. It's just a dream."

My husband Tom reached out to guide me back to bed and comforted me as I regained control of my breathing.

Nightmares like these are common, though fortunately less frequent in recent years since I moved to the city. They serve as painful reminders of the trauma that will not be easily forgotten.

Tom is my rock. We are a team, and very well matched. Together we own and operate three local businesses. As busy as we are, Tom likes to remind me that I always seem to find time for my "other" work. In 2011, I started the Newfoundland and Labrador chapter of Adult Survivors of Child Abuse and this year, 2013, was the inaugural year of Miles for Smiles, an organization I founded to bring much-needed awareness to the issues surrounding child abuse to Newfoundland and Labrador.

The work we did with the foundation made me proud. I had often wished there was an organization like Miles for Smiles when I was a young girl. Perhaps it would have made a difference.

I was lucky to have Tom. He was incredibly supportive, and he never judged me. If I needed an hour or a full day to myself, he made sure I got it. Some days were more challenging than others, and sometimes it would take hours to recover from the nightmares. There were many dark days behind me, but today was going to be a good one.

Once the fear and panic from the nightmare subsided, I got out of bed, headed to the bathroom, and splashed cold water on my face. I looked in the mirror and reminded myself that I was strong, that I was a survivor.

I remembered the gala happening that night and thought about my work at the foundation. Straightening my posture, I took a deep breath and remembered my purpose.

It was October 30, 2013, and the highly respected and influential Newfoundland and Labrador Organization for Women Entrepreneurs (NLOWE) was hosting its annual Entrepreneur of the Year award ceremony. I was nominated for the Community Impact Award in recognition of my contributions through Miles for Smiles.

Any leftover angst from the nightmare disappeared as I wondered who could have nominated me for the prestigious award. The thought of my work being a source of inspiration for others filled me with pride and gave me the strength to leave the horror behind, even if only for a little while. I was grateful to have the opportunity to turn my hideous past into something good—helping others.

The NLOWE awards gala was known to be a glamourous affair and I wanted to look my best. As the owner of a high-end fashion boutique, I had plenty of wardrobe options. The gorgeous gowns that arrived at the store were hard to resist and I often purchased samples for my own closet collection.

I narrowed my choices down quickly to something blue— the symbolic colour used to highlight child abuse awareness. I scanned the closet and landed on an elegant, one-shouldered, sapphire blue dress by Canadian designer Joeffer Caoc. Although we were well into the fall season, it was sunny and mild, and I would just need a light shawl to cover my shoulders.

October is normally one of my busiest months. Each year, my business partner and I organize a five-day trade show that is attended by thousands. The show's long days and fast-paced environment sometimes cause me to lose a little weight. For many, this would be welcomed news and barely noticeable, but for me, it triggers thoughts of the years spent struggling with an eating disorder and body image issues. After the trade show ended, I stepped on the scales to discover that I was four pounds lighter.

While I definitely had a little more room in the dress than the last time I tried it on, I was pleased with the way it delicately draped over my small frame. Tom was a lot less fussy over his clothing and joked that he dressed more to please me than himself. As we scanned his closet for suit jackets, we quickly realized that a trip to a nearby men's clothing store was in order.

It was a rare occurrence for Tom and me to have a non-work-related outing in the middle of the week and I was enjoying the leisure time with him. I urged him to model the outfits for me and he grinned sheepishly. He did a playfully dramatic runway walk and declared, "you're the model of the family." I had forgotten we were in public until I noticed the courteous employee smiling at our playfulness before taking our selections to the counter to package up.

With the wardrobe taken care of, I should have felt a little lighter, but I began to feel nervous as Tom headed back to work in one direction and I drove to the hair salon in the other. It was a last-minute request but lucky for me, I knew the owner and she was able to squeeze me in for a quick updo. At the salon, I was distracted by the friendly, light-hearted conversation between staff and clients and was able to relax a little.

Back at home, I grabbed a snack from the kitchen before heading upstairs to get ready for the evening. With almost 20 years of experience as a fashion model, I had no trouble applying my own make-up. My eldest, Jess (short for Jessica) often poked fun at how little make-up I wear. "No point in wearing it, Mom, if we can't even see it," she often said. Maybe she was right, I thought, and the NLOWE Gala was the perfect occasion to go glam.

As evening approached, Jess called to say she was on the way and would drive with us to the award ceremony. Not surprisingly, Jacob, our middle child, opted out after admitting he had no interest in a three-hour, sit-down gala ceremony, other than for the food. Sarah, our youngest, was upstairs preparing for her first formal event. She was happy to join us. She tried on most of her dresses and a few of Jess's before she settled on a charcoal spaghetti strap party dress.

Tom was ready in a flash. He got home from work and 30 minutes later was showered, suited up, and ready to go.

Smart and extremely eloquent, Tom could talk to anyone about anything. I didn't have that same worldly knowledge, though he always made me feel equal. Tom loved to socialize and was looking forward to the event.

I stopped to take it all in. From my morning nightmare, one of the lingering effects of my childhood trauma, to a scene from a fairy tale, my day had turned around –much like my life. Tom took my arm, I grabbed my shawl, and we headed out into the night.

The Fairmont Hotel was luxurious –the perfect setting for the event. We arrived early and the excitement was palpable as NLOWE members, special guests, and nominees along with their families and friends mingled in the lobby over cocktails. Everyone was dressed in their finest, and the conversation was cheerful.

Comedian and actress, Amy House, was larger than life, wearing a brightly coloured outfit, exaggerated makeup, and her signature glasses. She was in place on the red carpet where she conducted comedic interviews with award nominees. She pulled me in for a few silly questions and photos before sending me on my way. While the interview was theatrical, I felt honoured to walk the red carpet with my family.

Tom and I, along with our girls, made our way into the large, beautifully decorated ballroom. We quickly found our table, where my sister-in-law, Beth, and her boyfriend Jamie were already seated. Tom's parents, or as I usually call them, Mom and Dad D, are there too. They were all there to support me.

I looked around and was filled with gratitude for the love and acceptance that was so evident around the table - a love and acceptance that I had longed for my entire life.

The ceremony began with greetings from NLOWE's Chief Executive Officer. Kathy Dunderdale, the first woman Premier of Newfoundland and Labrador, and a regular at my downtown boutique, brought remarks on behalf of the provincial government. She congratulated all nominees and commended NLOWE members for their hard work and dedication. A quick scan of the room showed nods and smiles of approval as she talked about the positive impact female entrepreneurs have on the economy.

The room was buzzing with energy and I found myself getting progressively more anxious. I wondered how I'd stay calm if called to the stage. I looked around wondering if the other nominees were nervous too. I returned my eyes to the table and towards Tom for reassurance, but he was captivated by the speaker and oblivious to my discomfort. My glance caught Jess's eye and she was perceptive enough to notice my uneasiness. She whispered, "Are you okay?"

"Yes, of course, just a little nervous," I quietly responded. Jess, who has had to speak in front of her class on several occasions, had a newly acquired appreciation for public speaking. She had told me several times how much she admired my ability to speak in front of news media and large groups of people.

Three years prior, I would have never imagined myself speaking in front of a crowd. Throughout my life, I had always preferred to blend in. Being the center of attention made me uncomfortable. But a lot had changed recently, and I was most definitely not the same person.

As the nominees for each category were announced, a video featuring their work was projected on a large screen for the whole room to see. In hopes of getting tips, should I be fortunate enough to have my name called, I studied each winner as they made their way to the stage. Before long, it was here— the moment everyone at my table had been waiting for. We listened attentively to the presenter on stage, "The nominees for the Community Impact Award are..."

My face appeared on the screen in a pre-taped interview that highlighted the Miles for Smiles Foundation. I nervously forced a smile as Tom leaned in and proudly kissed my cheek. The other members of the family smiled with pride as I fought off the fluttering butterflies in my stomach.

The next moment was like something from a dream, a good one for a change. "The winner of NLOWE'S 2013 Community Impact Award is Bev Moore-Davis," revealed the announcer. I stood to the sound of roaring applause. My bracelets clinked together as I weaved through the aisles across the room and up onto the stage.

As I took a few short steps up to the platform, the award sponsor and presenter greeted me at the stage and congratulated me as they handed the award. I tried to contain my excitement as we shook hands and hugged while photographers captured the moment.

Admiring the thick glass sculpture in my hand, I was filled with pride. My name, the category, the award sponsor, and the year were etched into the glass surface, which was mounted on a silver base.

"Wow, this thing is heavier than it looks," I declared while speaking into and adjusting the microphone height at the same time. "Can I get one of you ladies to hold it for me, as I hold onto courage?"

The laughs from the audience relieved some of the pressure.

With one of the women on stage holding the award, I continued, "For those of you that are wondering, courage is this small bracelet wrapped around my wrist," I raised my hand and pointed to the bangles that symbolized strength and courage. I continued to address the room:

> My sister lives in Maine and last month for my birthday she went to a local jeweler looking for a birthday gift. When she sought advice on the perfect gift, the salesman - a quiet gentleman - asked her for more information about me. She talked about my personality, the Miles for Smiles Foundation, and she told him about tonight's nomination. She even told him that I was writing a book!

> The gentleman suggested an Alex & Ani sisters' bracelet and my sister was delighted with the idea. He wrapped the bracelet in a gift box and handed it to her.

Once the transaction was complete, he handed my sister a second identical box. "This one is called courage and I would like you to give it to your sister from me," he said.

So tonight, I am wearing both my sister's bracelet and the courage bracelet. And courage is a gift from someone that I have never met. How cool is that?

I cannot express how much I appreciate this award. It is wonderful to be recognized for something that has tremendous meaning to me and so many others...

Thank you NLOWE! From all of us. And now, I want to share a little bit about me and why I am here today...

At the age of 17, I remember a cold winter night in February. As most of my family slept, I opened a bedroom window and with nothing but the clothes on my back and the will to survive, I jumped out of the window and into the dark of night. I ran away from home. I was a runaway!

Having recently spoken with my sister about this night, I learned her recollection is a little different. Her memories focused more on seeing me run down the driveway and up the street. Apparently, I stopped briefly to wave before quickly disappearing into the dark.

It was very early into my adult life when I realized that I had survived the most horrific excuse for a childhood, and that I was one of the lucky ones. I have spent countless hours wondering how I could turn this horrible negative past of mine into something more positive.

About three years ago, I met someone from my past; he too was a survivor of child abuse. I remember after leaving the conversation, a light bulb went off in my head. I realized that we, as survivors, are all keeping secrets of our abuse. And by doing so, we hurt ourselves while silently protecting the perpetrators.

It was on that very day I decided I would no longer hide the secrets of my past. It was time to talk openly with the hope of helping others. I believe the first step to dealing with this issue is being able to talk about it. Over the past two years, I developed what I call my three-pronged approach to dealing with child abuse.

Support – I received training and subsequently started Newfoundland and Labrador's first chapter of the Adult Survivors of Child Abuse (ASCA), which is a peer support group for survivors of all forms of child abuse.

Awareness – This year we organized our first Miles for Smiles Community Awareness Walk in St John's and we were successful in having the city proclaim April as Child Abuse Prevention Month for the first time.

Prevention – This element requires the most effort and I hope to unveil a detailed plan within the next two years.

I turned to the ladies and asked for the award to be handed back. With the trophy in my hand, I proudly lean into the microphone:

I accept this award on behalf of all survivors of child abuse. For those who have had their innocence stolen. For those who grew up hearing and believing that they were not good enough, and for those who - as adults today – continue to struggle with these negative influences that have been cemented into our very foundation.

I leave this thought with you: there is no greater evil than those who willingly hurt an innocent child, and I assure you, our voices will make a difference.

Thank you, everyone.

As I turned to carry the award back to my table, the room erupted with loud applause. I smiled at the audience and the applause grew louder. I couldn't believe what I was seeing. People began to stand and by the time I reached my table, everyone in the room was on their feet.

My family was eager to embrace me. Tom's father wrapped me in a massive hug, then Mrs. Davis, Tom, and the rest of the family as everyone congratulated me.

When the final winner was called to the stage to accept NLOWE's Entrepreneurial Excellence Award, she began her acceptance speech by signalling to me and saying: "Now that will be a tough act to follow."

After the show, dozens of people gathered at my table. Friends, acquaintances, fellow NLOWE members, and strangers, thanked me for my courage.

My thoughts immediately went to the speech and the fact that I just disclosed to my peers, and the business community, that I was a runaway. For a second I flashed back to the events of my dark past but stopped myself as I graciously absorbed the energy in the room and was reminded of just how far I had come.

Bev - NLOWE Community Impact Award

Praying for a Rescue

As a small child, my mother would put me in frilly dresses and beam with pride as I was shown off to family and friends. I was a curious child with light hair, big blue eyes, and energy to burn.

My mother enjoyed challenging me with puzzles graded for older children and then boasted about the results by telling family and friends that I was already showing signs of intelligence beyond my years.

My father worked for a paving company. He was a heavy machine mechanic, and in paving season he operated the asphalt spreader. While in the family car with my mother, we sometimes drove through local areas that were being paved, looking to catch a glimpse of my father as he worked.

The asphalt paver, or spreader as it was more commonly referred to, was a large intimidating piece of equipment used to lay and lightly flatten asphalt on roadways in preparation for the roller. The spreader had a single seat for the driver perched on the top of the machine. It was high enough for the driver to have a clear view of everything happening below and around him.

My father was a hardworking and cheerful man. He sometimes seemed so focused that he would not notice us driving by. Other times, he was relaxed and would wave and smile at us, and all the other horn-blowing vehicles that drove past him.

We lived in Georgetown, a rural community of fewer than 200 people, in Conception Bay between Brigus and Marysvale. The closest hub was Bay Roberts, another rural community, though larger in size and population. There, in my childhood home, I lived with Mother, Father, my older sister and brother, my younger sister, and usually four other children who were in foster care. Mother and Father were foster parents and there were always children living with us.

Our property was large by most standards, but for us kids, it was massive. An old-fashioned three-rail wooden fence stretched out marking the borders completely around the property while a white picket fence enhanced the view from the front. As it is in a typical small town, everyone had a connection, and in the communities along Conception Bay, a lot of people knew Father.

Standing at approximately 5 feet and 8 inches tall, and carrying an average-sized beer belly, my father was not a big man. He wore Dockers work pants and shirts faithfully, along with work boots and short sleeve white undershirts. My mother would torment him for wearing an undershirt without fail, even on the hottest summer days.

Father's hair was jet-black and his eyes a soft shade of blue. He also had a jowl and missing teeth, and although their absence created visible gaps, he could not have cared less. Rapidly growing facial hair forced him to shave daily, and he would never leave the house without his signature navy blue baseball hat.

His grease-stained hands and dirty fingernails gave him the appearance of what some would call a "grease monkey". As much as he scrubbed, those stains would not come off. As a mechanic, he was well compensated for his work.

Other than the frequent cases of beer and the occasional box of Mary Brown's chicken, he didn't take much for himself. On Friday evenings, he would hand over his paycheck to Mother, most times already cashed. I knew nothing about the value of money but was always impressed by the number of banknotes stuffed inside the small banker's envelope.

My father also owned and operated the garage next to our house. The line-up of vehicles waiting to be serviced validated his exceptional work. Customers would often drive from distant communities to have Father repair their vehicles.

The garage was a single bay with only a couple of windows and a deep rectangular pit that enabled him to safely work underneath any type of vehicle. He worked in that garage almost every evening and weekend.

Father seemed happiest in the garage and loved to hear from locals whenever they visited him. He had a couple of buddies who regularly dropped in with beer. Mother was not a fan of any of his drinking buddies and often cursed on them when she noticed their vehicles parked outside the garage. The garage was far enough from the house to allow privacy yet close enough to see the comings and goings from our bathroom window.

Some days, Mother would instruct one of us children, "Go to the garage and tell your father to come home for the evening," while other nights she would leave him alone.

On one particular day, she seemed concerned and eager to get him out of the garage after she noticed a drinking buddy's vehicle parked nearby. When Father eventually walked into the house, his glassy eyes, big grin, and disgusting smell instantly told us he was drunk. He sat at the table where Mother laid a plate of leftovers with cutlery on either side, sliced bread, an empty mug, and a large glass of cold water.

She poured boiling water from the kettle and tossed a tea bag into his mug. "Long enough day in the garage, don't you think?" While watching TV, I heard the phone ringing. "Hello?" My mother answered from the kitchen. Father entered the living room and silently took his usual spot on the sofa.

After a few minutes of silence, I glanced away from my toys and up in his direction to find him watching me. "Come over, lie down with me," he said with a soft smile on his face.

Following his instructions, I walked to the sofa, climbed up, and lay down next to him. I briefly tossed and turned before finding comfort as I faced outward and away from him, using his arm as a pillow. A small batch of toys remained scattered on the floor close to the television and I noticed darkness beginning to fill the large living room window. While watching television with Father, my eyes were increasingly heavy and eventually closed.

I was startled by the movement of my mother when she wrapped a homemade quilt around the both of us. No words were exchanged as my father was engrossed in a television program and I was visibly sleepy. Mother returned to the kitchen to resume her telephone conversation. Her phone calls often lasted for hours.

At five years old, I had no interest in anything my father watched on television. In boredom, I scanned the room for objects of interest and listened to the sound of my mother's voice as it travelled from the kitchen. More tossing and turning until I found comfort, this time resting on my back as I once again closed my eyes.

Aside from the television and my mother's distant conversation, the house was silent. I was startled awake once again but this time, I did not open my eyes. I felt a tickling sensation as my father's fingers gently caressed the area between my legs. I pretended to sleep as the tickling continued.

Bedtime was regimented. I slipped into my nightgown and waited on the bed for Mother to come and listen to my nighttime prayers. I knew the drill. As soon as she came in she would tell me to kneel on the floor beside the bed. Keeping my body straight and rigid, I clasped my hands while my elbows rested on the bed and I began to pray.

> Now I lay me down to sleep,
> I pray the Lord my soul to keep.
> Guide me safely through the night and

wake me with the morning light.
God bless mom and dad.

I then followed with a list of others I hoped God would bless, including my brother, two sisters, and all my foster siblings.

And finally, "make me a good girl, Amen."

We were not a religious family, but Mother was strict about the nighttime prayers. She told me that God knew everything, that he could hear my thoughts, and see everything that I did.

It was around that same time that, without warning or explanation, I recall life suddenly changing. Mother was no longer proud of me and could barely tolerate my presence. I was punished daily for trivial incidents such as walking too slow or fast, not combing my hair properly, or not holding my fork the right way. According to Mother, I was loud, I was bad, and I was hateful.

Typical childish transgressions were met with severe discipline. Punishments varied from open-handed slaps or punches with clenched fists to full-fledged beatings for misdemeanors such as spilling something on the floor or responding to Mother with the wrong words. Depending on her level of anger, she sometimes decided to get an object to beat me with.

Belts, extension cords, hairbrushes, and broom handles were some of the weapons that left marks on my body. The more I cried, the more severe the beatings were. To stop the tears, I learned to hold my breath as soon as possible once the attack started. She worked hard to convince me that I was not good. If I felt a pain of any sort, such as a belly or headache, Mother said it was 'the badness coming out' and the beating would continue.

I was a prisoner in my childhood home. I had to follow strict rules that didn't apply to the other Moore children. Unlike my siblings, I wasn't allowed to open the refrigerator or cupboard doors or help myself to treats like the Purity cookies that were often left on the kitchen counter.

I was told to eat whatever was placed in front of me, whether I liked it or not. I sometimes plugged my nose to help get food down and I forced myself to keep swallowing when food tried to come back up. I was envious of my little sister, Tracey, who got to eat whatever she wanted, including French fries almost every day.

Bath time was terrifying. Mother yanked and pulled my head in all directions as she washed my hair. Her contempt was obvious, as she dug her fingernails into my scalp and threw water over my head from a pitcher.

With my eyes burning from the shampoo, I would blindly reach for a facecloth, but she wouldn't let me have it. Instead, she ordered me to sit still. Crying only added to my misery, so I squeezed my eyes tightly closed and waited for it to end.

My sister's bath time was much more joyful. It made me sad to hear Tracey laughing and singing as she played with toys and pretended to swim in the tub. Rather than throwing water in her face, Mother would give Tracey a neatly folded facecloth to protect her eyes from the gently cascading water and ask her to tip her head back to let the water softly flow down her back. I didn't understand why our lives had suddenly become so different.

***

"I will not say it, I will not say it, I will not say it..." I chanted to myself over and over as I rocked back and forth in a fetal position under the heavy blankets of my twin bed. Mother did it again - she said the H-word. I didn't want to hate anyone, not even mother. Hearing the word always made me sad. I would not allow myself to repeat it - not even in my mind.

Mother talked to her friend Louise on the telephone for hours. I would hear her telling Louise that she hated me. Louise must not have believed her, as Mother always followed with, "Yes, Louise, I really *hates* her," and "No, Louise, it's not a sin."

Louise was an older, gentle, grandmotherly-type woman. She was taller than my mother, had auburn hair, and was always smiling. Like Mother, Louise was also a local foster parent. I visited her house only a couple of times and enjoyed being there. It was very different from ours. The children were allowed to walk around and didn't get in trouble for laughing out loud or making noise.

Louise didn't work outside the home, but rather stayed home to take care of her children as well as the children in her care. She had a gentle disposition and was respectful when she talked to my mother and us kids. I assumed she was kind to everyone.

Anne was my older cousin who lived with us to help Mother with the children. She was in high school and planned to move away after graduation. Anne had short dark hair, pale skin, and a small frame. She was soft-spoken and pleasant, and always kind.

I imagined, like me, Anne was afraid of Mother, who sternly directed her to help the children with their homework after school. Anne was also assigned daily chores. If those chores were not completed the same day, she was sometimes forced to do them in the morning before school. Unfortunately, this sometimes meant she missed the school bus and had to walk five kilometres to the school in the nearby town of Brigus.

I loved Anne. She stood up for me when Mother was not home, and my father was teasing. Father would sometimes say, "Tell Anne what you are going to be when you grow up."

I'd proudly respond, "I'm going to be a teacher." Father chuckled, "No you're not, you're gonna be a *whore*, like your mother."

Being young and naïve, I didn't know what that word meant but given Anne's reaction, I knew it was not good. She warned my father to not say it, telling him that it would confuse me. This made Father laugh harder. I wasn't sure if he was laughing at me or Anne. Maybe he was laughing at both of us.

I was happiest when I was at school. While most of my friends looked forward to breaks like Christmas and the summer holidays, I dreaded them. For me, those holidays meant more punishments. School was my escape. My third-grade teacher was Ms. Dwyer and although she didn't know it, she was my favourite teacher.

I often daydreamed about having a different family during class. Ms. Dwyer never mentioned it to me, but she noticed the distraction and noted it on my report card before midterm break. I couldn't explain it, but I never felt a connection to my parents and wondered if there had been a mix-up at the hospital when I was born.

After all, real parents don't hurt or hate their children. I had spent countless hours dreaming about what my real family was like and what life would be like when they finally came to get me.

I imagined they were nice people. I thought about having siblings that looked like me, and grandparents too. Friends from school talked fondly of their grandparents and I wished I could relate. Mother's father had died and she was not on speaking terms with her mother. I barely knew my father's side of the family.

When the report card came home, Mother was furious. I was punished for daydreaming and warned to never let it happen again. It was one of the many times she would try to put an end to my dreams.

One sunny summer day when I was playing outside, I noticed an older couple slowly drive by. They smiled and waved at me, I waved back and watched the car drive away. I didn't move a muscle until they were completely out of sight. Convinced it was my parents, I excitedly ran to the house and into the kitchen where my mother was busy making bread.

Without stopping to breathe, or think, I blurted something that I immediately regretted saying, "I saw my real parents. They just drove down the street. They stopped and waved to me."

"And who the *hell* do you think we are?" she blasted. I turned and walked away, this time with much less enthusiasm.

Our large, five-bedroom house was constantly under

construction. Walls were moved to make rooms larger or smaller, windows, doors, flooring, and wall coverings always seemed to be in a state of flux, even the kitchen cabinets changed location at least once. As for the furniture, it was moved on a regular, almost weekly basis.

The house was modern for its time with shag carpets and matching curtains in every room. The family room, where we spent most of our time, was a large open space with a sofa and matching armchair, a wooden rocking chair, a recliner, and a floor model television. There was also a large shelving unit that was splattered with pictures of all the children in the house.

When we were not in school, my foster siblings and I were usually sent outside. Mother forced us to stay behind the house and not go near the front, where we could be seen.

Outside the back entrance of our house was a large area of loose gravel. The boys spent hours playing there, creating roads for their dinkies. They had car races and played smash-up derby.

Beyond the gravel, and up a slight embankment, was an open, flat, grassy area and a shed we used for play. The shed was perfect for playing house and especially useful for shelter on cold days.

Behind the shed lay a stretch of land with hills, open areas, plenty of trees, and well-beaten paths that zigzagged throughout the property. The adjoining properties appeared safe, except for the one directly behind ours. It led to a deep forest and Mother told me if I went beyond the gate, the fairies would get me. That was enough to keep me away.

Playtime inside the house usually involved sitting quietly in front of the television. Tracey had a lot of cool toys including Barbie dolls, games, and a Holly Hobbie Kitchen. I enjoyed playing with Tracey and her toys.

April, my older sister, had the best collection of dolls, though I never actually saw her play with any of them. In her bedroom was a dark wooden rocking crib that she slept in as a baby and now used to organize the dolls. The dolls were perfect. Their clothes and hair were never out of place.

I remember the walking doll with flawless porcelain skin and long white hair. She wore a pink pantsuit with white lace sleeves. My favourite, though, was the one with long, reddish-brown hair. She had a creamy complexion with a few painted freckles and a knee-length white silky dress. I always wanted long flowy hair like that doll.

April's bedroom was off-limits, so I was always careful when sneaking in to see her collection. I had some dolls of my own, but not pretty ones like April's.

17

Perhaps it was because everything was off-limits to me, or maybe it was just childhood curiosity, but I once wandered into Mother's bedroom where a picture book caught my attention. It was the size of a regular school journal and had an image of a child on the front cover. Inside was filled with graphic images of children, including horrific photos of babies and young children who were severely injured.

One page of the book featured a child with rope burns on her wrists and ankles where they had been tied together. Another showed a baby with cigarette burns on its body. Several other photos displayed the red hand mark left behind from an obvious slap to a child's face and plenty of pictures of children with multiple bruises. The most traumatizing photos were of the children with serious burns that also appeared to be deliberate. Equally scared and disturbed, I carefully left the book in the same place I had found it.

***

At some point, Mother stopped listening to my prayers. I still prayed, though I no longer knelt on the floor and the prayers were now more like one-sided conversations with God. I begged him to rescue me.

"If you are real God, and you can hear me, why are you not helping me?"

I wanted a way out so badly; I would sometimes plead with God to give me cancer. I didn't know much about the disease other than the fact that it made people really sick, and they died. I had heard my mother talking about people she knew who were dying from cancer and I thought if I could get it too, I would finally get away from this wicked house.

"God, you know my family won't mind; they won't even miss me so please give me cancer instead of someone else. Please! I am strong and I am used to pain. I can take it and I won't ever regret asking, I promise."

I imagined what life would be like when I got sick. I wondered if my family would be nice to me then. Would Mother regret being so cruel to me? Maybe she would make a bed on the sofa and allow me to watch television from there. The very thought brought a smile to my face as I visualized her being kind and affectionate.

Days and weeks went by and I did not get sick. There were no signs of cancer. I was devastated. I made the conscious decision to stop praying and rejected the notion that God was real. After all, if God *was* real, he would have saved me by now and not allowed my mother to hurt me as much as she did.

Nights went by without any conversations and at some point, I realized that if I didn't have God to talk to, then I was alone. There was no one else.

I profusely apologized to God and started the cycle once again – Praying for a rescue.

Bev, age 4

Bruises Fade

Mother was ten years younger than Father. She was a shapely woman with large breasts –a characteristic that my father undoubtedly appreciated, as demonstrated by his teasing. She stood at about five feet and four inches tall and had fair and flawless skin. Her dark hair was short and always permed.

Mother dressed for comfort over style and never wore makeup. Her hands were strong with sharp pointy fingernails. The two silver wedding rings that she wore dug deeply into her finger causing the skin to plump up around the edges, telling me she had gained weight since their marriage.

She did not drink or smoke and was not interested in socializing. At home, Mother was vulgar, sarcastic, and quick to react, whether verbal or physical. She was aggressive and ruled the household with an iron fist.

She walked heavily with her heels loudly pounding the floor with every step. The sound of her approach was enough to paralyze my body with fear.

Mother put most of us on edge. We all seemed to breathe a little easier when she was not around. I sought solace in spending time with my neighbour, Bride. She was a petite friendly lady and the mother of seven boys. They lived in a beige bungalow on the opposite side of my father's garage. I looked forward to seeing her each Saturday evening as we walked to the Marysvale Church Service together.

The service started at 5:00 p.m. and I would routinely leave my house at 4:30 p.m. so I could spend time at her house before church. I'd sit on a chair in Bride's kitchen patiently waiting for her to get ready. I enjoyed watching her scurry around applying finishing touches to her hair and makeup.

Bride appreciated having me around almost as much as I appreciated the respite of being in her house. She often spoke about not having girls of her own. Taking a last look in the mirror before we'd leave, Bride would ask how she looked while applying a few more strokes of lipstick. With perfectly curled hair, fine clothes, and makeup, I would readily smile while telling her, "Good. You always look good."

I was genuinely flattered that she even asked, and then as a bonus, she seemed to value my opinion. If there was any indication of adverse weather - be it rain, snow, fog, or even a mild mist - Bride would take a plastic head bonnet to shield her hair, which would remain in place until we were under the safety of the church's roof. I felt safe with Bride and I yearned to spend more time with her.

Our departure for the service was typically around 4:45 p.m. With no time to spare, Bride led the way with her brisk walk. I'd strive to keep up with her pace, saving our casual chat for the leisurely walk back home. We'd talk about Bride's family or things happening in her life. The conversation was often one-sided as I knew better than to discuss anything that happened inside our house.

During summer vacation, I spent most days outside with my foster siblings, exploring the backyard as we looked for ways to entertain ourselves. We had plenty of land to explore, berries to pick, and no lack of space for our make-believe games. Sometimes, we would just lay in the grass and watch clouds morph into shapes as they floated by.

When ordered outside, we were told not to come back in until we were called, unless we needed to use the washroom for number two. Otherwise, we were told to find a place outside to relieve ourselves - girls and boys alike.

In the evenings, we watched television until bedtime. My all-time favourite thing to do while inside the house was to play with Barbies. It allowed me an escape as I spent hours in an imaginary world. I had some of my own Barbie's and I once got a Barbie convertible for Christmas, but I preferred Tracey's collection. Her dolls had bendable limbs and they could easily sit in my convertible or her Barbie camper van. Mine were basic plastic with no bendable limbs.

Tracey's collection included Ken, Barbie's boyfriend, as well as children and baby Barbie dolls. She even had Annie, the little red curly-haired Barbie from the movie. April had been given Donnie and Marie collectible Barbie dolls when she was younger but had since outgrown them. Tracey was the lucky hand-me-down recipient of these collectables. I longed to own them but at least Tracey didn't mind when I played with her toys. Tracey and I sometimes played together but for the most part, I played alone.

April always had animals – specifically, a horse and dog. I remember that one of the horses once kicked April. Mother often reminded her about the incident and cautioned her to be careful around the animal.

The horse's stable was located behind the shed and from the door, I sometimes watched April brush down the horse's coat, tail, and mane. Of all the horses she had, my favourite was a brown one with a white patch on his face. April called him Star, and although he was somewhat intimidating, I adored watching her as she interacted with him. She loved those horses, and I am sure each one of them loved her too.

As I was finishing grade three, the Roman Catholic School Board announced changes for students living in my community. Instead of busing to the nearby town of Brigus, my siblings and I would now attend a school closer to home.

Our Lady of Peace was a smaller school and accommodated students from kindergarten to grade five with only one class for each grade. There was no gymnasium, cafeteria, or bus service. Students had no option other than to bring a packed lunch and eat from their desks before heading outside to play.

I was going to grade four and Mother declared that I would walk the distance. Tracey was younger, just starting kindergarten, and although we were going to the same school, she got a ride.

The thought of the long walk to my new school made me nervous, especially when the cold winter weather set in, but I was looking forward to a few extra hours away from home. I didn't have many friends at my old school, so there wasn't much for me to miss. I looked forward to the new school and was excited at the thought of making new friends.

Mother spent hours every day on the telephone talking to friends. In fact, she was usually still in her nightgown when the first call of the day came in. During one such conversation, I overheard that her brother's wife, Linda, was teaching at the Marysvale School. I wasn't sure if that was good or bad news.

Although I didn't get into trouble at school, the thought of Aunt Linda reporting my every move back to Mother frightened me. Mother found something wrong with everything I did and I was learning to do what I could to avoid her punishments.

I did not remember meeting Aunt Linda before now and anxiously awaited the opportunity. Friends told me she had a reputation for being the strictest teacher in the building, but I wasn't worried. After all, if I could live in the Moore house, I could handle anything. I didn't know many of my relatives and thought friends would think it was cool that one of the teachers was related to me.

When I first saw Aunt Linda, I was struck by her formidable presence. She was one of the tallest people I had ever met - even taller than the male teachers. Her short pixie-style dark hair completely exposed her earrings. Being fond of long hairstyles, I wondered why any woman would want such short hair. She had long polished fingernails and wore a lot of jewelry.

It was her stature that intimated most of the kids, but for me, it was her voice. It projected with great authority and when she spoke, even the rowdiest kids stopped and listened.

Aunt Linda was my fourth-grade teacher and although I never gave her reason to single me out or even raise her voice, she wasted no time in telling Mother of the profanity I had scribbled inside a textbook.

Aunt Linda and her friend, another teacher from the school, often came to my house to eat lunch with Mother on school days. It was during one of the luncheons that she told Mother of my rebellious act.

In the evenings, I sat at the kitchen table and worked on my homework. While trying to concentrate, I became agitated as my mother screamed profanities at Father. This was not uncommon, and when my father remained visibly unaffected by her tirade, she naturally became irate.

It usually occurred when he came home drunk, which was often. She started by stampeding around the house, banging cupboard doors, roughly handling dishes, and practically throwing his food on the table in front of him.

I did not like vulgar language and was bothered by hearing the F-word repeated over and over again. I guess that's what prompted me to write it on the inside back cover of my textbook. In small letters, I wrote *F-U-C-K*. I felt a certain satisfaction when I wrote it – almost as if I had stood up to defend my father. I would never really do that; I was too scared of Mother. But writing the word on the textbook at the time seemed like I was doing something to stand up to her.

Because I was always on the receiving end of Mother's bullying, I knew what it felt like to be insulted and shamed. According to Mother, children were meant to be seen and not heard. However, I never understood why Father didn't defend himself. Maybe because he was intoxicated and felt guilty. Maybe he didn't care, or maybe he was afraid of provoking her further.

Whatever the reason, I was sympathetic. He never fought back or said mean things to her. He didn't say mean things to anyone, and occasionally he stood up for me. He sometimes walked in while Mother was beating me and tried to intervene by saying "Just leave her alone, will ya?"

Mother didn't take orders from anyone. Her response was consistent: "You mind your own business; this doesn't concern you."

She usually continued with the attack while he sheepishly retreated. Although nothing changed, I recognized and appreciated his effort.

Although I sometimes pitied him, Father and I didn't have a great relationship. He rarely paid attention to me other than to tease or torment when the mood hit. But when he drank, he always paid too much attention to me.

From across the room, he would warn me of another late-night visit by scrunching his nose and lips, raising his eyebrows, and nodding his head while pointing to my vagina.

It was awkward, and I felt uncomfortable, but he always ensured that no one else saw the look. I didn't like his expressions or the visit, but most of all I didn't like the smell that was left behind when he was finished with me.

Father was an alcoholic and drank several times a week, which meant frequent bedroom visits. As often as he came to my room, I could never get used to that smell. But he was a parent and I had to do what I was told, even if I didn't like it.

My siblings and I were not close either. They were all aware of my mother's feelings toward me. She certainly never tried to hide her contempt and I assumed they didn't want to antagonize her. Siding with me or even being friendly could be misconstrued by Mother and they too could become subject to her vicious and vindictive behaviour. Mother treated my siblings differently. She didn't express love, but they were never harmed or verbally abused. They had a freedom that I could only dream of.

I had completely forgotten about the offensive inscription on my textbook when Mother questioned me about it weeks later. I was embarrassed and immediately faced the consequences. I never swore, and yet I was foolish enough to inscribe a supremely offensive word on a book that would most certainly be seen by someone. The punishment was severe; I was beaten with an extension cord, and this time, it was my own fault.

I came to realize that the few kilometres I had to walk to and from school weren't so bad. It gave me time with my new friends. Several of Bride's boys accompanied me, and Gordon, another friend, would join us along the way. On days with nasty weather, we weren't fond of the trek, but we did it just the same.

The boys knew a shortcut and called it the hill path. It took us through a wooded area, away from the main road. The route began in an open field across from the Marysvale church. Some areas along the walkway were more open than others and the path itself broke out just minutes from our school. The path offered some protection from any inclement weather and shaved some of the travel time of the trip.

Tracey continued to get a ride every day with Aunt Linda. I realized she was younger and too small for the long hike, but I didn't understand why I had to walk in the rain or cold weather when there was a vehicle stopped at our driveway to pick her up in the morning and drop her off at the end of the day.

I didn't complain despite having to watch them cruise past me every day. The walk kept me out of the house longer and that made it worth it.

Tracey was extremely shy, and I sometimes worried about her in the other classroom. Students weren't permitted to leave classrooms during recess or lunch breaks without permission from the on-duty teacher. The washrooms were halfway down the corridor, close to Tracey's classroom so, with permission to go to the washroom, I sometimes crept down to peek in and check on her. Most times she never even noticed me. I watched as she played with other children and that always brought a smile to my face.

During those long walks to school, Gordon and I became fast friends, and it wasn't long before he was calling me his girlfriend. I was in the fourth grade and he was in the third. Gordon was taller than the other boys that walked with us to school. He was cute with brown wavy hair and unlike most of the others, he had no freckles. I was shy and apprehensive when he not only offered but insisted on carrying my backpack.

Once, when Gordon brought me a gift, it made me incredibly bashful. As we walked through the hill path, he proudly handed me a silver necklace with a burgundy pendant. It was beautiful and such a kind gesture, but my thoughts immediately went to Mother's potential reaction.

I worried about her response especially given the gift was from a boy. I refused it in the name of self-preservation, telling Gordon I couldn't accept it. He was visibly disappointed and after only a brief pause, pushed the dangling necklace and my hand away from him.

"It's for you, I'm not taking it back," he said in a wounded tone.

"But I can't take it," I implored.

"Okay, but I'm not taking it back," he repeated while walking away from me. I released a deep sigh before I ran to catch up.

I knew his feelings were hurt but I was too embarrassed to make myself vulnerable with an explanation. I accepted the gift and Gordon triumphantly smiled with his success.

At the end of the hill path, Gordon and I would always part ways. He would turn left for another two- or three-minute walk to his house, while I walked in the opposite direction towards mine. I was silent for the remainder of the trip as I thought about the necklace. I was flattered but used the time to strategize how I could hide it. I did not own a jewelry box and worried my mother would be even more furious if she ever saw me wearing it or found it in my bedroom.

I ran several different scenarios through my head and talked myself in and out of showing her the gift. Upon entering the house, I pulled out the necklace and let it dangle from my hand as I exclaimed, "Look what I found!"

April and Mother were both in the kitchen and turned toward me –walking closer to study my "treasure." As Mother took the necklace from my hand to examine it, April leaned in and cooed, "I like it."

Without another word, she handed it to April and walked away. While admiring her new piece of jewelry with a dotingly fixed gaze, April retreated to her bedroom and as I heard the sound of her jewelry box cover close, I fought to hold back the tears.

I wasn't allowed in April's bedroom, which up until then had always been fine with me. But now I had a reason to go in. Of all bedrooms in the house, April's was the largest, even larger than the master bedroom. It was also the nicest. It had a double bed with a matching highboy, mirrored dresser, and a night table.

There was also a walk-in closet and on the opposite side of the room, a large window that faced the street. The carpet was a thick pink, fuchsia, and white shag. Her bedspread, wallpaper, and curtains all matched the carpet. The dresser tops were protected by fancy doilies. On her mirrored dresser sat a brush with a matching mirror, plus a collection of perfumes that included a large bottle of Avon Soft Musk.

Her jewelry box had two tiers: a pull-out drawer and a top that lifted to reveal compartments with a mirror in the lid. The box was lined with light gray velvet fabric. My necklace now sat in one of those compartments.

I walked away from the room's entrance thinking about my pretty pendant. My thoughts turned to Gordon and how he would feel when he noticed I wasn't wearing it. I hoped he wouldn't ask about it.

I was sensitive and that made Mother angry. She insulted, belittled, hurt, and humiliated me in front of the other children. I dared not respond as I took every comment to heart. It felt even worse when she summoned a sarcastic voice to mock my hurt response.

"I've got more feelings for April's little pinky than I have for all of you," she would say. Sometimes it was, "I care more about the water in that pot than you."

I realized that was true, but the constant reminders were painful. Tears silently ran down my face. I wished she would just hit me and get it over with instead of going on and on about her lack of feelings for me. Bruises faded, but the impact of the words never did.

During Mother's lengthy telephone conversations, I sometimes slipped into her bedroom. Each time, I found myself drawn to her graphically illustrated book of battered children. Sitting on the floor, I flipped from one page to another studying the pictures. Why would someone tie the hands and feet of a child together? How could they burn a baby with a cigarette or other hot objects? I scanned through the book and felt worse each time I saw it.

Carefully, I always returned the book to its original spot on the floor beside Mother's side of the bed in the same position I had found it. These horrifying images have haunted me my entire life.

On another occasion when my childhood curiosity led me into Mother's room, I noticed the large brown faux leather chest. I had seen her looking through this chest before and I knew it was where she kept her important files. While lifting the cover, my eyes darted across the top layer of papers. I was convinced there was something in this chest to explain her hostility towards me. As I heard her hang up the phone, I quickly closed the chest and like a startled mouse, scampered out of the room. I genuinely believed the answer lay in that chest and someday I would find it.

Christmas is supposed to be the happiest time of the year, and for my school friends, it was. Every year, I was hopeful that our Christmas would be better than the last. Getting the tree into the house was a messy job. April followed Father and the freshly cut tree as it was dragged through the house, frantically cleaning the trail of pine needles left behind. Mother complained the entire time while always threatening to not have a tree in the house next year. When the tree was finally hoisted into position, I could barely wait for April to decorate it. I wished Mother could be happy with the sight of the tree, even just for one day.

Christmas Eve was full of excitement and enthusiasm as we anxiously awaited a visit from Santa. There were classic Christmas shows to watch and treats to eat. I was also given a treat, but once everyone was in bed, I sometimes sneaked out for an extra cookie, or *two*!

Christmas Day kicked off early as my brother Evan and I woke up and tiptoed to the family room for our first peek of the presents. Mother heard us and demanded I return to my bed until she gave me permission to come out. I lay in bed crying and wishing I could be in the family room with my brother as he opened his gifts from Santa.

The Christmas dinner included a turkey with stuffing, homemade gravy, lots of vegetables, and, as a treat, drinks of Purity syrup. It should have been a happy day, but Mother always found something to fight about. The constant bickering left little room for holiday cheer.

I mentally blocked the turmoil by playing with toys and trying to stay out of sight. When the opportunity presented itself, I crept into the bedroom to grab the bag of Barbie dolls before finding a quiet space in the living room to play. While drowning out background noises, I divided the Barbies into families and imitated the fun happy life I dreamed about, like the ones I saw on television.

At the end of the day, I'd put away the barbies and head to my bedroom. If Father had been drinking, he was not long behind.

The Barbies reminded me of my sisters who both had long hair. I was envious of their long locks. Mother always made sure mine was short and I sobbed every time it was chopped off. April's hair was long enough to reach her belt, while Tracey's hair covered more than half the length of her back. I would have been happy with just enough length to fit in a ponytail. Sometimes I wondered if Mother wanted to make me look ugly.

Inside my bedroom, I often pretended to have long hair. I would sometimes slip into a turtleneck sweater then pull the sweater back up over my head, keeping the neckband tightly wrapped around my head. With the length of the sweater falling against my back, I pretended to flick it from side to side while watching in a mirror. With an elastic, I tied my "hair" back in a ponytail, or sometimes, I'd loosely fold the sweater arms behind while I pretended to have my hair in an up-do.

When January finally came, I was thankful to return to school. I listened to my classmates talk with excitement about their holidays, family traditions, and new toys.

Red Flags

By the time I was nine, I was extremely flexible. I could replicate a bridge by balancing myself on all fours face up with my belly pushed high into the air, and I could easily wrap my legs around the back of my neck and comfortably sit cross-legged with both feet on top of my opposite thighs.

The other kids in the house were amused with my elasticity. I often slept on my back with my feet tucked up under my bottom to keep them warm at night.

One cold morning in early spring, as Mother snapped her usual "get up" order, I tried to spring out of bed, but something wasn't quite right. My eyes immediately flew open, but the rest of my body was resistant. I wasn't ready for the day ahead, but I didn't want to trigger a second wake-up call either.

Gradually I rolled to the side and propped myself up by shifting my upper body weight onto my right forearm. At the same time, my legs fell to the floor over the side of the bed and I felt an unusual tightness in one of them.

As I attempted to stand, excruciating pain registered in my right knee. It was intense and I quickly sprang back onto the bed as I tried to comprehend what was going on. Sitting on the edge of the mattress, I tried to lift and slowly stretch out the leg, but extreme pain stopped me from extending it.

I continued to try to straighten my leg, but I couldn't. Normally, the thought of Mother's wrath was enough to motivate me to push through even the worst physical pain, but today it was just too severe. I worried as I thought about telling her.

She probably wouldn't believe me, I thought, and I worried she would force me to walk on it. Barely able to move, I had no choice but to call her. As she entered the room, I explained what was going on with my leg. With tears in my eyes, I tried standing once again to demonstrate my discomfort.

"What did you do to it?" she demanded.

"Nothing. I slept on it and now I can't straighten it all the way."

With a perplexed look, she said, "Get back in bed. I will make a doctor's appointment," and she turned to walk away.

Her voice did not have the usual harsh tone. She hadn't directed me to get ready for school, nor did she suggest that this was my fault. Never wanting to miss an opportunity to appease my mother, I did exactly as she said. I quietly lay in bed and waited for the next command, wondering what was wrong with my knee.

It was April 24th when Mother brought me to see the family doctor. On my left foot, I hopped from the car through the parking lot and into the clinic waiting room. After my name was called, I hopped all the way into the doctor's office, periodically leaning against the walls for support.

"She went to sleep with her legs wrapped up underneath her last night and this morning she can't straighten one of them out," Mother told the doctor.

I offered a meek smile affirming the details. Mother always did all the talking and given how shy I was, I didn't mind. It was how she wanted it anyway.

Following the doctor's physical exam, he noted that my right knee had become locked and that it was unable to flex past 90 degrees. He offered a couple of explanations (none of which I understood) and then sent us home with instructions for me to stay off my feet.

The next couple of weeks were some of the best ones of my life. I was permitted to lay on the sofa watching television for most of the day with my leg propped up on top of a thick pillow and Mother would regularly ask how it was. It was the most affectionate she had ever been with me. During this time, when Mother spoke to her friends on the telephone, she had stopped talking about me in negative tones and even expressed concern about my injury.

Once the two weeks had passed, I was still unable to completely bend my leg, so she brought me back to the family doctor. This time we were sent off to get an x-ray, routine blood work, and see an orthopedic surgeon.

According to my medical files, on May 11th, I was admitted to the hospital.

Mother sat next to me in the waiting room of the Janeway Children's Hospital while I watched children play in a designated area. A large plastic house big enough for several children to crawl inside sat on cushioned flooring. There was a small wooden table and chair set with crayons and colouring books scattered about. It looked inviting, but I wouldn't dare ask to play.

There was also a mishmash of plastic cars, horses, dolls, and toys suitable for children of all ages, and a large bookshelf filled to the brim. I loved to draw and was captivated by the life-size murals painted directly on the walls surrounding the large open area.

As my studious gaze swept the space, I saw more sick children than I had ever seen before. The ages ranged from newborns to teenagers. Some were sitting with their parents while others roamed independently. I smiled as I watched the smaller children play together.

My attention was drawn to a small boy. He was standing back from the group while watching a couple of children play. With a big grin, he anxiously shifted weight from one foot to the other. He was totally engrossed in the other children's activities. I imagine he wanted to play but was probably too shy to join in. Upon closer examination, I noticed that all the exposed parts of his body were covered with scars including his face, neck, two arms, and hands. I looked at my mother as I noticed she had spotted the same child.

"What's wrong with him?" I asked.

"He was burned in a house fire," she quietly explained.

My eyes widened and I quickly shifted my attention back to the smiling little boy as my brain raced with thoughts. I envisioned firefighters rescuing him from a burning house. The thought was scary to imagine. I wondered if there was anyone else in the fire. I hoped they were all okay. Looking at the burn scars made me sad, but he was smiling.

Mother interrupted my surveillance, "How's the leg?"

"It's fine," I replied.

"It's not fine or you wouldn't be here," she snapped in an authoritative voice that most would not question.

"Tell them it hurts, and where it hurts, or they will send you home. Do you hear me?"

I nodded my head in compliance.

"Now go over and get a book to read," she added.

With infection ruled out, Dr. Collins, the orthopedic surgeon, told my mother we were left with two likely alternatives. He suspected there was either a lesion and a cyst, or a displacement of the meniscus. His recommendation was to have me admitted to the hospital that day and placed on traction. Physiotherapy and heat applications would help reduce the restriction and the doctor was confident that traction would help completely straighten my leg.

Mother escorted me to the admissions department where she answered questions from a nurse, while a second nurse measured and recorded my temperature, blood pressure, height, and weight. I was fitted with a personalized plastic armband and asked to sit in a wheelchair before being pushed to the elevator and the ward upstairs.

I was frightened as the nurse wheeled me to my room. Inside

were four strategically placed twin beds. They were higher than normal, and each had a portable table over it. There were two other girls in the room, and I wondered why they were there. One looked like she might be close to my age while the other, I suspected, was a couple of years older than me. The girls were occupying the two beds that were closest to the windows. The remaining two beds were empty, and I was wheeled to the one on the right side of the room.

I fought to hold back the tears when my mother told me she was leaving to drive home. This was my first night outside the Moore house. I didn't know anyone at the hospital, and I was scared. The attending nurse, probably recognizing my apprehension, took the liberty of introducing me to the other children in the room. She then asked me some ice-breaking questions. She wondered if I had any brothers or sisters and if I had any pets. She asked if I enjoyed school and what grade I was in. I could choose the details I wanted to share, and surprisingly, life felt a little normal.

I changed into pyjamas and settled in for the night. Two more nurses, a male, and a female entered the room with ropes, pulleys, weights, and other equipment and announced they were there to set my leg in the traction.

The right leg was securely wrapped and suspended high over the bed with three to five pounds of weight dangling outside the foot of the bed. The traction was to remain in place while I slept, ate, and did everything else until the doctor decided to remove it. I was already uncomfortable with the constant pull on my leg. I expected sleeping would be impossible.

Visiting hours ended at 9 p.m. I flipped through a couple of comic books that Mother purchased at the hospital gift store as my roommates said good-bye to their visitors. The room lights were turned off and the headboard lights came on.

I noticed that one of my roommates had a corkboard that was covered in "get-well" cards with a few more on her nightstand. I also noticed she wore her own pyjamas and not the generic hospital ones like the rest of us. She had a blanket from home on her bed and I thought perhaps she had been in hospital for a long time and her family had brought personal items to make her feel more comfortable.

With restricted movement, I tried to find comfort with my leg suspended. Tears rolled down my face and onto my pillow as I looked toward the noise that came from the hallway. Embarrassed, I kept my head turned in that direction so the other girls wouldn't see my tears.

By May 14th, records indicated that I was making "slow progress" with the traction device that was being used to extend my leg. The nurse's notes indicated that I still had 30 degrees to go to fully extend my leg.

I should have been happy with the progress, but the thought of getting better scared me. What would Mother think, I wondered. She had been so focused on something being wrong with me, would she be mad with me if I was fine? I didn't want her anger toward me to return.

After a couple of days with little additional progress, the medical team made arrangements for exploratory surgery. I panicked at the thought of having my leg cut open. I became agitated and upset as I told the nurse that the doctor should not operate. "There's no need, I can straighten it out myself now," I said as I demonstrated a full leg extension.

Surgery was cancelled and on May 18th I was sent home wearing a full leg cylinder cast to keep my leg extended. Dr. Collins' had noted in my file, "There is something in her manner that suggests la belle indifference."

La belle indifference happens when patients aren't concerned about the symptoms they're experiencing. It's a characteristic of Conversion Disorder. According to the National Institutes of Health, Conversion Disorder is when a person experiences symptoms affecting the nervous system that cannot be explained solely by a physical illness or injury.

Symptoms usually begin suddenly after a period of emotional or physical distress or psychological conflict[1] and are thought to be caused by the body's reaction to a stressful physical or emotional event.[2]

On May 30, I returned to the hospital to have the cast removed and follow up with the Orthopedic Surgeon. Dr. Collins noted in my file:

I find this case to be extremely confusing and think all we can do now is do a bone scan to make sure we are not missing a lesion like an osteoid osteoma. I have considered psychological causes but find her to be a quite cooperative little girl who does not really

---

[1]Berger FK, Zieve D, and Conaway B. Conversion disorder. *MedlinePlus*. November 18, 2016; http://www.nlm.nih.gov/medlineplus/ency/article/000954.htm.

[2] Marshall SA, Landau ME, Carroll CG, Schwieters B, and Llewellyn A. Conversion disorders. *Medscape Reference*. November 9, 2015; http://emedicine.medscape.com/article/287464-overview

impress me as there being any underlying physiological disturbances.

By my next visit on June 27th, the pain had returned but this time it had moved to my groin, down the back of my leg and along the side of my calf. Dr. Collins ordered a flexion body cast which would remain in place for a month.

With a body cast, it was quite difficult to rest comfortably and although I had trouble sleeping, I took comfort in the fact that Father's late-night visits to my bedroom stopped for a little while. I didn't feel like playing and spent most of my time just laying around. Mother continued to ask about my pain. Sometimes I forgot until she reminded me of it.

On July 19th, the body cast was removed. My mother was vocal and complained to the doctor that I had experienced more pain while wearing the cast than before. I hadn't told her this, nor was it true, but I would not dare correct her.

Once the cast was removed, Dr. Dawe examined my leg and decided to admit me to the hospital for further investigation. That same day, records indicate that a requisition was sent to the Department of Child Welfare, for a home investigation.

I was in the hospital for twelve days, during which time nurses noticed that I only sometimes limped on my right side. Upon closer examination, they noted that I only limped when I knew I was being watched. It was also noted that I didn't complain of pain when left alone.

According to medical records, officials followed up on Dr. Dawe's home investigation request on July 30th.

> Spoke with Mrs. Moore by phone today. She was very positive about Beverly as a child. She is outgoing, many friends, no school problems. There are two siblings older than Bev – two children younger (they are foster children). Beverly is close to them all.
> Beverly was adopted at the age of 1 year. (Beverly does not know this and is not to be informed). This is the first illness (apart from the common cold) that Beverly has had.
> Conclusion: As a result of phone conversation only - there would seem to be no relationship between Beverly's social environment and her present symptomatology. I would be happy to do a more thorough study of the family should the situation warrant it in the future.
> R.T. S.W.

I was sent home the next day. On August 15 I saw Dr. Collins again.

Beverly is still on the go. I have been trying everything to investigate her quite fully but have been unable to find any cause for her pain which seems to be intermittently in the knee and groin. During my absence on holidays, Dr. Frank Dawe had her admitted and she was seen by Dr. Janes. She had a repeat arthrogram done which was negative. It is beginning to look very much as if Beverly has some deep-seeded emotional problem at the bottom of this and if mother agrees, I will refer her to a psychiatric clinic and see if we can find the cause of this.

Dr. Collins

Less than a week later, I met with a psychiatrist at the Janeway Children's hospital.

August 21
Dear Dr. Collins:

Thank you for referring Beverly, she was seen with her mother today.

On the morning of April 24th, Beverly is said to have complained of pain in her right knee on waking in the morning, she couldn't extend her knee which was apparently tender. For this problem, she was an inpatient at the Janeway in May and again in July for up to 12 days at a time. No abnormality was discovered and on one occasion she was able to extend the knee after an examination under anesthesia was proposed. The usual supportive measures apparently have not worked, and she continues to complain with pain. Beverly is said to be waking 2 or 3 times a night and crying with pain. She has always been a good student and has been promoted. Since the knee problem started Beverly tends to want to stay inside and not go out and play. In turn, mother is constantly asking her how her leg is.

Beverly is an adopted child having first been placed as a foster child at age 1 with Mrs. Moore. Mrs. Moore has never told her that she is adopted and is now very anxious about how to tell her. Beverly has been an exceptionally easy child, and this is the first time her mother has had any problems. Mother is 35 years old and married at 21. She worked as a waitress before but prefers her role as a housewife and foster mother. She takes foster children regularly and after having 2 of her own children has adopted Beverly and Tracey, a 6-year-old child. Neither of these children have been told that they are adopted. In addition to the 2 natural and adopted children, there are 4 foster children in the home. The father is 45, works as a mechanic and spends some time with the children in their leisure activities.

Beverly was a pleasant, cooperative child and talked freely and was somewhat overly affectionate. According to her description, there are 2 sharply demarcated bands of pain across her knee and upper thigh on the right side. The pain did not seem to bother her at all except when she is reminded of it. She wants to finish high school and become a nurse. The pain did not seem to limit her movement in any way.

I found the main problem to be Mrs. Moore's attitude. She has had behavior problems with foster children which she regards as attributable to their natural homes. If Beverly should be regarded as having psychogenic pain, she feels that this will reflect on her and she seems unable to accept the idea that Beverly may not have an organic disorder. She complained that the whole situation is getting on her nerves now, but she won't accept any suggestions. I have suggested that Beverly should come into psychiatry for a period of observation, but this again was not acceptable to her. The social worker will be telephoning Mrs. Moore in 2- or 3-days time to try and change her mind.

Yours sincerely,

U. Smith, M.B.,F.R.C.P.

Director of Child Psychiatry

On September 19th Dr. Collins did another follow up examination and noted that Mother felt it was "absolutely essential" that something be done so he ordered me a brace to wear in the day and a splint to wear at night.

On October 24th I returned to the Janeway and was admitted to the Child Psychiatry unit. Unlike past visits, this time I knew in advance that I would be admitted, but I wasn't aware that this stay was about more than the physical pain I felt in my leg.

I looked around and didn't see the familiar site of kids in wheelchairs or patients with broken bones. People here seemed to be mobile. No one was confined to a bed or attached to an IV. I was sure the kids had ailments such as mine, but they were not obvious.

On this ward, we wore regular day clothes, not pyjamas. The kids gathered in a common area to watch television. Here, academic lessons were compulsory five days a week and there was an optional church service on Sundays. We had movie nights and we were told to respect each other's personal property. I was uncomfortable here and longed to go home.

After a full month in the hospital, I was happy to be discharged and going home. Things settled down and my mother stopped asking about my leg and I stopped thinking about it.

Hot Water

As a licensed foster home, we always had children in our house. I especially loved the babies, although their stays were usually the shortest. Mother seemed to enjoy the babies as well.

I watched her dress, feed, and change them all while talking lovingly to them, but sometimes when a baby continued to cry for no apparent reason, she would place them in the crib and just leave them. "You're not hungry and you're not wet, a little crying won't hurt you," she would say as she closed the bedroom door on the way out.

I did not like hearing the babies cry. I wanted to sneak in and soothe them, but couldn't risk the possibility of Mother catching me in there.

Mother often cared for children with special needs and once, one of the babies staying at our house died. Mother was devastated when she found the 14-month-old's lifeless body in the crib one morning. The police were called and in no time, RCMP officers and two ambulance attendants were in the house asking questions.

The baby's small body was prepared for transport and taken away. Tracey and I sat at the kitchen table listening to the commotion as our mother told a police officer about the baby's preexisting health conditions. "Like the other boys in his family, he wasn't expected to live long," we heard her say.

Our foster siblings ranged in ages. Lorraine was seven years older than me and lived with us for five years. She was tall, had long brown hair, brown eyes, and a clear olive complexion. She was absolutely radiant. She was also kindhearted, mild-mannered, and soft-spoken.

Mother would sometimes make negative comments toward her but she never physically hurt her. Lorraine's age probably protected her from most types of abuse. I remember that she sometimes helped me with my homework and always did chores around the house.

My sister April was three years younger than Lorraine. They got along well, so I was surprised when I overheard April talking to

Mother about Lorraine one day. April was repeating something that I knew Lorraine would not want Mother to know. It bothered me so much that I told Lorraine about it. Lorraine confronted April and Mother became furious at the news of my involvement in the whole mess.

She stomped her way into the family room and with a pointed finger demanded that I go directly to her bedroom. There was no dispute from me. The aggressive tone only meant one thing –I was about to be punished. I had never been ordered to go to her bedroom before though and that scared me.

I hurried down the hall with Mother trailing directly behind. The sound of her heavy footsteps made my heart pound hard. As I entered her bedroom, she remained right behind me and was quick to swing the door closed behind her. I stepped further into the room, but only to remain out of her reach. With both hands planted firmly on her hips, she demanded, "What the fuck did you tell Lorraine about April?"

"I don't know what you're talking about," I fearfully replied.

Mocking me, she repeated my answer with a childish voice, "I don't know what you're talking about."

I nervously bit my lip, waiting for her next move.

"Oh yes, you do. You repeated something that you had no business repeating," she sneered.

Memories of the recent conversation with Lorraine resurfaced in my head as a knot tightened in my stomach. Maintaining my silence, I slowly and carefully stepped back to gain more distance while gravitating towards the closet. Unlike standard built-in closets, this one was free-standing, more like a fancy dresser with a full-length mirror covering half of the unit.

The closet was positioned about two feet from a dresser. I had misjudged my safety in stepping back to this area of the room. Without warning, my mother shoved me into the gap between the two pieces of furniture. She had me cornered. The side of my face struck the dresser with a hard thwack. Before I could process what was happening, I felt the pain of her dragging me by the hair, yanking me back out into the vulnerability of the open room.

She firmly grabbed my shoulders and began to shake my body back and forth, banging my head and back against the wall between the closet and dresser. Fear intensified as I saw the rage in the black pools of her eyes. I have never seen this level of anger before.

Words were coming out of her mouth, but they failed to register. I was trapped with absolutely no escape. Her fists and feet became brutal weapons. Trying to shield my face from her uncoordinated punches, I twisted and turned with the impact of every punishing kick.

Terror gripped my soul when I felt the strength of her fingers wrapped tightly around my throat. My cries went unheard, or at the very least were unacknowledged and I realized no one was coming to stop her. I was scared and thought I was going to die.

The assault seemed endless. I couldn't shield my body and the pain was undeniably intense. My brain only focused on sending signals to my hands and arms in the name of protection.

The punishment finally came to an end and she stomped out of the room, abandoning my battered and quickly bruising body on the bedroom floor. The carpet cushioned my face and muffled my wails as it soaked up tears. My body screamed in pain as I attempted to move.

A few days later, I overheard Mother on the phone with one of her friends. I learned that two new children were on the way. They were two sisters, who were ten and twelve years old. They were from Quebec and bilingual, I heard her say. I couldn't wait to meet them.

Christine was my age. She was tall, slim, and very pretty. She had shoulder length-brown hair, a bright smile, and perfect teeth. We immediately discussed common interests. I asked her about her family and told her everything about her new school. We were instant friends.

Guylaine was twelve years old, and although she matched Evan's age, his shyness prevented him from helping her adjust to the new school. Guylaine readily took on a big sister role and bonded with Tracey.

Mother was nice in the beginning but that changed quickly, and the girls started to see glimpses of her darker side. When their father called to chat on the phone, they spoke with him in French for a long period. When the call ended, Mother was fuming. She declared that if they wanted to use her telephone, their conversations must be in English or they wouldn't happen at all.

The girls' parents had separated, and Mother speculated whose fault it was as she spoke about it to her friends. Christine and I talked about her previous life before the separation. It was evident that she already missed her family.

She had photos of both parents with her. They were attractive people who appeared to be far more sophisticated than most folks I knew. The photos reflected a happier, and vastly different reality than what the girls would experience while living with us. I felt sorry for them.

Like our other foster siblings, Christine, Guylaine, and I were booted out of the house to entertain ourselves anytime that the weather was nice, and we weren't in school. The Moore kids were free to do as they pleased. Admittedly, April was older, more mature and she did most of the housework. She also looked after the kids whenever Mother went out, which was for a few hours most days or evenings.

Evan was independent. His best friends were a pair of brothers and as a teenager, he spent most of his time at their house. Mother made her irritation about his absence evident by saying, "Maybe you should go live with them," which she expressed quite often.

As frustrated as she was, she never grounded him or made any attempt to restrict his outings. I considered him to be lucky in that regard.

Tracey was the baby of the family. Being the youngest, she was always treated special. As a child, I assumed it was "the norm" for the youngest member of all families to get special treatment. Sometimes she joined us outside, but she was never forced out the door.

As Christine and I headed off to grade six, I was excited to introduce everyone to my new sister. She was not only pretty, but she also had the "city vibe" and could speak two languages, so I knew the other kids would find her interesting.

There were two grade six classes at St. Edwards, and I was disappointed to learn we landed in different classrooms.

We still spent a lot of time together outside of school and on one specific Saturday afternoon while Mother was shopping, we found ourselves in the bedroom with Father. It was unusual to be in the bedroom because once the beds were made, we weren't permitted back in there until bedtime. That ensured the bedrooms always remained clean and tidy. It was even more unusual for our father to be home. If he wasn't working, he was usually in his garage.

On this day, however, Christine and I had been in the bedroom when Father entered and closed the door behind him. He sat on the edge of the bed and opened his trousers, exposing himself without a second thought. With his penis fully erect, he held it upright and repeatedly said, "Touch it," while having a great laugh for himself.

It turned into an awkward game as Christine and I leapfrogged one another to avoid his reach while sacrificing the other. We pushed each other toward him; "No, you," and then, "No, you," we argued, each fighting to escape his reach.

This bedroom was on the ground level of the house. We were both startled once we spotted one of the older kids standing outside the window peering in. The game abruptly ended. Father fastened his trousers and immediately left the room.

While this type of incident happened often to me alone, it was the only time that I witnessed someone else being involved in

Father's sexual games. We never spoke of it again. I anticipated that Christine and I would be punished once Mother heard about it. To my surprise, that never happened. No conversation about the incident occurred or if it did, Christine and I never knew about it.

The two sisters only lived with us for a year. I was heartbroken the day they left, but I was happy that they would return to a life of normalcy, whatever that meant for them. That same year, Lorraine completed high school and also moved out.

At the end of the school year, my grade six report card reflected declining grades and came with comments from my teacher about incomplete homework and assignments. It was difficult to study at home. Most nights, when I tried to study at the table, she'd send me to bed.

Mother couldn't handle being around me and often cut my study time short. I was upset every time I wasn't allowed to finish homework because of Mother, and I wasn't able to explain the situation to my teacher. Instead, I just accepted the teacher's disappointment and Mother's punishment.

On the bus ride home, I nervously picked at the protective plastic cover on my binder. I noticed the three half-circle marks on the underside of my forearm, distinctive marks left by Mother's long fingernails. Sometimes they cut deep enough to draw blood. If I pulled from her grip, the nails would rip through, stinging, while taking a layer of my flesh with them. Her nails were a sharp weapon that she often used to inflict pain.

Mother had two distinctly different personalities. In front of teachers, doctors, social workers, or anyone else outside the house, she spoke in a friendly, caring tone and even had a sense of humour. I could see why people liked her and I wished that she would be that person at home too. At home, she was a monster.

Public perception was extremely important to her. Every child - from small babies to teenagers - was dressed in only the finest clothes. Nothing was ever stained or wrinkled. Hair and nails were trimmed regularly, and footwear was always in top shape. Our house was also always kept in immaculate condition.

We had strict cleaning rituals. The dishes were to be washed and dried, and the floors swept after every meal. The kitchen and bathroom floors were to be hand washed twice a week.

On Saturdays, there was a list of chores that included cleaning the bathroom, dusting the entire house, changing the beds, and vacuuming the carpets. If time allowed, the furniture sometimes got moved around as well.

Our home was licensed to take up to four foster children at any one time. We were a family of six, and with four additional foster children, we became a family of ten. A shortage of foster homes in the province ensured we were usually at capacity.

Not long after the sisters left, our mother received a call requesting that she take another set of siblings. This time it was two brothers, and they were much younger. She accepted the request and within days they arrived with a social worker.

Four-year-old Leonard was an adorable child with olive skin, brown eyes, and brown hair. He was quiet, shy, and seemed nervous around strangers. He didn't say much, though he was very protective of his baby brother, two-year-old Clarence, who had big blue eyes and a full head of blonde curly hair. Clarence was energetic, curious, and full of life.

Within minutes of their arrival, Clarence was running around, eagerly exploring every room in the house. Attempting to keep them occupied, Mother prepared snacks as she continued her conversation with the social worker. Leonard was content to sit and eat but as soon as he noticed his little brother having no interest in the snack, he returned to following him around the house.

"It's okay. Let him explore but keep an eye on him," she said.

I thought that Leonard following so closely behind, watching his brother's every move, was endearing. The boys were delightful, and I envisioned it being fun to have them around. Mother spoke affectionately to them and I assumed she was excited to have them as well.

That same year, Katie joined the family. Katie was born to a drug-dependent mother and as a result, she was saddled with a broad spectrum of health challenges. She had been taken away from her mother immediately after birth and placed in child protective services. We were told that her biological mother was not capable of taking care of her.

Katie weighed less than two pounds when she was born and had spent the first seven months of her life in hospital. Once she had gained sufficient weight and was strong enough to live outside an incubator, she was declared a miracle baby and placed in our care.

I refer to it as *our* care because I immediately became attached to Katie and although I was only twelve, I was caring for her full time when not in school.

Katie was born with cerebral palsy. She was fed through a tube and was blind. I enjoyed the responsibility of looking after her and caring for her special needs.

Although she couldn't speak, Katie had exceptional hearing and her own way of communicating. When I came home from school, Katie would make loud gurgling sounds to get my attention until I picked her up in my arms. If she was excited, she would kick her legs back and forth almost as if she was on a bicycle, demonstrating great strength. She used the same attention-seeking strategies for Mother and Father.

Most evenings, upon returning home from work, Father would take Katie in his arms and walk around the house until she settled down enough for him to eat dinner. Otherwise, she would continue to make her attention-seeking noises and they would get louder and more persistent until he finally gave in. Katie loved being with him, especially after he'd been away all day. It appeared he loved her too.

Katie started having seizures and with time, they became more frequent. She would be given Phenobarbital and Dilantin both in the morning and night to control them; these medications seemed to work until she outgrew the prescribed dose. The doses were based on her weight and had to be adjusted regularly.

Katie was two when Adam, a one-month-old infant, came to live with us. Clarence was now five and in kindergarten while Leonard was seven and in grade two. Adam had been given up for adoption by his birth mother and was temporarily placed in our care. Tracey was ten years old by the time Adam arrived; she immediately bonded with him and referred to him as her baby. She helped our mother dress and feed him, and she was proud to help in that sort of way.

Although there were many children in the house, noise levels were strictly controlled, and cleanliness was enforced. Everyone obeyed. Mother would only have to speak once and everyone in the room would be quiet. Mother didn't mind low-decibel chatter, but she wouldn't tolerate a volume much louder than that. Depending on her mood, some days the volume had to be kept to a whisper, or a child (usually Clarence) would end up being removed from the group and sent to lay on a bed while others continued to play. When the weather was suitable, they were sent outside to play. I no longer joined them because of my responsibility to care for Katie.

Figuratively speaking, Katie was placed on a pedestal. Both parents showered her with affection. Her special needs required a lot of attention and they were happy to deliver.

Leonard often appeared nervous and seldom took chances or did anything that might land him in trouble, while Clarence was unable to avoid it. His abundance of energy, or hyper disposition, did not diminish with age. Mother considered him a challenge and was determined to control him. The punishments became extreme and I cried every time I heard Mother beating him. I wished I could take the punishment for him.

Adam was still quite young, and given that he was Tracey's favourite, I believe he was spared from most punishments.

Mother never expressed hatred towards Clarence but showed no mercy when punishing him. His inability to avoid trouble put him in the same category as me. The only difference was that the rationale for his punishments was usually justified, at least in Mother's opinion. For me, however, she needed no reason and seemed to find pleasure in my misery.

Once, Mother's friend dropped in for a visit while Clarence was taking a bath. Leonard had already finished his bath and was in his pyjamas watching television. Mother was enjoying her cup of tea when she overheard Clarence splashing around in the water. Politely excusing herself from her company, she headed to the bathroom to help Clarence out of the tub.

Mother dried him off with a towel, then took the towel away and directed Clarence to go to the porch and put away his sneakers which he had left in the walkway. She had told him that he would receive his clean pyjamas once he'd returned from completing the task.

To get to the back porch, Clarence had to walk through the kitchen. As he walked naked past Mother's friend, he was horrified to discover that the friend's young daughter - a little girl from his school - was also sitting at the kitchen table. Clarence was humiliated when he saw the little girl looking at him as he scooted past.

Once children were toilet trained, our mother had no tolerance for accidents. While enjoying his playtime, Clarence sometimes held off going to the bathroom to extend his moments of fun. Even though he was in primary school, he still had the occasional accident. One of the many punishments Mother inflicted was spanking his bare bottom.

While playing outside one day, Clarence once again held off until it was too late. I remember him sheepishly walking in the house, both of us knowing that he would surely be punished for having another accident. Mother was furious as she grabbed him by the arm and dragged him through the kitchen and into the bathroom.

I had been sitting in the rocking chair with Katie when I heard the bathwater running. Mother came out of the bathroom for a moment and when she returned, she left the door slightly ajar.

I heard her scream at him, "GET IN THE BATHTUB!"

My stomach flipped, folded, and went in knots as I heard him bawl before his cries quickly turned to screams. This wasn't like Clarence. It sounded like he was boldly refusing to obey her.

I was nervous as I wondered why he wasn't listening to her demands. I stood and anxiously paced the length of the family room.

The screams continued over the running water. I was terrified and felt compelled to go see what was happening as her voice got louder and more demanding.

My heart pounded as I walked towards the door with Katie in my arms. Taking pause just outside its threshold, I saw Clarence standing naked in the tub struggling to get out. Mother was yelling at him as she blocked his desperate attempts to exit the tub. I suddenly felt sick to my stomach as I saw excessive steam rising from the water.

I couldn't bear to watch. I was angry at myself for not being brave enough to speak up for Clarence. I tearfully and quickly moved to a safe distance from the bathroom. I walked around the house tormented by the image of Clarence fighting to escape the burning water. My heart hurt.

When I heard Mother emerge from the bathroom, I returned to the family room to resume my position in the rocking chair with Katie. I avoided eye contact with her as she brushed past telling Clarence to wait where he was for her to come back with pyjamas. Clarence was standing naked next to the bathroom door with noticeable bright red watermarks highlighting any areas of his body that had been submerged in the scalding water.

With his wet hair slicked back and in clean pyjamas, Clarence sat with his back pressed into the sofa without saying a word.

I whispered, "Are you okay?"

His bottom lip quivered as he stared at the television screen without saying a word.

Clarence and Leonard

White Underwear

I was startled by the sound of movement in my bedroom. My eyes popped open, but I couldn't see anything in the pitch-dark room. With both hands, I slowly scrunched the comforter close to my throat. I held my breath hoping my nightgown was pulled down and that it still covered my body underneath the blankets.

I felt his presence at the bottom of my bed. I remained motionless as his hand ran the length of the mattress before grazing along the contour of my body as I lay in the fetal position. The hand briefly paused on my shoulder before a gentle shake and the whisper of my name. "Beverly. Beverly. Beverly."

I resisted any response, physical or verbal until he started to shake me and say my name louder. I desperately wanted him to leave but I knew that would not happen.

He was drunk.

Like a wild animal, focused only on his prey, he would persist until I completed the chore. With a tormented moan, I acknowledged his presence. He removed the bed covers and I quickly sat up in a silent move that denied his clear intention to get in my bed.

I hated his white underwear.

I hated his man-parts.

I hated that he exposed himself to me.

I hated touching him and I hated his hands on me.

I hated the pressure to perform his disgusting acts.

I hated my obedience.

I hated his disgusting smell... God, I hated that smell.

I always smelled it, even when he wasn't in my room. I could even smell it when he was nowhere near me.

When he left, there was only that smell. The odour sickened me. I scrubbed my hands over my nightgown and blankets compulsively. I wiped the fabric over and over until I could no longer smell his manhood and then I would bury myself under the covers, tightly holding the comforter up to my neck as a means of trapping any remnants of the stench underneath.

**

I looked forward to entering my teens and attending grade eight at Bishop O'Neill Collegiate in the fall. It was where I would experience my first year of high school and although I was nervous, after a summer at home, I couldn't wait to get back to the sanctuary of school.

Among other perks, I looked forward to not having to wear a school uniform this year. During the summer holidays, my mother had given me the newest Sears Fall/Winter catalogue and said I could pick out a couple of new outfits for school. This was the first time she had allowed me to select my own clothes. I was shocked and hoped it wouldn't be the last time.

When I was able to get breaks from Katie during her feedings and bedtime, I would take advantage of the time by going through the catalogue, trying to find styles that Mother would approve of. It took me a full week to narrow down my options. At age twelve, I thoroughly enjoyed choosing my own clothes for the first time, even if my options were restricted to Mother's judgement.

In the end, I picked a pair of aqua-coloured capri dress pants with side pockets and a matching sleeveless sweater. The sweater was ivory, dotted with small specks of aqua. It had a back scoop neck and matched the pants perfectly. I also picked out a pair of Jordache jeans and a few basic tops. I was pleased with the selections, and even more pleased when my Mother agreed to order the specific items.

The first day of school was nothing like I had imagined. The two-story building was large and had multiple classrooms for grades eight to twelve. Most of the students arrived by bus, while others were dropped off or walked. To my surprise, some were even driving themselves.

Bishop O'Neill Collegiate, or BONC, as many students called it, had divisions of junior and senior male and female teams in several sports. I liked volleyball and basketball and desperately wanted to play. Over time, I built up the courage to ask if I could try out for the school volleyball team. Mother said I could play during school, but she wouldn't allow me to participate in any after-school activities. After lunch, I'd often make my way to the gymnasium to take in the games, secretly wanting to join in.

During the first week of school, two guys approached me. "My friend thinks you are cute," one of them said.

I felt myself blush. I smiled as the shy guy nudged his wingman before they walked away, pushing and shoving each other. There were a lot of good-looking guys in the new school, and I developed a crush on two - a preppy guy from one of the other classes and the shy guy from the first week's interaction, who happened to be in the next grade. Unfortunately, I was too nervous to speak with either of them.

School jackets were available in our distinctive school colours - black with golden yellow trim. The school's name was embroidered on the front left chest and we had the option of having a name embroidered on the arm of the jacket.

We were one of the 'fortunate' families that didn't have to worry about being able to afford the jacket. Without hesitation, Mother took the order form and said she would order a size small for me. I smiled at the thought of being able to wear the same jacket as many of my fellow students. It would surely help me fit in a little better with the crowd.

Excitement diminished when the jacket arrived, and I saw my mother had specified "Beverly" to be embroidered on the sleeve for my name. My friends called me Bev and, although I was grateful for the jacket, I wished she had considered using "Bev" or had just omitted the embroidered name altogether. I usually only heard my full name at home and didn't want to encourage other students, or friends, to call me by that name.

It wasn't until high school that I realized just how different my life really was. I heard friends as they talked about the hours they spent on the telephone, hung out at each other's houses, and stayed up late to watch movies. I wasn't allowed to do any of those things.

When my friends talked about their weekend activities, I said I had to babysit. I loved caring for Katie, but I certainly would have preferred to hang out with friends. The more I hung out with friends at school, the more I resented my lack of freedom at home.

After wearing the Jordache jeans only a couple of times, Mother took them back, claiming they were too tight. I tried to explain that this was the style and that all the girls wore skinny jeans to school, but she wasn't interested. "I don't care what all the other girls wear, you won't be wearing them." She firmly announced.

I desperately wanted to fit in. So much so that I took a needle and thread and hand-sewed the inside seams of another pair of jeans to make them a little more fitted in the legs. I only wore the jeans to school and not around the house, in hopes Mother wouldn't notice.

The Jordache jeans sat for weeks on top of a basket of clothes in my parent's bedroom. One Friday night when Mother permitted me to go out, I crept into her bedroom and grabbed them. I put the Jordache jeans on and another looser pair over them. Once safely outside, I got rid of the decoy jeans.

I checked the windows and door to be sure Mother wasn't watching before tucking the loose jeans in the back of Father's truck. The risk of getting caught made my nerves rush but wearing the same style of jeans as all the other high school girls made me feel a little more normal – even if it was just an illusion.

I headed to the local snack bar for a couple of hours, keeping a close eye on the time. I couldn't be late, and I had to make sure I had time to jump into the loose jeans before going inside. Thankfully, I was able to grab the pants from the truck and slip inside without Mother noticing.

Father loved women and didn't try to hide his attraction to the women on TV. He was usually sprawled out on the sofa after dinner, as I sat with Katie in another chair. He would sling sexist remarks at many of the women that graced the screen and laughed anytime I frowned or expressed a disapproving look.

I became immune to the crude comments but was bothered by certain remarks. "How's your cunny?" He'd sometimes ask. I despised hearing that word. Whenever I was in the truck with him, I would notice him straining his neck to watch women walking on the street. Once we passed by, he would continue watching them through the rearview mirror, talking about her "ass" or "breasts." My well-intended suggestion that he shouldn't say such things only made him laugh dismissively.

Despite the chaos and constant fighting in our house, Father was typically happy. I sometimes wondered how he managed to smile when our house was such an unhappy place. Mother usually called him an alcoholic and she was right, but I couldn't help but wonder if the drinking was his escape. Maybe he spent the sober time laughing and joking to compensate for the excessive drinking.

Mother's mood could nosedive at the drop of a hat. Trying to cheer her up was never easy, but Father tried, nonetheless. In his own silly way, he tried to bring levity to situations. I felt sorry for him when Mother refused to acknowledge or appreciate his efforts.

On another Friday evening, Mother was out for a drive with her sister, while Father worked late. I watched TV with the smaller children and took care of Katie. When Mother got home, she was annoyed that Father was still out. Her voice blared throughout the house as she accused him of being out drinking again. She was probably right. Normally, when he was late, it was because he was drinking with his work buddies.

The smaller kids were immediately sent to bed. When his truck finally pulled into the driveway about thirty minutes later, Mother bolted to the kitchen and waited for him to walk through the door. She was furious when her assumptions were confirmed –he had been drinking. To make matters worse, he drove home.

It always amazed me how he was even capable of driving home drunk because once he was inside the house, his feet could barely navigate through the space. Mother's words fell on deaf ears, as they always did. There was no point in talking to him when he was drunk. It was a complete waste of time.

Father took a seat at the kitchen table while Mother stood next to the woodstove with her hands on her hips. The cast iron wood stove had two heavy round burners on top with a steel handle for lifting them. Without hesitation, she grabbed the steel handle and launched it directly at Father.

I had never seen my mother show any sign of remorse or regret for anything she did or said before. On this occasion though, she immediately felt the implications of her action as Father fell to the floor with blood spilling out over his face, staining his clothes.

"Oh my God, I've killed him," Mother shouted. I could hear the fear in her voice as she rushed to the bathroom and returned with towels. Cradling Katie in my arms, I watched from the hallway as she knelt on the floor and began wiping blood from his face.

Father was conscious and moaning in pain as blood continued to pour from his body. While crying, Mother cleared away enough blood to see that the cast iron had struck him on the bridge of his nose.

He bled profusely, probably because of the alcohol coursing through his veins, thinning his blood. Panicked, Mother left him on the floor and grabbed the telephone to call her sister. Aunt Carol didn't drive but lived close enough that she could walk to our house in five minutes. "I've done the job on him Carol, come quick! He's bleeding to death," Mother confessed.

Within minutes, Aunt Carol barreled into the house and in a calm, firm voice she took control of the situation. She directed Mother to get cold cloths as she rushed to Father's side on the kitchen floor. Holding his head up and cradling it in her lap, she applied pressure to the wound. In a soothing voice, she reassured him that he would be okay.

I was sad when I heard Mother crying. She didn't apologize, but I knew she felt bad for what she had done. Aunt Carol tended to Father and did what she could to calm Mother. When the bleeding finally stopped and Aunt Carol confirmed there was nothing to worry about, I felt relief. Although still visibly upset, Mother's tone changed as she explained to my father that it was his fault this happened.

Although I loved school, I was envious of the other students' seemingly normal lives. The attacks continued at home and my resentment toward Mother was building. I was becoming more confident in standing up to her. Not physically, of course –that was far too dangerous. But mentally, I was learning how to push back.

One Sunday, I was sitting on the armrest of one of the sofas while Mother scurried around preparing to take Katie out for an afternoon drive with Father. I was waiting patiently for them to leave, looking forward to a peaceful afternoon. Without notice, Mother swatted me across the leg with a large paddle hairbrush.

"Don't sit there. Armrests are not made for sitting on," she complained.

The plastic handle of the brush snapped into two pieces. I jumped to my feet as she began viciously hitting me with the broken handle and yelling that it was my fault that the brush was broken.

She determined that the handle wasn't inflicting adequate pain, so she threw it on the floor and continued the assault by slapping me with an open hand. With each smack, there was more force in her hand as she repeatedly struck my face, the side of my head and shoulder. I tried blocking her swings with my forearm though it offered little protection.

Taking a firm mental stand, I refused to give in and let her see me cry. Not this time, I told myself, as I blocked any sign of emotion. Mother's irritation intensified. As my father walked in, he asked, "Leave her alone, won't you?" She told him it didn't concern him and to mind his own business. Father turned and abandoned his meagre effort to help me as she took another swipe at my face.

I refused to give in. Maybe she felt my will, the sheer determination to be stronger and not allow tears into my eyes. She stopped and looked at me with contempt before she walked away. "God damn the day you came here wrapped in a pink blanket," she said, taking one last emotional stab.

Although she never said it, I believe she noticed my improved mental resistance. I wasn't immune to her just yet, but I was getting better at inwardly blocking the physical pain she inflicted. The next day, standing face to face with Mother in the family room, she confronted me about an incomplete homework assignment. "I didn't have enough time to finish it, you sent me to bed early," I daringly reminded her.

Through clenched teeth, she formed a fist and without saying a word, it launched directly into the pit of my stomach. The pain was intense, and it felt like an explosion within my core. I instantly folded over while gasping for air. Mother yelled, "Get up! Get up!"

I couldn't get up. I couldn't breathe. With both hands, I firmly clasped my legs for support. Her screams echoed above my head as I repeatedly gasped for air. I was red-faced when I was finally able to stand upright and breathe again. Mother showed no reaction at the sight of my tear-stained cheeks. She simply turned and walked away. I made my way to the armchair and cradled my stomach.

In high school, I had gained some freedom. Mother now allowed me to go out on Friday or Saturday night –although rarely both. Additionally, I was able to go out on Sunday afternoons when my parents took Katie out for an afternoon drive, provided there were no chores or homework to do.

By the time I had reached 14, I was allowed to walk to Poole's Snack Bar to hang out with my cousin (Aunt Carol's daughter) and her friends. There was a pool table there, as well as a jukebox and a couple of pinball machines. Georgetown had a lot of summer cabins which meant the snack bar was busiest from late May to early September.

My cousin was free to go out after school and on weekends, I assume that's why she had so many friends. She also befriended many of the cabin owners in the area. So anytime we got to hang out, I was able to meet some of those folks.

On weeknights, Aunt Carol routinely visited our house, sometimes to chat over a cup of tea. Some nights she and Mother would go visit friends, go shopping, or simply just drive around.

During summer nights, I regularly seized the opportunity to ask Aunt Carol where her daughter was, already knowing she was likely out with her friends. I always asked strategically within earshot of Mother, hoping Aunt Carol's answer would motivate her to let me go out too.

Sometimes she would say, "If you are going out, go - but, be back in this house at 10 p.m. and that's not five after ten." Other times she would say, "Well you need not think you're going anywhere," totally dismissing my clear desire to be a normal teenager and hang out with my friends.

In our small community, there was very little for teenagers to do. We spent time at the local hangouts or went to the weekly teenage dance in Marysvale, the neighbouring community.

By the time I was 15, I would yearn to attend the teenage dances or to hang out at Ryan's Convenience (also a snack bar) with friends from school. Although I was permitted to go out on occasion, Mother's preference was to have me stay home and take care of Katie most of the time.

I really did love Katie and didn't mind the responsibility, but I also wanted a social life like every other teenager I knew. I socialized with friends as much as I could during the weekdays at school. One day, during a conversation with a couple of girls in the washroom, one asked me about being adopted. I interrupted her and said, "I have no idea what you are talking about." "You should, you were adopted," she replied.

I was shocked, but suddenly things started to become clear. My entire life, Mother had treated me differently than the other kids. She hated me and never tried to hide it. It all made sense to me now. When Mother referenced me as "someone else's dirt," she wasn't referring to Father. At home later that day, I boldly stated "Someone in school told me I was adopted." Mother's response was sharp, "So what if you are?"

April, who was ironing clothes at the time, spoke up, "But, you're not." Disregarding April entirely, Mother repeated herself, "Well, so what if you are? It's not like it changes anything. Does it?" Feeling confronted, I backed off. "I guess not," I said quietly. I sheepishly retreated as a voice in my head screamed "It does change things. It changes everything!"

What's in the cat, is in the kitten. Someone else's dirt. A lifetime of Mother's negative comments now replayed over and over in my head.

I was obviously someone else's child. Somehow, Mother ended up with me and she had been burdened with raising me when clearly, she didn't want to. How had I not figured this out? I had never felt a connection to my parents, and I was very different from my siblings.

From the time I was a young child, I had convinced myself that there must have been a mix-up in the hospital at birth and I was mistakenly taken home by the wrong family. For years I had prayed for my real parents to realize the mix-up and search for me.

My feelings were finally confirmed, I was not part of this family. I should have been happy, but surprisingly, I was heartbroken. Feeling even more like an outsider, the words "someone else's dirt" ate away at my soul. I felt like my life was over.

Life changed after I found out I was adopted. I was lonely and desperate. I thought about ending my life. One evening, when Mother was out, the kids were in bed, and Father was asleep on the sofa, I locked myself in the bathroom, shutting the world out. Looking at myself in the medicine cabinet mirror above the small pedestal sink, I watched as tears spilled from my eyes and trickled down over my cheeks.

While silently sobbing, I reflected upon what I felt was a pathetic life –A life that was not my own. With only two years of high school remaining, I worried about what my future held. My friends talked about college and university— options that likely wouldn't exist for me. I was sure I'd be promoted to Katie's full-time caretaker once high school ended. I didn't foresee much of a life outside the confines of the Moore home.

I thought about running away. I considered running into the forest as fast as I could. In this scenario, I would keep running as long as I could before stopping to catch my breath. By then, I'd be far from the house. But I snapped back to reality when I thought about being in the woods alone in the dark. And what would happen when I was found? What would Mother do to me?

I needed a way out and concluded that ending my life was the only option. There were plenty of medications in our house, so I imagined using them to escape. That might be an easy way to go, I thought to myself. But then I worried about what would happen if the overdose didn't work? I thought about the sharp edges of soda cans we had lying around the house. Maybe that would work, I thought.

A marketing stunt from a local soft drink company prompted consumers to cut open cans to reveal a letter at the bottom. We had been collecting the letters in hopes of spelling out a word and winning the contest. The cutouts had jagged edges, and some were so sharp I imagined they could easily slice through the skin.

I looked down at the pale pink and green checkered tiles on the bathroom floor and imagined them covered in blood. The window faced our back driveway and Father's garage. I glanced out through the white lace curtains. There was no one in sight.

My hands trembled as I rested the serrated edge of the soda can cut-out on the bare skin of my wrist. Slowly applying pressure, I imagined pulling it along the track of my veins, tearing layers of flesh and severing the artery so that life would drain from my body.

I was only fifteen at that time, yet I felt as though I had lived forever. My life was worthless. Other than a few superficial relationships at school, I was alone. I was nobody's best friend; I wouldn't be remembered by any of the sports teams or clubs. Most of my relatives didn't even know me. If anyone remembered me at all, it would be as "that girl" from Georgetown, "the one who died by suicide."

I purposely ignored the knots gathering in my stomach as I rested the blade on the underside of my wrist. I looked for the courage to apply pressure and forcefully yank the sharp aluminum towards the floor. If done properly, one good rip would do the job.

My shaking hands slowed me down. Mentally, I believed I had prepared myself for this, but physically my hands were not cooperating. I looked around the room, maybe an unconscious way of buying more time. This room, like all the others in the house, was full of dreadful and unpleasant memories. If these walls could talk, I believe they would likely ask to be destroyed.

As I sat on a built-in seat next to the foot of the bathtub, I remembered being bathed as a small child. I could still feel Mother's sharp fingernails digging under the surface of my scalp as she lathered shampoo. I felt the sting from the shampoo in my eyes as if it were happening now, and I remembered her asking if I wanted a reason to cry. I thought about Tracey's happy bath time experiences and dwelled on how unfair my childhood had been.

I remembered the time Tracey had tried to shave her legs in the bathtub using Father's razor. She ran the blade up the front of her leg, cutting into the flesh and removing about three inches of skin from her shin. She was eight at the time and cried hysterically as blood pooled in the bathtub.

I wasn't in the room, but somehow it was my fault. Mother beat me badly for that. My mind wandered and I shifted my weight to sit more comfortably, pulling my legs into my chest, hugging myself for comfort.

Once again, I positioned the blade on my wrist and applied pressure. The sharp metal cut into my skin, though it was more of a graze than a slash. I continued to push the blade against my skin, but now the motion was more of a rocking back and forth as I hoped the blade would cut through on its own. I was scared.

Feeling defeated, I threw the blade into the sink. I was disappointed I couldn't finish the job. I had the chance to end my misery and squandered it.

Suddenly I heard the sound of Mother's voice as she entered the house. I quickly dried my eyes then brushed my teeth in an attempt to buy a little time as the flushed colour left my cheeks. I hoped Mother wouldn't notice my sombre mood. "Take that face off you before I do it for you," she would usually say when I appeared sad. I didn't know how to adjust my expression, so I usually just sucked in my lips or pulled them to one side of my mouth until her attention shifted away from me.

With a deep breath, I unlocked and opened the bathroom door. Another deep breath as I stepped forward - back into my pathetic world.

Mother's punishments and threats continued to escalate. One day, not long after the suicide attempt, she placed a knife to my throat and threatened to take my life. Part of me wanted her to just do it and get it over with. I stood frozen with my heart pounding as I waited for her to lower the knife, signalling the threat was over, at least for now.

The third time Mother threatened me with a knife, she held it to my face rather than my throat. I held my body rigid and mentally dared her to just go ahead and kill me. I internally challenged her:

"Go for it!" When it was over, I commended myself for being brave.

Father was already in bed when Mother ordered me to change Katie's diaper and get her dressed for bed. I followed the instructions and put Katie in a long-sleeved nightgown and carried her into their bedroom.

In the bedroom, Father had his arm under the blankets and was shaking his leg. Although I was 15, I was naïve, and I didn't know what was happening. I had seen him do this before and assumed he was vigorously rubbing his groin or upper leg. With a slight movement of his head and no spoken words, he gestured for me to go ahead and place Katie in bed next to him.

When Katie first moved in with us, she slept in her crib. As her seizures became more frequent, Mother decided it was safer to have her sleep in their bed. This way, Mother would wake if Katie seized during the night.

Like always, I did what I was told. I had not told anyone about Fathers nighttime visits to my bedroom, although they had been happening my entire life and I knew they were wrong. To get through, I would remind myself that he only visited when he was drinking and because he never seemed to remember the events when he was sober, I wondered if he even knew it happened at all.

I believed he had two distinct personalities - one when he drank, and another when he was sober. Given that no one else knew about it, I was the only one that could stop it. I was the one who had to stand up to him for this nightmare to end.

At 15 years of age, I was ashamed of myself for allowing him to continue to sexually violate my body for as long as I could remember. "It was over," I told myself.

I was only lightly sleeping when I felt the presence of him entering my bedroom. My heart raced as my eyes opened to the darkness. As per the norm, my comforter had been tightly clenched by both hands under my chin while I slept. Without breathing or moving, I waited in silence.

His hand landed on my shoulder and he began to shake me as he whispered my name. I dared not reply. He continued to shake harder, repeating my name. I held on tight refusing to acknowledge his presence. The shaking went on for what felt like an eternity. Finally, he gave up and I listened as he walked away.

What a relief! I was happy I avoided the assault this time, but I knew he'd be back. I committed to do the same thing the next time - and every time - until he stopped entering my bedroom at night.

On the following Friday evening, Mother gave me permission to go out for a couple of hours. She warned that I should behave myself because she always found out what I did. As I got dressed to

go out, her words resonated in my head.
	"I find out everything."
	Everything? I wondered...

Age 16

Runaway

During my senior year of high school, my friends were consumed with princess-style graduation dresses, hairdos, and dates. For many of my friends, the biggest concern was showing up at graduation wearing the same dress as another classmate. I, however, had much bigger things to worry about.

As I slowly rocked back and forth in the wooden rocking chair, I stared out our family room window. As usual, the TV was on, though I had no interest in watching it. Katie was already in her nightgown and ready for bed.

She was laying in my arms and stretched out across my lap, peacefully drifting off to sleep. Her long blonde hair was draped over my forearm and swayed back and forth with the rocking motion of the chair.

Katie was six years old now. She was tall for her age and although her body was slight, she was getting heavier all the time. At home, I spent most of my time walking around with her in my arms because she liked to be moving. Sometimes we'd just sit together in the rocking chair continuously swaying back and forth.

I didn't mind spending time with her. Being blind, I imagined her world would be quite lonely without constant auditory stimulation. Katie had blue eyes and pale skin. I affectionately called her "my girl" and I was flattered when I heard her gurgling sounds to win my attention whenever I walked in after school. Her eyes followed sound; for anyone who didn't know her, they could be easily fooled into thinking she could see.

I was dressing, changing diapers, and caring for Katie before I was twelve and by the time I reached fifteen, I was confidently feeding her through a feeding tube. This included checking the tube with a stethoscope before each feeding to ensure the tube was in the correct position leading into her stomach. I administered her medications, knew how to care for her when she had seizures, and regularly helped her with her daily exercises, as prescribed by her physiotherapist.

The feeding tube was inserted through her nose and ran all the way down into her stomach. Two pieces of medical tape secured it in place, on her nose and cheek. The fastened tape ensured the tube stayed in the correct position as it carried liquid nourishment and medications from a syringe directly into her stomach.

Seizures weren't the scariest moments when taking care of Katie. I knew what to do to protect her, but I was more alarmed when she pulled out her feeding tube. To pacify herself, Katie usually sucked on her thumb and pointer finger. Often when a finger slipped underneath the tube, she would, in a body-jerking motion, yank and pull out the feeding tube. That was especially unnerving, and it happened quite often.

If it happened when Mother wasn't home, I'd quickly get the stethoscope and put the tube back in place before she returned. I'd start by measuring the amount of tubing needed to go down the length of her torso from her nostril; I had watched or held Katie during this process so many times that I knew exactly what to do.

Similar to using a measuring tape, I started by aligning the tip of the feeding tube with the edge of her nose. Then I stretched out just enough to reach the middle of her cheek. From there, I pivoted the tubing to change direction and measured the length required to cover the remaining distance to a predetermined spot in her stomach.

With my fingers, I firmly pinched the exact measured length on the tube, then I would loop a piece of medical tape around that spot to represent the distance needed to go inside her body.

As I gently inserted the tube into Katie's nostril, it was evident that this was an unpleasant experience for her, and understandably so. The tube was forced past the back of her throat and down the esophagus until it reached its final position in her stomach. I continued to guide the tube inside until the piece of white tape reached the edge of her nose.

The looped tape was then fastened to the bridge of her nose, securing it in place. A second piece of medical tape attached the tube to Katie's cheek and added extra protection as it kept the tube securely in place.

I performed this procedure numerous times and fortunately for both of us, I was good at getting it back in the correct position without issue.

Katie was such a special child and very much loved. Her pictures were proudly displayed throughout the house. Mother showered her with toys and gifts, and she had a closet full of beautiful clothes. Her crib was full of expensive toys, including a $200 talking doll named Cricket. Cricket was the rage, and Mother was determined to ensure Katie had one for Christmas that year.

Cricket sat in the crib with other dolls, musical toys, and stuffed animals. All were in perfectly new condition. Sadly, the toys were never played with because of Katie's disabilities and because they were her toys, they were not to be used by the other children. The toys remained unused and pristine in Katie's crib.

Because Katie slept between Mother and Father every night, the crib was also preserved in its original condition. I usually took care of Katie after school and in the evenings, until Father was in bed himself. Then, I would wait for Mother to tell me when to put Katie in bed with him.

Our house was always spotless. April was obsessed with keeping it in perfect order. She seemed to be Mother's right-hand woman and although she had the freedom to do whatever she chose, April opted to spend hours cleaning. I wasn't sure if it was her way of being distracted from the family drama, or if she just preferred to keep a clean house.

Although most of my time was dedicated to caring for Katie, I did have a handful of chores. Washing the kitchen and bathroom floors every Wednesday evening and Saturday was my job. It was a time-consuming chore because I wasn't allowed to use a mop. Instead, I had to scrub the floors on my hands and knees with a washcloth and a bucket of soapy water. Mother believed a mop only partially cleaned the floors, and her standards had to be upheld.

We had a large kitchen, and it was swept three times a day, after every meal. Being left-handed, I held the broom differently and Mother seized yet another opportunity to bully me about it. "You don't have sense to sweep the floor; you look like a cat covering shit," she ridiculed.

Mother was well respected in the community and within the Department of Social Services for her many years as a dedicated foster parent. The children in her care were clean and nicely dressed - just the same as her own kids.

Visiting social workers were always suitably impressed with the cleanliness – the "eat off the floor" standards, the well-behaved children lazing about, and the walls that looked more like a shrine that proudly displayed the most recent school photos of each child.

Ms. Rose, a social worker who visited regularly, seemed to be impressed each time she came to our house. She would repeatedly offer Mother praise, "Mrs. Moore, you are so good to the children. You know, there is a place reserved in heaven for you." All of this happened as my foster siblings and I sat on the sofa with our eyes glued to the television set, too afraid to speak.

Perception was of the highest importance to Mother. People

saw her as friendly, compassionate, and easygoing. I wished she could be that person at home.

I spent most evenings with Katie as she lay resting in my arms. One particular evening, I apparently looked sad, though I had no idea why tonight's sad face was any different than last night's sad face, or last month's for that matter. Father read something into my look as he towered in the hallway calling out to Mother to come and have a look at me.

She walked past him into the family room, obviously begrudging the interruption. "What's wrong with you?" She asked as she impatiently stood in front of me with her hands on her hips, waiting for me to respond.

"Nothing," I said. "I am tired."

She snorted a sound without opening her mouth. "Well, take that face off ya, before I does it for you," she said.

Father pressed his concern though. "Something's wrong - I can see it in her face."

After a lengthy pause, his gaze flipped from Mother back to me. "Not pregnant are ya?"

My eyes widened with surprise as I wondered where that comment came from.

I uncomfortably replied, "No!"

"Well, something's going on," he said and walked away.

I was seventeen and I was dating a 22-year-old guy. I suppose the five-year age difference may have caused Father some worry. His name was Joey and we met at one of those Marysvale teenage dances. I was fifteen and he was twenty. Joey had been hanging out at the Town Hall entrance. I couldn't tell if he was actually working or just helping out with the community dances.

He was friendly and had a sense of humour. I was nervous, naïve, and desperate to fit in. It didn't take long for my parents to find out I was dating an older guy and they were quick to vocalize their thoughts. In typical fashion, Father asked inappropriate questions like, "Is Joey getting lucky tonight?" or "How does he touch you?"

Mother threatened, "If I ever catch you with Joey Martin or in his car, he won't have to worry about you again." His car was sporty and distinctive and any time he drove it past our house on the main road, Mother would chide, "What a pile of dirt." Their disapproval only pushed me further away from home and closer to my boyfriend.

Joey seemed to understand the dysfunctional nature of my family and he never pressured me on the lack of freedom or limited social time I was afforded. His understanding probably stemmed from his past circumstances. As a child, Joey had lost his father in a tragic accident. That led to Joey, along with most of his siblings, spending time in foster care.

Joey's experience was not pleasant. His foster mother wasn't nice to him. She treated Joey and his foster siblings differently than her biological children. Perhaps this is why he understood my home life. At some point, he returned to the community and moved in with his grandfather.

Joey was about an inch taller than me. He had dark straight hair, a mustache, and freckles. He usually wore jeans and his signature black leather jacket. Having my first real boyfriend made life much more exciting and dangerous at the same time.

I wasn't allowed to talk on the telephone, so I would wait until everyone in the house had gone to bed before sneaking to the family room to call Joey. I would sit in the dark whispering, and also listening for the sound of footsteps. Although I was scared, I risked getting caught so I could talk to Joey on the phone.

Joey didn't have to worry about curfews. Some nights he would go out with friends and then call my house once he'd returned home. He would call and let the phone ring only a half ring and then hang up. This was our signal – it meant he was now home, sitting by the telephone. Otherwise, I wouldn't call out of concern that I might wake his family members.

During my senior year, I was sometimes permitted to go out on the weekends once Katie had gone to bed, which was usually between 8:30 p.m. and 9 p.m. There was no guarantee I would be allowed out, but once I finished taking care of Katie for the evening, I would wait and hope for the best.

I was never brave enough to directly ask permission, but while watching the clock, I would walk past Mother as she talked on the telephone. This was my way of getting her attention and usually an answer. Approval was dependent on the weather and more importantly, Mother's mood. Once she saw me walk past, she would give one of her usual two comments, "If you are going out, go, but be back in this house by 11 p.m. and that's not five after eleven." Other times she would crush my hopes by telling me, "You won't be going anywhere tonight."

Sometimes she allowed me to stay out later while attending the teenage dance, however since Joey came along, Mother became strict about the 11 p.m. curfew. My friends were allowed to stay out later than me and I found this embarrassing, but I wouldn't dare ask for a later curfew. Now that I had a boyfriend, I wasn't interested in teenage dances. They weren't really Joey's thing either.

Joey pressured me about sex. I figured it was normal, considering his age. He talked about it being safe and said he always had a condom in his pocket. My innocence was evident when the subject of condoms was raised. I knew they had something to do with sex, though I had never seen one or even knew how to use it. I prolonged it for as long as possible, but when he talked about moving on to date other people, I gave in. I yearned for affection of some kind – any kind.

I wasn't sure if Mother actually thought I was pregnant or if she thought something else might be wrong. Nevertheless, she went ahead and scheduled an appointment for me to see Dr. Power, our family doctor.

Dr. Power was tall, thin, and soft-spoken. He was young, early to mid-thirties, I estimated, but he had been our family doctor long enough to know how to handle Mother. At the start of our visit, he asked, "What brings you here today, Mrs. Moore?" In her natural state of irritation, she fired back, "I think this one's pregnant."

I believe Dr. Power saw the fear in my eyes and asked to examine me privately. Mother remained seated as I followed him into an adjoining examination area, and as per his request, I hopped up on the table. I laid down and he pulled up my shirt to examine my barely noticeable belly.

He quietly whispered, "You are pregnant, aren't you?" I nodded my head in confirmation. His tightly pressed lips and half-smile comforted me as he signalled his recognition of my fear.

I had learned about the pregnancy a few weeks earlier after Joey had gotten me in to see his family doctor on a Sunday afternoon, outside regular clinic hours. I had been consistently nauseous, and I suspected this was why. Once the doctor confirmed my suspicions, I hid the sickness from my mother, worried about how she would react.

Dr. Power motioned for me to follow him back into his office where Mother was waiting. "We're going to need blood work. Someone from my office will call when the results come in," he explained to Mother as he settled down into his leather chair. Mother was satisfied with that. She watched as he wrote out the requisition and then directed me to exit the office in front of her. Now she had a mission. Blood work would be done immediately; we headed directly towards the nearest hospital in Carbonear.

On the drive home, Mother informed me that I was not allowed to see Joey anymore and I was not to go to school or leave the house until the test results came back. Then, depending on those results, she would deal with me accordingly.

Several days passed and during my confinement to the house I took care of Katie around the clock. I managed to keep Joey updated through our late-night phone calls. I was absolutely terrified. I knew

I was pregnant, and I worried helplessly about what Mother would do once this fact was revealed. Joey was also worried and encouraged me to leave the house. He had never met Mother and had no idea what I was up against. I couldn't simply walk out. Besides, where would I even go? Where would I live? What would I do with a child?

The day the phone call came was not a good one. The clinic confirmed the pregnancy and before Mother even had time to process the news and react, she noticed a woman walking up our driveway. It was Mrs. Manning, Mother's least favourite social worker from the Bay Robert's office. Social workers normally called ahead with advance notice of home visits, but clearly, this check-in was not scheduled, or welcomed, by Mother.

"Get in your room and do not come out until I tell you to," she ordered.

Horrified, I desperately needed to know what was going on. Mother was already angry, but the visit pushed her over the edge. Why was Mrs. Manning here? Why now? Did it have anything to do with the phone call from Dr. Power's office? I had to know. I strained to hear the conversation between the women from my slightly ajar bedroom door.

Minutes later, the conversation was over. Mrs. Manning left the house, and Mother was now enraged as she screamed, "Beverly! Get the fuck out here." Her commanding voice, even after all my years there, still forced a lump in my throat and a thick knot in my stomach.

Not wanting to keep her waiting, I hurried out to where she was standing in the family room. April and Tracey were also in the room wondering what was going on. I stopped in my tracks, standing just outside Mother's reach - an old habit. If I kept enough space, I could at least see a fist or arm swipe before it hit me.

"Yes?" I asked, in a panic-stricken voice.

"Mrs. Manning wanted to know why you're not in school," she said with a sarcastic undertone.

Without warning, she barged toward me and before I had time to react, my hair was tangled in her fingers and my body yanked to the floor.

Once I hit the floor, I was usually quick to crawl away or at least create distance to allow myself time to get back on my feet, but not today. Mother was livid and her speed only proved it. "I told Mrs. Manning it was none of her concern," she snapped, as she kicked me repetitively.

Turning to my side in the fetal position, I quickly pulled my arms and legs inward to cover and protect myself.

65

"You slut! You are nothing but a whore!" she yelled.

My body twitched with the impact of every kick.

The kicks came fast and furious and April tried to intervene.

"Mom! Let her go, you are going to hurt her!"

"Hurt her? I will do more than hurt her," she said as she punched me first in the ribs, and then she hit me in the back of the head.

"Mom, she's pregnant!" April exclaimed. I could hear the concern in her voice.

"Pregnant?! The likes of that coming home pregnant. I hope you experience the worst labour; I hope you have forty-eight hours of labour. The likes of you with a baby. I hope the baby is born with two heads!"

At this point, Mother was panting, obviously overexerting herself.

Tracey, my thirteen-year-old sister, stood backed into a wall with her hands tightly clasped over her face covering all but her eyes. She watched with horror, too scared to say a word. Tears streamed from her eyes.

Determined to hurt, if not kill me, Mother paused briefly to catch her breath before the kicks resumed with even greater intensity.

April's voice had found authority and was now raised, "Mom, you are going to get in trouble."

Mother finally stopped and stepped back. She turned and walked away.

"She's not worth the trouble," she mumbled.

I released the tension from my tightly wrapped extremities. My entire body throbbed.

The following days were difficult. Every part of my body hurt. Mother instructed me to now sleep with April. I had no idea why, but I certainly wasn't about to complain. April had a large bed in the biggest and nicest room in the house.

Up until now, April and I had not had a close relationship. She was the oldest biological child, four years senior to me, and she was the second in command when Mother wasn't home. April actually seemed better at being a parent than a sibling. A couple of days after the attack, April came home with a tray of sweets for me as a means of trying to improve my mood.

Mother had calmed down somewhat, but she still showed no mercy. She wailed threats at me, anything she knew would hurt. She threatened to make me abort the pregnancy, she threatened to send me away, and she threatened to put the baby up for adoption. I was not doing well, emotionally or physically.

Three months into the pregnancy, I had gained about three pounds. I was pale, exhausted all the time, and looked like death. No matter how hard I tried, I could not get past Mother's threats of forced abortion or adoption. I knew first-hand what could happen to an innocent child if placed in the wrong home. I was tortured my entire life and I feared the same fate for my unborn child. It became clear to me that I had to escape. I had to get out of this house, and I had to do it as soon as possible.

I spoke with Tracey and enlisted her help in my escape. "I have to do this," I explained. "I have to protect the baby and I cannot do that here." After witnessing the latest brutal beating, she knew I was right, and she agreed to help.

April was out with her boyfriend and the rest of the family was in bed. Tracey and I rehearsed one last time. Like a scene from a movie, I stuffed towels on my side of the bed under April's quilt to simulate the shape of a body. Tracey stood guard in the family room as I ran to my bedroom and bundled up in layers, with a warm winter jacket over the top.

I couldn't leave through the door; it would surely wake them up. As quietly as possible, I slowly opened a bedroom window. The bitter February wind took my breath away and made my body shudder. Carefully, I pulled myself up onto the dresser where I paused to listen for any sound from within the house. There was only silence.

I took one last look around the room, held my breath, and nervously jumped out of the ground-level window into the garden. As I turned to close the window, I felt the heaviness of the glass. From this angle, the window was much more awkward to manipulate, and it didn't slide quite as smoothly.

My heart pounded at the thought of lights turning on inside and me getting caught outside. I considered leaving the window open, but the frigid winter night would fill the house with cold air in short order.

Tugging with all my strength, the sliding window gave way, but slowly and only a third of the distance. Now, I was scared. With all the effort I could muster, and every bit of determination left inside of me, I pushed and pulled until the window finally slid the rest of the way.

I breathed a sigh of relief and ran to the front of the house and down the driveway. I ran for a minute or two before I stopped to look back. Tracey was in the window watching me. She looked sad. I forced a smile and waved to her one last time before turning to take flight, disappearing into the dark, cold night.

Teen Mom

I was relieved to be out of the house, but at the same time anxious, nervous, and scared about the future. I had run away from home. Mother would find out in the morning, if not before and she would be livid. The embarrassment of people knowing that I ran away would only fuel her rage.

Once I got out of the house and made it down the street, Joey was there waiting for me in his car, as we'd discussed. We didn't take the time to develop a plan beyond the getaway. I could not risk another day in that house. Mother was dangerous and unpredictable.

Without options, I felt completely helpless. Joey knew that was the case too, and he intuitively offered reassurances as he drove me to his sister's house in Colliers, another small community located less than ten kilometres from Georgetown.

Cathy and her husband lived with their two children in a three-bedroom bungalow on a quiet street. Despite our unexpected late-night arrival, we were welcomed and made to feel at home.

The house was located off the main road and I felt a little better once I noticed their driveway extended to the back of the house. That meant that Joey's car could be hidden from view and I would be safe, at least for that night.

I presumed Joey would have forewarned his sister about my situation, or at the very least, he would have asked for permission before he brought me there. I was visibly shaking and quite fatigued with worry about what Mother would do once she discovered my empty bed. I imagined her driving through the community with ferocious determination to find me, or Joey's car.

Cathy did her best to comfort me.

"Bev, you're out of there now, you are safe. They can't make you go back, and they won't hurt you again."

I folded my arms tightly and leaned back against the kitchen counter, quietly nodding my head. My apologies for the late-night disruption were hushed as Cathy showed me to her daughter's bedroom where there was an empty bed.

"This is not an inconvenience," she insisted; "Now get some rest and we can talk in the morning."

Cathy closed the bedroom door behind her on the way out. Sleep didn't come easy though I did my best to relax, if not for myself then for the baby's sake. The room was dark with minimal light that seeped in through the window. When my eyes adjusted to the darkness, I was able to see the room layout, and most importantly, I could see the door.

My mind was incapable of blocking thoughts of Mother. With my hands cradling my belly, I acknowledged that I was okay, and most importantly, my baby was safe.

Early the next morning, I heard a vehicle speeding around to the back of Cathy's house. I was sitting in her family room when I heard Joey announce that it was a Chevy pickup and that my father was behind the wheel.

On high alert, I hopped to my feet and ran into Cathy's bedroom in a state of terror.

As I ran past the kitchen, I heard Joey and Cathy's husband debate over who should answer the door. Meanwhile, in the master bedroom, I climbed into the closet and swiftly closed the folding doors behind me. I stood in the dark closet with clothes dangling on hangers all around me. With my hands clasped together and pushed over my mouth, I held my breath.

I struggled to remain silent as the lump in my throat swelled. If he got into the house, he would surely start searching for me, and it would only be a matter of time until he made his way to the bedroom.

I was terrified at the thought of anyone opening the closet door to expose the sanctity of my hiding spot. I feared being told I had no choice but to leave with Father. Visions of Mother beating me to death flooded into my head as I remembered the pregnancy beating. I imagined her anger had intensified now.

Although I could hear voices, I wasn't able to make out what was being said and was far too afraid to even crack the closet door open. With my hands fastened to the sides of my neck, I crouched down to an upright fetal position and rested my forehead on my knees. There was nothing to do. I could only wait and hope that he would leave.

While swaying my body ever so slightly I waited for the closet door to be opened. Finally, I heard the door slam and that meant one of two things: Father had left, or he was now inside and coming for me.

I couldn't take the pressure any longer as I returned to a standing position and pushed my back against the closet wall. The internal sound of my heartbeat was deafening.

I heard footsteps walking down the hallway towards the bedroom. The sound of Cathy's voice raised a flurry of emotions as she declared, "He's gone Bev, you can come out now!"

Joey was standing on the other side of the closet doors as they opened. Overwhelmed with emotion, I completely broke down and began weeping out loud.

"It's okay, they can't make you leave. You're okay," he said.

I spent the next few days at Cathy's house. Emotions resurfaced in a swell when a cardboard box was delivered with some of my belongings. There wasn't much inside, some clothes and a few childhood photos. On some level, I was relieved.

I would never be brave enough to go back and ask for my clothes and I didn't have any money to buy more. The pictures made me cry. I knew Mother well enough to know there was a hidden message. This was her way of showing me that I was cut off—amputated from the family. By sending these photos, she was removing all reminders of me from her house.

As bad as things were in the Moore house, now that I was gone, I was overwhelmed with sadness. I realized that I had lost the only family I had ever known. Good or bad, they were still the only family I had ever had. Guilt set in as I thought about how my abandonment had upset the family.

With only four months of my senior year remaining, Aunt Carol offered to let me stay with her until graduation. She was married to a pleasant man, and I graciously accepted their invitation, though I would come to constantly worry about whether Mother would show up at their house.

Aunt Carol was Mother's older sister. They were close and spent a lot of time together, but they were very different. Mother was high-strung, easily agitated, and volatile. Aunt Carol and her husband were both calm and easy-going. They were not pretentious, on any level, and never seemed to be overly stressed.

Two weeks had passed since Mother had prohibited me from attending school, so I was grateful to return to classes. Mr. Mahoney, the school principal, and I discussed my situation. I only offered the briefest level of detail - revealing that I ran away from home and wouldn't be returning. I expressed concern about my safety and disclosed that I was pregnant. I also shared my worry that Mother may come to the school to try and drag me out of there.

Mr. Mahoney was very professional. He wore a suit and tie every day and was respectful in the way he communicated with both students and teachers. He was calm and assertive, and I was comfortable sharing some of my concerns with him. He was approachable and never appeared to be stressed.

Mr. Mahoney was a patient man and listened attentively before he offered advice. It was his engagement with students, along with his interest and unwavering compassion, that easily made him one of the most popular teachers in school.

Although I gave limited details of my life from hell, Mr. Mahoney seemed to already know or suspect something. He told me I would be safe anytime I was on school property. I left his office feeling better than I had in a long time.

With graduation quickly approaching, I listened to classmates enthusiastically chat with one another about their plans for the big day. There was excitement over dates, parties, and especially the elaborate ball gowns the girls would be wearing.

I knew what to expect. A year earlier, I had accompanied a high school senior from Avondale, a neighbouring community, to his graduation. I met Gary at one of the Marysvale dances and I was tremendously excited when he asked me to his high school graduation. I waited for Mother to be in the right mood before I asked for permission to attend.

When the moment finally arrived, I nervously explained that Gary was just a friend and he needed a date for his school graduation. I remembered being completely dumbfounded when she gave her approval, with the caveat that I was to be home by 11 p.m.

Gary was pleased when I finally gave him an answer.

A week after I had accepted, on a Sunday afternoon, he walked to our house to visit. I was sitting in the rocking chair with Katie and became instantly nervous when I saw him walking up our driveway.

With a pointed finger, Mother told me not to move or say a word. I overheard as she abruptly told him that I wasn't home. As he walked down the driveway dejected, Mother gave me a piece of her mind. How dare I have a guy come to her door?

Surprisingly, she still allowed me to go to the graduation. Gary and his dad drove to my house to pick me up and I had no idea what to expect. I told Gary that I had to be home by 11 p.m. to babysit my younger siblings. He was disappointed but happy I could still attend. We drove to his house for family pictures before heading to Roncalli Senior High.

Dressed in a black tuxedo, Gary looked sharp. He presented me with a corsage, and I blushed when he told me I looked beautiful. I could see he was excited about the event and he proudly smiled as he introduced me to his mom. She was kind, though I noticed her looking at me oddly as I walked into their home. She didn't say anything out of the ordinary, but I sensed something was off.

It wasn't until we entered the school gymnasium that I understood the look on her face. I was underdressed. I was wearing a cobalt blue, knee-length dress. There was a shimmer in the fabric; it had cap sleeves, a buttoned front with a small collar, and a stiff belt was covered in the same fabric. Every other girl there was wearing a fancy floor-length ballroom gown.

The blue dress was one of only two that I owned. When Gary asked me to the graduation, I innocently thought the blue dress would be a good choice. I smiled through the awkward situation when all I wanted to do was take refuge in a washroom stall and cry.

How could I know so little about something so important? I suppressed my embarrassment and was actually relieved to leave at 11 p.m. I was devastated and felt humiliated for Gary, though he showed no sign of being even remotely bothered by my attire.

This time around, I wouldn't make the same mistake. But because I had no money to buy a dress for my own graduation, I decided to skip it. Cathy offered to help, telling me her friend Marilyn had a beautiful knee-length party dress and she was willing to let me borrow it for the graduation. The dress had a fitted bodice, a flared skirt, and fit perfectly. It was a gorgeous dress, but I couldn't get past the length.

I refused to roll the dice on once again being the only girl in a knee-length dress. My mind was made up; I would not attend my high school graduation.

In June, I completed my final school year still showing minimal signs of a baby bump. The school year had been incredibly stressful, and I was thankful to now have it behind me.

I was even more thankful for the parts Joey and Aunt Carol played in helping me get through that final year of high school. I could easily have been a pregnant drop-out. Even with the missed school time, I was still able to graduate with grades high enough to get into university.

I had been sick for the entire pregnancy and looked as bad as I felt. I gained only twelve pounds, but experienced significant pain as my tilted womb "shifted" in preparation for a natural birth. My pregnancy was considered high-risk and my gynecologist suggested I stay close to the hospital for the final two weeks.

I was eventually admitted to St. Clare's Mercy Hospital in St. John's, the capital city. Due to a bed shortage, I was assigned a room with women who had already delivered their babies. Because of my size, I was always explaining to other patients that I had not yet delivered. Their questions and reactions weren't surprising as my baby bump was barely noticeable through to the end.

Five days beyond my expected delivery date, I was brought to the delivery room to start induced labour. Joey came to the hospital but chose to wait outside as he wasn't comfortable being in the delivery room. Judy, a close friend of Joey's younger sister, offered to come in so I wouldn't have to be alone.

The labour lasted over nine hours, and it was brutal. Without realizing my strength, I crushed Judy's hand so hard that I embedded it with ring marks. Judy was patient and tried her best to keep me calm. She casually moved her rings to the opposite hand and announced that she wasn't going anywhere. I was thankful she chose to be with me and to stay until the very end.

At 8:14 p.m., baby Jessica finally made her way into the world. She was 7 lbs, 6 ½ oz., and had the tiniest fingers and toes. She came with a full head of hair. I beamed with pride as nurses fussed over her telling me, "She is beautiful!"

It hurt to remember Mother wishing that she would be born with two heads or some other abnormality. As she was wrapped and laid across my chest, I saw for myself - she was absolutely perfect! Nothing in life could have prepared me for that moment. I was one month shy of my 18th birthday. In the eyes of most, I was a child with a child. It did not matter because above everything else, I was now a mom.

Jessica and I found a temporary home in Colliers, not too far from Cathy's house. Since Joey spent most of his time at his sister's, he was able to visit us daily. The house was fairly big, and although I was renting just a bedroom, I had access to other common areas.

Our bedroom was small, just big enough for a twin bed and a small crib. The size didn't matter to me; I was content to simply have a home. The homeowners were a young couple with two small children of their own. I was respectful of their privacy and happy to spend most of my time in the bedroom watching my baby.

Tracey managed to connect with Joey and together they arranged a secret meeting. I was excited and nervous, as Joey offered to drive Tracey to visit us in Colliers. At age fourteen, Tracey was proud to hold her niece for the first time.

She relayed how different things were at the house since I had left and in turn, I talked about my new life with a baby. We also spoke about the process of choosing godparents. Tracey was disappointed but understood that she couldn't officially take on the role of godmother. We were lucky to sneak this visit in. It was Friday and she told Mother she was hanging out with friends.

Tracey said that since my sudden and unexpected departure, Mother had revealed to Tracey that she too had been adopted. Apparently, I was the first foster child for them. I arrived at their house on my first birthday. They became attached and petitioned to adopt me. Three years later, Tracey had been delivered there as an infant, and once again Mother and Father decided to adopt, giving them four children in total.

Keeping an eye on the time, we realized it was getting late and Tracey had to get back to Georgetown. I removed the tags from a new pair of tiny yellow socks belonging to Jessica and gave Tracey one to take with her. It would serve as a memento of her niece and a keepsake from their first visit. I kept the other sock for Jessica and promised to tell her about Aunt Tracey just in case they didn't get another opportunity to visit.

Cathy was very considerate and always looked for ways to help others. When her neighbour and good friend Rose offered us a new home, I suspected that Cathy had something to do with it.

Rose had four daughters, the youngest was a twin and one of them had been born with cerebral palsy. Rose's husband, Bill, worked in construction and was often away from home for weeks at a time, which left Rose alone to care for the four young children.

I had amassed a fair amount of experience with cerebral palsy because of my time with Katie. Rose offered up a room for Jessica and me in exchange for some assistance with her children. Her kind offer felt more like a gift.

My excitement was palpable, and I could barely wait for the move. I spent a lot of time with Rose and Bill and appreciated the "normalcy" of their home. Rose was kindhearted, patient, and so very selfless. She was very much like a big sister to me, and I noticed that even with four children, she was never too tired or busy to help others. She was a good mom. Bill worked a lot and during his time off, was usually found at home with his family - hanging out with his girls or watching sports.

I was anxious to move and pleased to see our new bedroom was much bigger than the one we were leaving behind. It enabled me to move Jessica into a larger crib and still have plenty of room for my twin bed and a sizable play area.

On Christmas Day, Jessica was four months old. I dressed her in a frilly blue dress with a white cardigan over the top and snow-white tights. With her abundance of hair, I pinned it back in lightly clasped pigtails. The length and thickness of her hair made her look older than she was.

The room was full of excitement as the girls unwrapped gifts, pausing briefly to display items to each other. Rose, Bill, and I chatted as we enjoyed the holiday happiness. Then we propped the girls up on the sofa for photos before tucking Jessica in for an afternoon nap. This was my first Christmas without hostility, conflict, or any level of stress. It felt so strange, but so welcomed.

By March, at eight months old, Jessica needed to be hospitalized for a gastrointestinal issue. As I watched her lethargic body lie in my arms, I was worried and felt helpless. I refused to leave the hospital until she was discharged and slept in a chair next to her crib. Thankfully within days, she was released and back to herself. She was a happy child; always smiling, climbing, and exploring.

Joey encouraged me to search for information on my biological family. I had never inquired before, but he stressed the importance of it now that we had a child. He wanted to know if there were any genetic health issues to concern ourselves with. I agreed and started my search at vital statistics by requesting a copy of my birth certificate. I received that document the same day and learned that I was born in Grand Falls-Windsor, a town in central Newfoundland. I also learned that I had been baptized as Beverly Rexine Thomas.

This was particularly interesting because I had been raised as Beverly Roxanne. I realized then that the Moores must have changed my middle name during the christening or adoption process. The name Rexine added a whole new element of mystery, leaving me to wonder if I was named after someone.

I contacted the provincial government's adoption agency to request a copy of any pre-adoption information they might have on file. That process took longer than the birth certificate acquisition. I was anxious and nervous while I waited for a reply. When the envelope arrived via Canada Post, there was a lot less information than I had hoped.

Birth History:

At the time of your birth, your birth mother was two weeks from her thirtieth birthday. She was in excellent physical health during her pregnancy. She was, however, under severe emotional strain and contemplated suicide on three occasions. At birth, you weighed 9 pounds, 8 ounces and you were healthy.

Birth Mother:

Your birth mother was described as an attractive, well-groomed woman with blue-green eyes and a light complexion. Her natural hair colour was light brown; however, it was dyed blond. She was 5'5" and weighed 130 pounds.

Although it wasn't the details I had hoped for, I was happy to have some information about my birth mother. Within months of receiving the initial package, we surprisingly found ourselves on the receiving end of more information. While visiting his grandfather at the hospital in St. John's, Joey had a conversation with a priest from the Grand Falls area.

Joey spoke with him about my situation and our quest to find my biological family. My birth certificate had confirmed I was born in the Grand Falls area and although there was no father listed, my biological mother was registered as Marie Thomas. That name was familiar to the priest who grabbed a pen and paper to jot down a note. He then handed the paper to Joey with the instructions: "Tell Bev to call this lady."

I hesitated about making the call. What if this woman didn't want to hear from me? For all I knew, she could be related and how awkward would that be? I was also nervous about what I might potentially discover about my biological family.

Several days passed as I debated making the call. Joey was right, I should want to know if we - Jessica and I - were predisposed to any health issues. I did want to know my background. I wanted to know about my parents, if I had any siblings, and why I was given up for adoption in the first place.

It was early in the evening and Jessica was already sleeping when I finally decided to make the call. A friendly voice identified herself as the lady I was seeking. "Yes, this is Lulu," she confirmed.

I am sure she heard the nervousness in my voice as I explained who I was and how I received her contact information. Rose and I had talked about this moment and I was mentally prepared for any rejection I might have received.

To my absolute surprise, Lulu expressed that she was happy to receive the call. She had plenty of questions, although I remained a little reserved with my answers.

I asked if we were related. "Actually, we are related, "Lulu said. "Your mom is my husband's first cousin."

I learned that Lulu lived in South Brook, Green Bay, which was approximately 45 minutes west of Grand Falls, and my mother worked for her at the time of my birth.

The conversation was exciting, and at the same time, a little overwhelming. Lulu asked if she could meet me in person on her next trip to the city. I wrote down a date and time and we agreed to meet at the Irving restaurant on the Trans-Canada Highway, closest to the community I was living in.

A few weeks later, Joey and I walked into that restaurant and scanned the space looking for Lulu. Fortunately, it wasn't a busy time of day and I didn't have to stand very long before our eyes met. Her gentle smile and wave confirmed I had found the right person. As I walked towards her, I observed what an attractive and stylish woman she was. She sat with a younger man leading me to wonder if they were related.

As I approached the table, Lulu pointed to her right and offered me the detail I needed to satisfy my curiosity, "This is my son Rocky," she said.

Rocky reached out to shake my hand. I introduced them both to Joey as I sat down across from Lulu, smiling through my nervousness. I broke the ice by asking about their five-hour drive to St. John's.

"I don't mind driving. I could drive from one end of the province to the other, then turn around and drive back again," Rocky said.

The attendant excused her interruption to take our order and once we had that out of the way, we returned to the conversation. There was small talk before Lulu interrupted.

"Bev, I am so happy you called. I didn't want you to go up for adoption."

A silence followed as we waited for her to continue.

"Your mother worked for me; I begged her to let me keep you. You were such a beautiful baby..."

Lulu wiped a tear from the corner of her eye. "I cried when they came and took you. I don't know why she would not let me keep you. I offered to pay for everything."

"That was a long time ago Mom," Rocky interjected. "We really don't know what her reasons were."

In an attempt to lighten the conversation, I asked Lulu about her children. Her face lit up as she told us about her four children, now fully grown. She had two sons, two daughters, and seven grandchildren.

I was surprised to hear Lulu also had a daughter named Beverly. "Your mother was quite fond of my Beverly," she explained. "And, I couldn't say for sure, but I wouldn't be surprised if you were named after her."

The tone of the conversation shifted when Lulu asked about my family - the people who had adopted me.

"Unfortunately, I was adopted by monsters. There's no polite way to explain or talk about it. They were just not nice people," I shared.

Lulu's eyes widened and she was visibly taken aback. "I am sorry to hear that."

"It's okay," I replied, "Jess and I live with a really nice couple now and we are happy. Life is much better."

I reached for my handbag to pull out photos of Jessica as Joey spoke about my adoptive mother. "She's evil," he said bluntly, "pure evil."

Teen Mom

Breaking News

After living with Rose and Bill for a year, we decided it was time for Jessica, Joey, and I to move into our own space. After all, we couldn't stay with them forever.

We found a reasonably priced apartment in Georgetown and ventured out on our own. The apartment was basic. It was the centre unit of a triplex and had just one bedroom with just enough room for a double bed, Jessica's crib, and a dresser. There was a small, combined kitchen and family room, and a bathroom.

It had been nearly two years since I ran away from home and I was working to put the horrific nightmare behind me, but not long after we settled into the new space, a news story brought it all back. Joey and I were watching the evening news when Mother's face suddenly flashed up on the screen. The headline read: Children in Care removed from Georgetown Foster Home.

I couldn't believe what I was seeing. Things were bad, no doubt, but Mother had a way of making people believe she was an upstanding citizen. I wondered what had happened since I left. Mother responded to the accusations, saying she was outraged that after 18 years and 42 foster children, the Department of Social Services had taken her children and revoked her foster license. She said that the department didn't give her a reason and reassured the public that she was a good mother.

My thoughts went to the children. I was sure Clarence was happy to get out of that house, but I was concerned about Katie. She was unable to communicate, and I worried she was feeling scared.

We watched the supper hour news and read the local newspaper, for updates. Mother was interviewed regularly. Not surprisingly, no statements were being issued by the Department of Social Services.

Mother told reporters that she had hired a lawyer and would be suing the Department of Social Services for wrongfully taking her children. The media interviews became less frequent as time passed, and a date was announced for the trial to commence at the Supreme

Court House in Brigus.

I tried to avoid getting wrapped up in the case, but I couldn't help myself once the trial got started. After all, this was my story too, even if I wasn't involved in the issues that were currently before the courts. Mother and Father hired a well-known lawyer from Bay Roberts, while the provincial government had its own team of lawyers for these types of cases.

As the trial went on, additional details emerged. School staff suspected the children in Mother's care were being medicated to the point where they were unable to function to their full potential. A report was filed by school personnel with the Department of Social Services and Mother was notified that the children would be removed from her house the following morning.

The children were taken to the Janeway Children's Hospital in St. John's. There, blood work confirmed the school's suspicions as outlined in the report. Some of the children were being over-medicated. They would not be returned to the Moore house.

Joey was working with the Department of Transportation and Works and I spent all my time with our little girl. When we lived with Rose, I had been working full-time and dearly missed having that time with Jessica. Now that I was unemployed, I appreciated being able to spend my days with her.

When Lulu called to invite us out to South Brook, a small community in central Newfoundland where she lived, I gladly accepted. Jessica and I did the cross-island trek on DRL's bus service and once we arrived at our destination, Lulu was there waiting for us.

While driving past some of the houses, Lulu pointed out the ones that belonged to relatives of my biological mother. Lulu's home was a modest-sized bungalow with a wraparound deck that had two levels. A wooden rocking chair that looked like it was crafted from an old-fashioned wooden barrel was positioned on the deck and made the home look inviting. The house was set almost at the edge of the property line, close to the road. A small fence around the home protected a perfectly manicured garden with lovely flowers in the front.

Once inside, Lulu introduced me to Sam, an older grandfatherly type of man. He had a round belly and wore a baseball hat, work pants with suspenders, and a white t-shirt. His face was weathered, and his hair was white. The smile on his face was contagious and prompted one from me in return.

"I fed you my darling," he said warmly. "I got up in the middle of the night and made your bottle when you lived here. I am so happy to see you," he shared, as he extended his arms for a hug with tears in his eyes. I could tell he was genuinely happy to see me.

Jessica was now tired and overdue for a nap. Lulu showed me to the spare bedroom and offered a pile of blankets to use as a makeshift bed on the carpet. That way, I could leave the room when she slept and not worry about her rolling off the bed. I laid on the blankets and coaxed her to rest next to me. It took a while for her to settle but eventually, she gave in, as I pretended to sleep myself.

I quietly crept out of the room and made my way to the kitchen. From a distance, I heard a new male voice which turned out to be Tom, Lulu's husband. He pleasantly said as he saw me, "You must be Bev! Another Bev... You know I have a daughter Bev? Though, she's older than you."

"Yes sir, I know."

Tom was probably in his mid-fifties. He was shorter than me with a petite, pale face, and graying hair. It didn't take long to see he had a sense of humour as he joked with Sam about anything and everything.

Lulu gave me a tour of the house and Tom interjected to say I should make myself feel at home. The house was beautiful, and I complimented Lulu on the gorgeous decor.

Over dinner, we discussed my biological mother's family history. Tom reminded me that Marie was his first cousin. Lulu talked about her life and offered information that I longed for ever since finding out I was adopted.

Marie was married at a young age and had five children before her husband left her for another woman. Apparently, Marie had been overwhelmed with grief. So much grief in fact, that she was unable to care for her children. Consequently, her children were raised by other people.

The oldest child, a girl, was raised by Marie's parents. A second daughter and one of the boys had been raised by their father and his new wife, and the remaining two boys were taken into protective care.

Tom stated, "Marie's oldest girl is now married, has two boys, and lives in South Brook. The others have moved to other communities and provinces," he added.

I wondered if I would ever have an opportunity to meet any of them.

Sam charmed me with stories about my younger years as an infant. He reminisced about how I had spent the first few weeks living in this very house. During that time, Lulu tried talking Marie into letting them raise me.

"I was broken-hearted when they took you away," he said in a quiet tone. I smiled at the realization that these good people had really wanted me, and they could have been my family.

Lulu's son, Rocky, and his wife lived in the neighbouring house with their three children. It was still morning when he dropped in and invited us over to meet his family. The visit to Rocky's house lasted over an hour and when we returned, we were greeted by Lulu who was bursting to pose a question.

"Would you like to meet your mother?"

"Seriously? How?"

"I just spoke with her on the telephone, and I told her you were in South Brook," she replied.

"Yes, I would like to meet her!"

"Well, we'll have to hurry," she explained, "Your mother lives in Triton and that's a 30-minute drive. Her husband is at work and she doesn't want him to know about you. We will have to leave the house before he comes home," Lulu warned.

I was a little taken back with the part about her not wanting him to know about me, but I still desperately wanted to meet my biological mother. I hurried to the bedroom to get Jessica ready for the visit.

On the drive to Triton, Lulu pointed to the Upside-Down Tree, which was protected by a small fence and appropriate signage.

"We can stop on the way back for photos if you like," she said.

I wondered if it had actually grown that way or if someone had pruned it into that shape. Lulu assured me that it was real.

As we knocked on Marie's door, I caught a glimpse of her looking out the kitchen window. I sensed she was probably as nervous as I was. After a brief introduction, in which Lulu identified us by our first names only, Marie offered tea and coffee before she proceeded to fill her kettle with water.

I carried Jessica in my arms as Lulu led me to Marie's family room. Jessica pushed herself out and away from me, letting me know she was ready to get down and explore the new surroundings. I was prepared. I opened her bag and took out some small toys for her to play with.

Sitting across the room from one another, I found myself studying Marie as I searched for genetic similarities. I noticed she had small lips and a small mouth, like me. My eyes were a darker shade of blue, however, and she was shorter in stature than me. She was well put-together. Her hair was light brown and neatly styled. Doing the math in my head, I determined she was in her early fifties.

Marie was quite soft-spoken. As I looked around the room, I was reminded of the previous comments made at Lulu's house about Marie being extremely orderly and clean. I thought this was interesting as I had that same characteristic. My thoughts were interrupted when Marie and Lulu pointed out that I looked a lot like Marie's oldest daughter.

Once the conversation was flowing, I bashfully asked, "Can I ask who my father is?"

"He's a trucker, and not from the province," Marie shared.

"Oh... But, what's his name?"

After a slight hesitation, she said she couldn't recall.

I was uncomfortable. Instinct told me she was not being honest. Lulu redirected the conversation and turned the focus to Jessica. Our time for visiting was coming to an end. Marie worried that her husband would be suspicious if he saw me because I did look so much like her oldest daughter.

I packed up Jessica's toys, and we left. I was disappointed that I didn't feel much of a connection to this woman— my mother. I was even more disappointed that she was reluctant to tell me who my father was.

Back at Lulu's house, her niece dropped in for a visit. She was obviously curious about my situation because she asked questions about my life growing up on the east coast of the province.

"Do you know who your father is?" she asked boldly.

"No! Though, I was christened Beverly Rexine and I think that might be a clue. I have never heard the name Rexine before," I commented.

"No," Lulu's friend disagreed, shaking her head. "Rexine is a common name."

I still had my doubts, but courteously didn't challenge her further. Once Lulu's niece left, I returned to the kitchen.

"Do *you* know any Rex's?" I asked Lulu.

"Well, yes actually," she said. "The lady you just spoke with has a brother Rex."

If Lulu could have read my mind at that point, she would have seen lights turn on. She may have just given me the missing piece of my puzzle! Her niece expressed interest in my life and asked a lot of questions. When the opportunity arose, she neglected to mention that she had a brother named Rex.

I didn't need her to say anything else. I figured I had enough information now to see the complete picture. My father wasn't a trucker nor was he from another province. I knew he was close. I could feel it. Still, I said nothing for the remaining few days but on the drive back to the DRL bus stop, I broke the silence and confided in Lulu.

"I am pretty sure I know who my father is," I stated, before explaining the conversation that had transpired between her niece and me.

Rex was Lulu's nephew, her brother's son. I understood why she was reluctant to say anything. Lulu's gaze remained on the road. "Bev, it's not my place to say. People talk but I can't say for sure."

"I understand, but I think I am right about this."

When I arrived back in Georgetown, I received an unexpected phone call from April. She had called to see how I was doing. The conversation was strained as she asked about Jessica and what life was like with a child. In a surprising twist, she shared that Father was sick. He was showing early signs of Alzheimer's disease. They believed it had been brought on by the stress of me running away from home.

"He worries about you. He often wonders if you have a place to sleep," she persisted.

Without allowing sufficient time for a response, she asked if Jessica and I would come for a visit. "Both of them would like to see you and meet Jessica," she said.

A day or so later, my heart raced as I walked up the driveway with Jessica in my arms. I never envisioned myself ever walking back into that house, yet there we were. I hoped this wasn't a mistake.

Tracey, in a deliberate attempt to soothe any tension, welcomed us as soon as we came through the door. We engaged in idle chat until Mother walked in and greeted us as though nothing had ever happened. Tracey held Jessica in her arms as Mother walked over to see her for the first time. I was nervous as we talked mainly about Jessica.

"Well, come on in away from the door," Mother said. "Is she hungry? Can I give her some apple juice?"

As we entered the family room, my eyes were immediately drawn to a family portrait. It was an extra-large photo of the four Moore children. I was about seven when the photo was taken. That framed portrait had taken up the same space on the same wall for the past twelve years. The only difference now was that my face was completely covered by a sheet of blank paper. I pretended not to notice.

Father sat on the sofa and appeared sedated. He said very little and responded only when spoken to.

"Is he okay?" I asked.

"Yes, it's his medication. It makes him dopey," Mother replied.

There was an uneasiness in the room but with Jessica's energy and activity, the focus remained on her. It wasn't long before I announced it was time to leave. Mother left the room and returned minutes later with a gift for Jessica. It was a short sleeve, layered blue dress with a matching cardigan.

I felt awkward. I had not seen Mother for almost two years, and at that time, she had wished birth defects on my child. Now, here she was presenting her with a gift. I blocked the memories from my brain and politely accepted her gesture. The visit had been uneventful otherwise, and despite my discomfort, it was fairly pleasant. There had been no mention of my foster siblings.

According to the small-town rumour mill, Mother believed that my running away had brought unnecessary attention to the family. Mother's situation had been further fueled by her suspicion that a bitter social worker with a preexisting axe to grind against her, caused the children to be taken away. Despite all this, the visit went well.

I walked away from the house feeling better. Maybe Mother had changed, I thought. Maybe she now saw me as an adult and regretted the pain she had inflicted on me as a child! Again, desperate for my mother's affection I wondered if maybe everything could be different, and we would have a normal mother-daughter relationship.

I wanted to start over and begin to rebuild a relationship with the Moore family. Joey, not really knowing all the details about my childhood, supported me. Tracey, now fifteen, was the youngest and only child still living in the Moore house. I wondered if they might benefit from visits with Jessica. Mother was being nice to me, so I concluded she must have changed.

With time, the visits became less strained. I ran errands for Mother and drove her to medical appointments. Family and friends were surprised when I mentioned the rekindled relationship. Everyone knew I had run away from home. Naturally, without specific details, they had speculated and developed their own theories. I resisted filling in the blanks, as I simply appreciated having family in my life.

While sleeping in our apartment, I began to have disturbing nightmares. They were always the same, I would wake up in a panic seeing someone standing next to my bedroom door. The silhouette was of a man, but I could not see his face. I was disturbed by the realness of the visions, as well as the frequency of these nightmares. I reminded myself they were just dreams, though I struggled with just how vivid they were every time.

Jessica spent almost all her time with me but one particular day, Joey offered to stay with her so I could run errands. As I drove home from Colliers, I braked to accommodate a car slowing down in front of me that had signalled a right turn. When I glanced in the rearview mirror, I noticed a vehicle rapidly approaching and it was not slowing down. My eyes returned to the front and I panicked as the road ahead of me hadn't yet cleared. I kept my foot firmly on the brake and braced myself.

SMASH!

The loud bang was significant, and both cars were impacted by the crash. The vehicle had hit me with such force, I expected to see the rear of my car spiralled up into the back seat. My brain immediately told me that I was okay, and I was comforted to see the other driver walking toward me, indicating that he was not seriously injured. My body was trembling.

"Are you okay?" he asked.

"I think so," I replied.

"I saw the child's seat from my car; I am relieved to see it's empty," he commented, as he pointed to Jessica's car seat in my back seat.

"Yes, me too!"

After inspecting both vehicles, we exchanged insurance information. We were quite surprised to see minimal damage on both cars. During the conversation, I learned that his family had a summer cabin in Georgetown.

Dr. Batten did a medical examination, diagnosed my symptoms as whiplash, and sent me home to rest. The pain was agonizing and prevented me from sleeping. Within days, I developed lower back pain, but I hadn't mentally connected the new pain with the accident until my follow-up appointment with Dr. Batten weeks later.

After completing another thorough examination, Dr. Batten recommended I see an orthopedic doctor, and that I should consider making a claim for the injuries. I had no idea where to look for advice on that, so Dr. Batten recommended a friend who was an attorney.

Resting, while caring for a rambunctious three-year-old, was not easy. Jessica was energetic and a fearless climber. In seconds, she could drag a chair from the table to the kitchen cupboards, then climb from the chair onto the countertop and sit with a grin, legs dangling, as she waited for my reaction. She scared us both one day when I came from the bathroom to find a chair next to the cupboards and Jessica sitting on top of the refrigerator!

From the countertop, she had used a canister to boost herself up the extra height. Once she was up there, she had limited space to turn her body and so there she remained, silently frozen in position, waiting to be rescued.

I was nineteen, and Joey was twenty-four when we decided to get married. He was the only guy I had ever dated, but given that we now had a child, I assumed we would always be together.

On the wedding day, Father wasn't quite as "foggy," although still obviously medicated. Mother was a little standoffish and seemed uncomfortable in a dress and heels. She also did not like crowds.

The wedding was a low-key affair with a church service, followed by a dance club reception for about 100 guests. There was no honeymoon. I, being the non-drinker, drove us to a hotel in St. John's for our wedding night, and our lives returned to normal the next day.

As Mother's trial continued, I heard the news that Clarence had come forward with additional claims of abuse from the time when I was also living at the Moore house. His claims included accusations of severe physical abuse from Mother.

I didn't attend any court proceedings, but Tracey continued to keep me updated. I knew Clarence was telling the truth, and I expected to be subpoenaed. I was 17 when I abruptly left the house. Social workers, schoolteachers, and essentially everyone in the community knew about it. Yet, to my surprise, I was never called upon for interviews nor ever questioned about what had motivated me to run away from home.

The trial had dragged on for 27 months in the Brigus Supreme Court. Mother spent a fortune on legal fees before she decided to abandon the trial. In a statement to the media, she said her decision was due to health problems suffered by both herself and her husband. They would not continue with their lawsuit.

Although blood samples taken at the children's hospital had indicated that several of the children were being over medicated, the only penalty Mother and Father faced was the removal of the children and losing their foster home license.

I had a hard time justifying this. It made no sense. Court documents confirmed that there was a criminal investigation into allegations that Clarence was abused. Everyone knew it was true, yet there were no charges laid. And although I had fled home two years prior, I was never questioned. Tracey, who was a teenager still living in the home, was also not interviewed. There were so many red flags, yet it seemed they were all ignored. Sadly, our horrific upbringing did not matter.

During a visit to Joey's sister's house in St. John's, I watched as she demonstrated a newfound enthusiasm for sewing. She was following a pattern, using an older Singer Sewing Machine.

I had never sewn before or even seen anyone use a sewing machine, yet I surprisingly found myself following along and seemingly knew what she was going to do next. I left her house feeling inspired and decided that I also wanted to try sewing.

Back at the apartment, I went through the Sears catalogue in search of an outfit to replicate. I settled for a blue and white crop top that had a matching skirt. The top was pale blue with white trim, and it had short sleeves. The skirt was blue with a white band. It was slightly flared with a side opening and slash-style pockets.

Excited, I purchased the material and waited for Jessica to fall asleep before I started the project. I used my own clothes as blueprints to make patterns before cutting out the actual fabric pieces.

With the catalogue opened to the relevant page, I laid it out on the coffee table to guide me as I hand sewed the pieces together. It took a couple of days, but I was delighted with the results. I modelled the outfit for friends, and they had trouble believing I made it myself. So, to prove these were my efforts, I turned up the hem and exposed the handmade stitches.

Motivated to create more, I bought a sewing machine, patterns, fabric, scissors, and other sewing tools and immediately got to work. I made clothes for Jessica, as well as curtains, and comforters. With the completion of every project, I was excited and couldn't wait to start the next.

Although my neck injury was slow to heal, it was improving; however, my lower back issue had worsened with time. After two years of unproductive visits to an orthopedic surgeon who was treating my "soft tissue injury," I requested a second opinion.

With a referral, I was scheduled for an appointment with Dr. Phillips, an orthopedic surgeon at St Clare's Hospital. Dr. Phillips reviewed my file and immediately scheduled a discogram. This procedure was set for Friday evening and involved the painful insertion of several fine needles into my spinal column.

As soon as the test began, I knew the excruciating pain meant there was a problem. Once the procedure was completed, Dr. Phillips requested I come back to his office at 8 a.m. on Monday.

I arrived at an empty clinic. Dr. Phillips had scheduled the early morning appointment as a means of fitting me into an already full schedule. Otherwise, I would have been waiting months for the test results.

He jumped right to the point and explained that I had damaged the lower three discs in my spine known as L3-L4, L4-L5, and L5-S1. We discussed the car accident and the certainty that it had caused damage to my lower spine. Surgery was recommended.

The recommended surgery was a three-level spinal fusion. For this procedure, Dr. Phillips explained, bone shavings would be removed from my hip bone; and, along with supportive hardware, these shavings would then be fused to my spine. After the surgery, I would have limited mobility, but if successful, I would have significantly less pain.

At age 21, aside from persistent lower back pain, I was healthy. I had been accepted into a nursing program and was anxious to get my life back on track, ideally without pain. I made the uncomfortable decision to undergo spinal surgery, mostly because I hadn't worked in two years.

In less than two weeks, I found myself back at the same hospital. This time, lying on a gurney being prepped for surgery. An anesthesiologist was doing his best to keep me calm by promising to take care of me.

My gurney was wheeled into a bright operating room where an IV was inserted into the back of my hand. Dr. Phillips, completely cloaked in green scrubs, entered the room. Without removing his surgical mask, he asked how I was doing. With a nod from the doctor, the anesthesiologist started the procedure. I felt a very cold solution entering my hand; it ran up my forearm as my eyes got heavy.

After the surgery, I was greeted by a nurse and although I was still groggy, she insisted on waking me every ten minutes, or at least that's what it felt like. Once I had been returned to my room, she explained that I had been given morphine for pain, therefore a nurse would remain by my bedside for 24 hours. I also had to stay flat on my back for the same amount of time.

I didn't feel any pain in my back, so after 18 hours, I begged the nurse to let me roll over. My chest felt heavy, and my lungs and ribs were aching from lying in the same position for so long. In the next hour, she agreed to check with the doctor to see if I could shift positions.

Minutes later, the nurse returned with two of her colleagues and explained how they would help me stand upright. I wasn't sure if I was ready to stand, or why it would take three nurses, but I definitely wanted to move my body.

With assistance from the team, I was rolled onto my side. I thought – it's not really that bad; maybe, I could stand up. One of the nurses helped move my feet to the floor while the second prepared to pull me upright into a seated position. When my body shifted, intense pain spread through my lower spine.

"Put me back, put me back," I cried out as the nurse lowered me back to a horizontal position. I continued to rest on my side but that was about as much movement, and pain, as I could bear.

Dr. Phillips visited me the following morning and talked about the surgery. He presented a small bottle from the foot of my bed and held it upright; "This is what came out of your back," he said. The bottle contained shavings of one of the discs from my back.

He also explained that once the surgery began, he had discovered that one of my spinal discs had been protruding much worse than the other two. He chose to remove the protruding disc and not perform the fusion, hoping that the disc removal would give me relief.

I was simultaneously surprised and relieved. I concluded that a second incision in my hip and the addition of hardware to my spine would have been significantly more painful.

"Can I now go back to school and complete the Nursing program?"

"No," Dr. Phillips said without hesitation. "You will never be a nurse. Most nurses hurt their backs while working. You already have a bad back; I would not recommend that career path for you." I was devastated.

After several days of hospital care, I was ready to go home. Jessica heard her father and I talking about my back surgery and after I explained that I wouldn't be able to lift her for a while, she asked to see my back. She wanted to see the "operation".

As she patiently sat on the bed waiting, I lifted my shirt to expose the fresh incision on my lower back that was being held together by 11 stitches. Jessica was immediately disturbed by the sight and began crying, "Take it off, Mommy. Take it off!"

Jessica and I still spent every day together. Our first trip to the grocery store, post-surgery, proved to be challenging and fun at the same time. At three-and-a-half years old, she was able to climb in and out of the car seat; however, I struggled while trying to get her in and out of the shopping cart and had to ask friendly customers for help.

From the seat of those carts, Jessica liked to play a game that we called "Missus". I had no idea how the game originated, but it entailed us talking to each other like old married women. While talking in her big-person voice, she asked, "How are you today Missus?"

"I'm good Missus, how are you?"

"Not good, my husband won't let me borrow the car," she said in her pretend angry voice.

I was fascinated with her imagination, and she thought up new details every time, as she talked about her fictitious husband and children.

The conversation continued as we slowly strolled through the grocery aisles. Other shoppers smiled or chuckled at our conversation and I smiled back, though Jessica remained in character, totally oblivious to anyone outside our conversation. Once we were back in the car and she was secured in her seat, the game restarted, always the same way, "How are you today Missus?"

Joey's brother and his wife had two daughters and these girls were just a few years older than Jessica. All three of them played well together but Melinda, the younger of the two, was closer to Jessica's age and had become one of her closest friends.

Marie, the girls' mom, joked that it was easier to have two girls than one. Together they played well and when apart, would constantly ask for the other. Marie also offered to take care of Jessica whenever I travelled to St. John's for appointments.

Based on Dr. Batten's recommendation, I hired an attorney from St. John's after my car accident. During a post-surgery meeting, I was relieved to tell him that my surgery had been successful. Although I still had some discomfort, my back pain had been significantly reduced.

He opened my file to a post-surgery follow-up letter from Dr. Phillips. After handing me a copy, he read out a section from the report highlighting where Dr. Phillips had classified me as being 22.5% disabled. Additionally, he had documented that I would never be able to seek work that involved prolonged sitting, standing, lifting, or bending.

Although sympathetic to the situation, my attorney stated and reiterated the obvious—the injury would prevent me from ever becoming a nurse. He outlined how an insurance settlement would help afford me the time to consider other options, while my back healed.

This was of small consolation to me, considering my back would be a life-long problem. With the surgery now behind us, a clearer picture was forming of the future and we agreed to settle with the insurance company.

Like most couples, Joey and I argued. Over time, however, the arguments became more frequent. Confrontations were quick to start and unfortunately, sometimes witnessed by Jessica. During one of our disagreements, she disappeared into her bedroom for a lengthy absence.

When Jessica emerged, she was wearing a bright pink baseball hat backward on her head along with a heavy sweater, pale blue striped pants, and her pink handbag dangling around her neck. While dragging an overnight bag across the floor behind her, she announced, "I am going to Aunt Marie's!"

Not quite four years old, Jessica was wise beyond her years and had opted to be absent for this argument. I didn't blame her.

Bev and Jessica

Rock Bottom

At age 21, I was tall, thin, and had very little shape to my body. Joey told me that he loved me being "plain and ordinary." I believed he meant it as a compliment but when he spoke about his curvaceous ex-girlfriends, I couldn't help but feel even more insecure about myself than I already did.

Joey and I were comfortable talking about everything, though I continued to keep most of the dark memories of my past to myself. I kept thinking if I resurrected the most horrible details, I may later regret sharing. I also thought that if I concealed my past and didn't tell people – or even think about it – it was "almost" as if it hadn't happened. I convinced myself that eventually, my past would fade, and I was okay with that.

Two years into our marriage, my relationship with Joey was changing. We had several friends with whom we regularly spent time. Several couples would meet for drinks before we'd all head out as a group to a local bar. Joey and I were the only couple in the circle that were married and living together so our apartment was the logical place to gather.

The bar scene was new to me and because I never drank, I was happy to serve as the designated driver. Jessica usually slept at her Aunt Marie's house anytime we organized a night out. One night after the bar, Joey was still feeling the effects of the alcohol he had been drinking, he confessed to having feelings for another woman.

"We grew up together and have a lot more in common," he confided. "She understands me better than you."

I was hurt and the conversation mutated into a heated argument. When Joey finally drifted off to sleep, I reflected on my life and considered the possibility of a future without him.

Six months had passed since the spinal surgery. I often thought about my back and the long-term prognosis. I recalled Dr. Phillips's advice and his comments about my limitations regarding work and I gently reminded myself that I was still healing. I would get through this; I had survived worse.

Joey, Jessica, and I had moved twice since our first small

apartment. Our initial move was to a larger home and although we loved the extra space, the high electrical bills during winter months did little to compensate for the spacious layout and beautiful decor. The second move was to a small bungalow in Marysvale.

We were in the new house less than a week when another heated argument erupted. Later, I talked to Mother about our relationship and the frequent fights. She suggested we consider time apart and invited us to stay with her. When Joey agreed that it might be a good decision, Jessica and I packed overnight bags and headed to Mother's house for a few days. I had truly believed Mother had changed and was hopeful about having somewhat of a "normal" relationship with her. And besides, I wouldn't be returning to the same house.

When the trial ended, Mother and Father were forced to come to terms with the fact that they had lost their licence to foster and the children would never return. Tracey had moved to St. John's to continue her education and the large house that was always so full was suddenly empty. They didn't need the big house in Georgetown, and I sensed they wanted to shed some of the memories of what happened there.

No longer able to work because of his health, Father spent the days at home with Mother. Life was very different now. They sold the Georgetown house and moved to another, fairly large, house in the neighbouring community of Brigus.

Mother suggested Jessica and I stay here with them as Joey and I made some decisions about the future of our relationship. "There's plenty of space and having you both with us will only bring more life to the house," she said.

I accepted the offer and the arrangement initially seemed to work for all of us. Jessica quickly adapted to the new home. I spoke to Joey on the telephone daily and reminded him that the move, and time apart, would be good for us. I didn't have a vehicle of my own and Joey agreed to let me use his car for the first weekend. He didn't mind me using the vehicle but requested that I come back to the house on Saturday night to talk.

When I walked into the house it was obvious things had changed. It was quiet and I felt awkward. Joey sat at the table and invited me to take a seat with him. I uncomfortably opted to stand. Joey asked if I had thought about our situation, and of course, I had. At that moment, I told him I wasn't ready to come back. As he stood up from the chair, he gave me an ultimatum.

"You have to make a decision, and you have to make it now. Either you leave this house and never come back, or you come back, and you stay here tonight."

I didn't appreciate the tone or being given an ultimatum. "Well," I said defiantly, "I guess I am not coming back."

The look in his eyes scared me. As I turned to walk away, he snatched my arm. I yanked it from his grip, then rushed to the bedroom. Joey was right behind me and as I turned to face him, he immediately shoved me onto the bed. I bounced back on my feet but just as quickly, his rigid fingers were on my chest and my body was pushed back onto the bed.

With sheer determination, I returned to my feet, only to be forced back down several more times as his fingers once again met the bony part of my upper chest. His anger intensified.

With my back on the bed, I raised both legs into the air and gave my body the momentum needed to change position, allowing my feet to access the floor from another side of the bed. Just as quickly, he was in front of me, and I felt the sting of his hand slapping my face. The physical assault continued as I struggled to find a way out of the bedroom. Holding a firm grip, Joey squeezed my arm as he yelled in my face.

When I escaped his hold, I ran outside the house, leaving the door open behind me. My eyes were drawn to two people walking along the road just past the house. I was horrified when Joey caught up with me and shoved me to the ground. The bystanders looked on but did nothing to intervene.

The next thing I remember, there were bright headlights from a car pulling into the driveway. Within seconds, Tracey and Mother appeared and pulled Joey off me. Mother distracted Joey telling him it was best for him to leave. Meanwhile, Tracey quickly helped me up off the ground and into the car.

During the drive home, Mother shouted, "He's a fucking madman. He would have killed you if we hadn't shown up when we did."

She couldn't have realized the irony of her own words.

I woke in the morning to back pain and overall soreness. Once Jessica was up, I waited for her to leave the bedroom before I gave my tender spots a proper examination. Bruises were starting to form on both sides of my arms, but the biggest and most painful ones were on my chest.

It was Jessica's fourth birthday and I had already picked up a special birthday cake. Friends had been invited over for a birthday celebration and I quickly decided that the party must go on. I mentally prepared to face guests, some of whom were Joey's close friends.

Against Mother's wishes, I chose not to press charges against Joey. I wanted out of the marriage, but I didn't feel there was a need to involve the police. When Joey announced his plans to seek sole custody, Mother warned I had no choice but to contact the authorities.

"He did this to you; would you really trust him with a child?"

She was right. I was left with no choice. I gave a verbal statement to the RCMP, and as they requested, Tracey took photos of my badly bruised body and handed them over for their records.

Tracey was living in St. John's during the week but came home on the weekends. Jessica loved to see her; she was sad whenever Sunday evenings came, and it was time for Aunt Tracey to go back to the city.

After about a week of living in Mother's house, Jessica had a bed-wetting accident. I explained to Mother that this didn't normally happen and promised to clean the sheets and mattress. Mother suddenly grabbed Jessica by the arms and swung her around so that her little body was turned inward towards Mother's knees. She yanked her pants down and firmly spanked her bare bottom. My body completely froze.

Familiar feelings of fear came rushing back. I was petrified of Mother. Jessica had never been slapped, spanked, or deliberately hurt in any way. I was devastated, and furious at myself for not reacting or speaking up at the moment. My heart broke as Jessica's bottom lip curled up and tears filled her eyes. Jessica was scared and I didn't know what to do. This painful event would play out in my mind for years to come. In fact, decades later as I write this book tears fall down my cheek. My heart still hurts to remember the incident.

I saw no difference in Father's health but noticed he was taking a lot of medication. When it was time for a doctor's appointment, Mother often left him home and headed to St. John's to see the specialist herself. She would describe his condition and the doctor would write a refill prescription or would prescribe new medications as he saw fit.

I wondered if the medications were doing more harm than good, as Father was dopey most of the time. I also wondered what kind of doctor wrote prescriptions without physically seeing the patient.

Joey would now take Jessica every second weekend. As the months passed, we developed new routines. I could tell Mother loved having Jessica around and she hadn't hurt her again since the spanking incident.

Mother encouraged me to go out on the weekends. She reminded me that she was quite capable of taking care of Jessica when I was not there; however, I obviously had reasons to be apprehensive.

Joey and I were also back on speaking terms. During his weekends with Jessica, I often hung out with my close friend Lori-Ann. Her boyfriend had been life-long friends with Joey and while Lori-Ann told him he could do as he pleased; she was my friend before anything else. I knew she meant it. Together we took Jessica out for drives or to visit her parents. When Jessica was with her dad, we would sometimes go out to the nightclubs in Colliers, the community we lived in for the first year of Jessica's life.

Lori-Ann was pretty. She had strawberry blonde hair that was always perfectly curled, and her makeup was always in place. She was the youngest member of her family and still lived at home with her parents. I admired the relationship they had. Her siblings had all moved out of the province, though she remained in constant contact with all of them.

One evening while at the Misty Moon Lounge with Lori-Ann and her boyfriend, I met Johnny. We chatted throughout the night and at closing time he offered me a ride home. I politely declined and minutes later watched his car drive off from the parking lot ahead of ours. Lori-Ann said she had gone to school with him, and he was a nice guy.

"He's definitely a good-looking guy," I added. I had noticed a few girls at the club checking him out.

Two weeks later, I headed out with Lori-Ann and her boyfriend once again and ran into Johnny. This time, I was a little more relaxed with the conversation and after an evening of dancing, I agreed to a date.

Johnny was charming and before long, he introduced me to his parents. I felt it was a little premature and told him so, but he felt I was reading far too much into a simple introduction.

Mother expressed interest when I told her I had started dating someone from Colliers. I was caught off guard when she suggested I bring him home to meet her, Father, and Jessica. The thought of starting a new relationship, one that Mother approved of, made me happy. I was grateful for any small life indicators that hinted at normalcy.

I invited Johnny to visit on a weekend when Tracey and her boyfriend would also be there. Johnny was about six feet tall with dark straight hair and blue eyes. He was very social with a laid-back, easy-going personality.

I liked spending time with him and enjoyed his sense of humour. Mother also seemed to appreciate some of these characteristics as she quickly warmed up to him.

Mother's mood swings were still unpredictable. Jessica had

been in bed sleeping one night and I thought she would be okay with me visiting a friend. When I asked Mother if she would mind, she shot back. "Yes. But make sure you're back in this house by midnight, and that's not five after."

I cowardly agreed to her terms though I was not happy to have an imposed curfew – especially now that I was 21 and a mother myself. However, it was her house, and she was watching over my child, so I didn't rock the boat.

I arrived home just a few minutes before midnight and to my surprise, the door was already locked, and all lights turned off inside. Mother hadn't given me a key, so I had no way of getting into the house.

I returned to the car where I ended up spending the night. It broke my heart to be locked out of the house while Jessica slept inside. I was also upset that I allowed Mother to break my spirit yet again. As dawn broke, I was startled by a loud firm knock on the car window. Mother was standing outside the car in a three-quarter length nightgown.

"Get in the house," she said sternly before she turned and walked away.

I did not waste time telling her that I had returned home on time. I quietly walked to the bedroom and got in bed with my sleeping child. My mind was in turmoil.

It seemed that Mother had reverted to her old self. I would overhear her talking about me when she was on the phone with her friends, and she often disrespected me in front of others. When I talked about moving out to get our own place, she threw insults and threats my way.

"You can go wherever you please, but you *won't* be taking that child with you."

Her words and tone scared me.

In desperation, I called Joey and asked for his help to get Jessica and me out of the house—again Joey knew it was for the best and agreed to assist me.

Our bags were packed and hidden in the bedroom. As Joey walked into the kitchen, I rushed upstairs and grabbed them. Guiding Jessica with my free hand, I carried backpacks and travel bags in the other. Mother was in conversation with Joey when we passed through the kitchen. She immediately noticed the bags.

Mother instantly turned hostile and left the room. Joey grabbed Jessica's hand and led her towards the door. When Mother reappeared, she threatened to scald me with boiling water from a kettle she was holding over my head. Joey jumped in between us and talked her down. He was able to get us safely out of the house.

In Joey's car, I cried and told him I thought she had changed.

"People like that don't change. Just be satisfied that you are out and do yourself a favour: don't ever go back."

I was comforted by his support and thankful that he had been there to help. I don't know how I would have gotten Jessica out of the house without him.

While at Joey's house, I was distressed and tried to hide it from Jessica. Joey occupied her with play until bedtime. Once she was settled in her bed, we talked openly about the situation.

I planned to start looking for an apartment in the morning. When I left Joey six months earlier, I left everything behind, except for our clothes. Now I needed to start over and furnish an apartment of my own. I asked for Jessica's bedroom set for our new home and Joey agreed to give it to her.

In the morning, I called Johnny and he was relieved to hear we had left Mother's house. He didn't know a lot about our life but knew enough to understand it wasn't a healthy environment for us.

Johnny immediately called a friend for advice, and she invited Jessica and me to stay with her until we found our own place. I accepted her kind offer; not just because I had limited options but because she was also a single mom and could give me guidance on a lot of things.

I was a single parent with no home, no money, and no way to support my child. I had reached rock bottom. I was left with no choice but to turn to the Department of Social Services and request assistance. I felt defeated. I knew I was a good mom, but I also knew Jessica deserved better than I was providing.

I met with a social worker and tearfully explained my circumstances. I was injured in a car accident and had undergone back surgery a year ago, and I was waiting on clearance from my doctor so I could work.

I had no family to turn to, and only a few friends for support. I explained I was due to receive a settlement from the car accident and prepared to pay back anything I could borrow. The social worker took notes as I spoke.

Once I finished, she proceeded to explain, "You will receive a predetermined amount of money for a single adult and one child. You will receive the money bi-weekly and by signing these forms, you guarantee to pay back all the money you receive, from now until that date." Without hesitation, I picked up the pen and signed my name in the highlighted areas.

It took about a week to find an affordable one-bedroom apartment. Between Lori-Ann and a few friends, we managed to find secondhand furniture and I worked diligently to make a comforter and curtains for each window. I was excited about moving in and felt a new sense of freedom.

Jessica and I slept together until we could manage to get a bigger living space. Until then, we would leave her bedroom set at Joey's. We were in the apartment for just a few months when a friend dropped by with an incredibly generous offer.

Her mom had recently moved into a retirement home and rather than leave her mom's furnished bungalow vacant, she suggested that Jessica and I move into it, paying only a nominal fee. The price was perfect, and I couldn't afford to pass up the offer. They also offered to deduct any home renovations I did from the rent. This arrangement truly was a gift.

Johnny and Lori-Ann helped us move. Unlike the apartment, there was a backyard for Jessica to play in along with a spacious bedroom of her own. Joey delivered on his commitment to turn over Jessica's bedroom furniture for the new house.

The home was dated in style though comfortable, plus the utilities were affordable. Both the house and property were simply adorable. I bought a princess-style comforter set for Jessica's bedroom and immediately began modernizing the house.

Shortly after we moved in, Johnny and I celebrated one year of being together. He was such a lovable guy with a charming personality. Johnny was from a respectable family and had already completed training for a trade.

He had everything going for him, including those good looks which earned him plenty of attention from the ladies. I loved him, but insecurity prevented me from completely settling into the relationship.

Johnny talked about moving to Toronto with his brother to obtain his journeyman hours as an electrician. I didn't want to hold him back. Johnny was upset when I ended the relationship and called several times to talk about it before he ultimately booked his flight and departed for Toronto.

***

My attorney called to let me know the settlement cheque had arrived from the insurance company. It had been over three years since the car accident, and the insurance company had challenged me every step of the way.

Before surgery, insurance adjusters treated me as though my injuries were not legitimate. I became irritated whenever I heard people nonchalantly talking about unwarranted insurance claims that people made. In their opinion, it was easy to get money for minor accidents. I was defensive when telling people that I had to fight for my rights because of those unjustified claims and having to explain it constantly made me somewhat resentful.

I was excited to finally receive the cheque but acutely aware of my status. As a 23-year-old single mother, with a 22.5% disability, I had to think long-term. The settlement would be enough to help me get back on my feet, but I certainly couldn't rely on it to take care of us for any amount of time. I knew I had to be careful with my financial decisions.

My first purchase was a secondhand black Pontiac Sunfire, it was a sport edition and about five years old. It was a major step toward independence for Jessica and me.

In a phone call, I told Joey that I had received the settlement and as promised, would repay our accumulated loans and credit card balances in full. I prepared individual cheques for each and kept records for my files.

To each of my three siblings, I gave a $1,000 cheque, and I wrote a $3,000 cheque to Mother and Father. Mother had talked about being financially strained since the court proceedings. They had paid an attorney to represent them for over two years and it had depleted their savings. I hoped my gifts to the family would help.

I called the Department of Social Services and requested a summary of the total amount I had borrowed and committed to sending a cheque in the mail. Lastly, I went out to purchase some furniture. I selected a bedroom set for my room, a sofa set for the family room, and a hardwood dining set for the kitchen.

Next, I sought the advice of a financial adviser. Although there were not a lot of options outside of St. John's, I had heard positive feedback about one in particular. Edmund was from the area, he was well respected for his work, plus I had gone to school with two of his three daughters.

Edmund was a small man with a lively and energetic personality. He was always professionally dressed in a suit and was quite personable as he talked about his family. He was a father before anything else and that point of pride beamed through.

During our initial meeting, Jessica coloured a picture for Edmund as he updated me on the status of his three girls. When the picture was complete, she gave it to him and he handed it back, "Jessica, I need you to sign this picture for me. It will be kept in your mom's file for a very long time. I'll show it to you once you're all grown up!"

I had limited knowledge of financial investments and was apprehensive about signing money over to an investment company. Edmund seemed to have all the answers, including how to make more money in interest. After an hour with him, I felt like I was in good hands.

Eventually, the brakes needed to be replaced on my car. The local mechanic sent me to an auto parts store in Bay Roberts with a list of the parts needed for my specific model. As I arrived in the parking lot my attention was immediately drawn to a sharp-looking white, Z28 Chevy Camaro. The T-bars were removed and as I walked past, I noticed the inside was as clean as the outside.

Inside the auto parts store, I was greeted by two employees. I walked to the nearest attendant and handed him my list. As he searched the inventory for the parts on his computer, I wandered to the large windows for another look at the Camaro.

"That's a gorgeous car," I commented out loud.

The second attendant was watching from behind the counter and was quick to respond.

"Want to buy it?"

"Is it your car?"

"Yes ma'am."

"How much?" I asked, just out of curiosity.

"You can't afford it," he confidently responded.

He was a slim, good-looking guy with a blonde clean-cut style and blue eyes. He was likely around my age, dressed in jeans and a designer t-shirt and oozing confidence. I blushed from his apparent playfulness.

I wasn't sure how to respond so decided not to. He leaned out over the counter and extended a hand, "I'm Chris."

I politely shook his hand and introduced myself.

"The car has a lot of money invested in it. I would never sell it. I have to run; nice meeting you," he said with a smile as he looked directly into my eyes.

As he walked out from behind the counter and towards the door, he announced, "Hey Randal, I am gone to do the bank deposit."

Without waiting for a response from his co-worker, he removed a pair of dark sunglasses from his breast pocket and slipped them on in a cool Tom Cruise sort of way. Not that I was a Tom Cruise fan, but something was interesting about this guy.

I purposely resisted watching him leave but couldn't help checking to see if he actually got into that dream car and, of course he did.

The employee returned to the counter with an arm full of parts, "I think I have everything you need."

"Can I pay by cheque?"

"Sure can."

Two days later, I received a phone call from Chris asking me out on a date. "How did you get my telephone number?" I immediately asked.

He reminded me of my payment method at the store. I was intrigued and somewhat captivated by his demeanour and agreed to join him for a casual Wednesday night game of pool.

Instead of allowing him to pick me up, I insisted on driving myself to Bay Roberts and meeting him at Tables Lounge. My heart raced as I noticed his car already in the parking lot when I arrived. I walked into the building, and when the door closed behind me, all eyes seemed to shift in my direction.

I tried to hide my nervousness as I scanned the crowd. There were clusters of people surrounding every pool table and after a few long dragged-out seconds, I spotted Chris weaving in, out, and around people as he walked towards me. With a big smile, he appeared happy to see me.

Chris led me to a pool table where he introduced me to several of his friends. I joined in the game but quickly declared myself a novice player, certainly not in the same league as any of them. The pool games were fun, and I enjoyed the group. The guys tormented each other as though they had been lifelong friends, and I soon learned that some of them were.

As Chris walked me to my car, he suggested going for a drive in the Z28. "After all, the car is what brought us to this point," he said.

We drove for an hour or more before Chris pulled off on the side of the road near the ocean. It was a beautiful night as we sat back and watched the waves. He led the conversation as I heard lots of stories from his past and learned he was the only child of a close-knit family.

"I have a little girl," I disclosed, waiting for a reaction.

I was pleasantly surprised when the conversation continued with him asking questions of interest about her. Maybe he was a player I thought to myself, as he seemed to know exactly what to say and when to lean in for a kiss. The kiss was impulsive and exhilarating.

Relationships usually progress at a slower pace for single parents. I was no different, and I remained acutely aware of the fact that I did not have the same freedom as others my age.

After a few more dates and plenty of phone calls, Chris asked if he could visit me at my house. I welcomed the idea but insisted that he not arrive until thirty minutes past Jessica's bedtime. I didn't see the need to introduce Jessica to boyfriends unless of course, the relationship became more serious. He was okay with that and showed up on time.

We stood outside her bedroom door as I allowed him to peek in to see her. She looked like an angel with her long blonde hair covering most of the pillow and her little body snuggled under a heavy comforter. There was a doll and several teddy bears strategically placed on her bookcase headboard plus one in her arms.

The next evening, Chris called and asked if I had any trouble around my house. Puzzled, I asked, "What do you mean by trouble?"

"While visiting last night, I was driving my dad's Jeep. I had no problems driving home but dad took the Jeep to work today and while driving down a steep hill, a tire came off."

Very calmly, Chris continued, "We brought the Jeep to a garage and were told the lug nuts were purposely loosened on a couple of the tires."

I was dumbfounded and asked, "Why do you think it happened at my house?"

"Our driveway extends to the back of our house," he explained. "The vehicles are hidden from the road and parked close to the house. We have never had an issue in our driveway."

I remembered that during his visit, Chris had parked the Jeep in my driveway, but it had been left fairly close to the street. I was still not convinced the lug nuts had been loosened in my driveway.

Jessica, or Jess, as I now called her, had settled in well and was delighted with our new home in Colliers. She had a beautifully decorated bedroom just across the hall from mine. She also had a new best friend. Gerard, a former high school friend of mine, had a daughter the same age as Jess. They were both in kindergarten and spent many afternoons and weekends together.

Holly was very shy, and Jess was protective of her. Holly and her family had just moved into a new house but when the school bus driver stopped to let Holly off the bus, it was at the old location. Holly, being timid, stepped off without protest. Minutes later, Jess got off the bus at her stop and ran through our back door in a panic. She grabbed and pulled my hand, then led me to the door saying, "We have to hurry mommy, we have to save Holly!"

I acknowledged Jess's panic and dropped everything to follow her lead. Inside the car, she sat and stretched her body tall to look out the window as she instructed me about where to drive. Within minutes, we pulled over to find Holly standing by her old house, as she held onto her school bag. Before getting off the bus, Jessica had instructed Holly to stay next to the house and assured her we would be right back to save her. Holly did just as Jessica had said. I was quite proud of my girl that day.

Jess and I lived in the house in Colliers for a year, and we loved it. We were not in any rush to move; however, when a friend suggested I look at a mutual friend's house that was for sale in Georgetown, my interest was piqued.

We drove on a side road to find the house in a quiet area of town. It was a two-bedroom bungalow with an attached deck and a small, paved walkway from the parking lot to the back door. The house had new siding and windows, and it looked to be in great shape. The inside was tastefully decorated and seemed to be the perfect size for us.

When we talked to the owner about the price, I was pleased to hear it was listed at a price that I could afford. I was careful with my money. If I spent too much on the house, there would be nothing left.

Before allowing my hopes to get too high I asked a friend, who was an experienced carpenter, to go through the house and look for any issues that I may have missed. I was excited when he came back to say there was nothing of note for him to share; in fact, he too thought it was perfect for us.

It didn't take long for the legal work to be completed and once again, we moved. This time, I was thrilled to be moving into our own house. With the help of a few friends, Jess and I settled in. It wasn't extravagant by any means, but to me, it was beautiful and would be our perfect home.

The Stalker

The morning sun beamed through the large kitchen and family room windows, warming the house and radiating positive energy throughout our new home. I felt so much pride as I personalized our humble little space. It was ours and with that brought freedom for Jess and me.

Jess had already made a new friend on our street, and she was thrilled to spend more time with her cousin Melinda. Not long after the move, my doctor cleared me to work, and I got a retail job in Bay Roberts. Things were finally falling into place. Life was good.

But that carefree, content feeling would soon turn to worry. Not many people knew we lived here so I was surprised to wake one morning to a knock at the door. On the other side stood a small-statured elderly man. I had seen him before in the garden next door and immediately recognized him as our neighbour.

"Good morning sir, how are you?" I cheerfully asked.

"Good," he said with a quick nod. "I heard a noise in my garden last night but when I looked out the window, I couldn't see anything. At daylight this morning, I looked out to see my ladder propped up against your window."

"What?"

"Come," he motioned with his hand. "I'll show you," he said, as he turned and began to walk away.

I jumped into a pair of shoes and rushed to catch up as he slowly made his way back toward his house. With a pointed finger, he directed my attention toward the ladder leaning on the side of my house, ending at my bedroom window.

Responding to my bewildered look, he quickly assured me, "I didn't do it, my dear, I can barely get around."

"Maybe some kids in the neighbourhood were checking out the new resident?" I speculated while trying to keep myself from freaking out. But deep down, I was worried. I thought about it on the drive to work. Who would want to look inside my home? I was uncomfortable and scared.

I was now spending most of my free time sewing. I made

curtains and valances for all the windows in our new home and a comforter set for my room. Once the house projects were complete, I went back to sewing and designing clothes.

People regularly asked where I bought mine and Jess's outfits and were always surprised when I told them I made the clothes myself. I received a lot of compliments and before long, was getting requests to make curtains, graduation dresses, and clothing for people I didn't even know.

I enjoyed the challenge of making different outfits and, as the work orders began piling up, I recognized an opportunity to turn my hobby into a home-based business. My retail position was reduced to part-time and the sewing business, which increased my income, became full-time. I did a little advertising on the community channel and as a result, had a constant flow of new customers.

As time passed and my work became more well known, an administrator from the local college invited me to consider teaching adult sewing classes. I was thrilled with the opportunity and although it wasn't required, took a Sewing & Designing Course through distance education to better prepare for the position.

My schedule was full. I was working retail part-time, teaching one evening a week, working full time from home with the sewing business, and to top it off, I was a full-time mom. Although there was little time left in the week, I also continued to foster a relationship with Chris.

Chris and his buddies were always playing pranks on one another. The pranks could be anything from drawing a mustache on an intoxicated friend's face to actually towing a friend's vehicle from one end of a parking lot to the other. With April Fool's Day just around the corner, I decided to get in on the action. I developed a plan and enlisted the help of my little sister, Tracey, who was delighted with the proposed shenanigans and as part of our plan, she was eager to call Chris at work.

"Hello Chris, my name is Tracey, and I am calling from the Department of Motor Vehicle Registration. My records indicate you have a list of outstanding fines, including several speeding tickets. Unless you can pay the complete balance by the end of the day, I will be left with no choice but to immediately terminate your driver's license."

Chris, taken completely off guard, tried to explain that there must be some kind of mistake and that her records were incorrect. Yes, he did have an outstanding speeding ticket, but that did not warrant him losing his driver's license. Tracey insisted firmly, "I am sorry sir, I have no time for this. Please confirm that the fines have been paid by end of the day or your driver's license will be revoked."

As Tracey ended the conversation, Chris hung up the phone fuming with anger. I waited about ten minutes before calling to remind him that it was April Fool's Day. Then I told him that Tracey was my sister. "I watch you play pranks on your friends all the time. Today, finally, the prank is on you!"

He was relieved to hear the call had been a joke and admitted to being totally taken in by it. A couple of days later, while we were out for a drive, he approached his own residence. Chris pulled into his driveway and all the way up to his house. He turned off the engine and grabbed the keys, motioning for me to follow.

"No, I am not going in there. Your mom is home."

"Exactly, you can meet her."

I protested, "No Chris, I am not ready for this."

"Bev, she doesn't bite, trust me. She knows we're here and if we leave now, she'll wonder why you didn't want to meet her. C'mon, the sooner we go in, the sooner we leave."

Chris proceeded to walk ahead. I begrudgingly got out of the car and followed him into the house. "What is it with guys wanting me to meet their moms," I mumbled under my breath.

Once inside, I smelled a sweet distinctive scent and assumed his mom had been baking. I followed him into the kitchen and almost immediately, his mom appeared from the family room. She smiled with a big ear-to-ear grin as Chris moved out of her sightline to expose me standing behind him.

"Are you the young lady that played the April Fool's joke on my son?" she asked.

I bashfully smiled wondering how to answer the question. I couldn't quite tell if she was pleased or disappointed.

"Yes, that was me," I sheepishly responded.

"Well done. Chris is always the instigator, and no one seems to ever get one up on him. Well done my dear," she said.

She extended her arms for a hug, "You must be Bev."

I reciprocated and immediately felt the warmth of her personality.

"I have heard good things about you. It's nice to finally meet you," she said.

"I have also heard good things about you," I replied.

Chris's mom was a professional woman. He told me she had been a teacher until he finished high school. Once Chris graduated, she left teaching and now worked with the provincial government.

She was petite and attractive, and her voice was quiet and calming. I noticed that her eyes lit up when she smiled. I was still smiling when we drove away. Without breaking my stare from the traffic ahead, I announced, "I love your mom."

"Yeah, me too," he said, without taking his eyes off the road. I was delighted it had been such a pleasant experience.

Since buying my own car, Jess and I had returned to Lulu's house in central Newfoundland every summer. Sometimes, if the weather was favourable, we got a second visit around Christmas.

We loved spending time with Lulu and her family. We also enjoyed the road trips and "girl-time" in the car. Jess and I talked, played travel games and we stopped regularly for food, bathroom breaks, or just to look at sights. Every trip was a new adventure.

Based on what I had learned on that first visit, I was convinced Lulu's nephew, Rex, was my biological father. Rex was a miner and had worked all over the world. He was always travelling when I visited South Brook. I asked about him each time I visited and was pleased to learn more about his life.

From my conversations with Lulu and others, I learned that Rex was 21 years old when I was born. Even as a young man, he had spent a lot of time working away from home. I was told that his relationship with my mother was brief and she had not told him about me.

Several years later, he met and married a nurse from the area. They settled and raised three daughters and now lived in one of the larger homes in the community. Driving past his house, I always wondered what life was like inside.

While enjoying a beautiful summer's day, I sat on Lulu's deck with Sam, Jess, and a few family friends. We had visited enough that I felt comfortable around family members who had stepped forward to introduce themselves.

Ernie, my cousin, flashed a mischievous smile and asked if he could take Jessica for a short drive. There was a look in his eye, and I knew he was up to something, though I had no idea what it was. When Ernie returned, he carried Jess from his truck and placed her on the deck next to me.

"Jessica just had ice cream, and she met her grandfather," he declared.

"Really? How did you manage that?" I asked in amazement.

Ernie winked and proudly nodded his head. I could see how pleased he was with himself.

Within the hour, another truck pulled into the driveway. I had never met my father before or seen pictures but, somehow, I immediately knew it was him walking towards me. With dark hair and a mustache, he was younger than I had imagined. He was close to my height, wearing jeans, a dark t-shirt, and looked to be in decent shape.

He stopped right in front of me after walking up onto the deck.

"I heard you wanted to meet me."

Without thinking, I replied, "That would be nice."

He continued by asking where I lived, how often I visited South Brook, and a few more random questions. I was nervous but politely answered each one. "How long are you here for?"

"I plan on heading back later today," I told him.

"Well, I have to go home and talk to my family. They will want to meet you," he shared. I was surprised and somewhat taken back. We talked for another few minutes before Rex noticed Sam.

"Hello Skipper," Rex said with a nod. His attention and conversation then turned to Jess. Shortly after, he stood up and said, "I have to go but I will see you girls later."

As my father drove away, I recalled my introduction to my mother. I remembered her desire to keep my existence a secret. I was sure she had her reasons and couldn't imagine my birth father's family accepting the news either. I decided not to wait around for possible disappointment.

I headed into the house to tell Lulu that I had just met my father. I could tell by her smile that she was genuinely happy for me. I then told her we had to leave. The five-hour drive was long, and I wanted to get home before dark.

Sam helped me pack our bags into the car before Jess and I said our goodbyes. Two hours later, I received a surprising phone call. A female voice asked if it was Bev on the line.

"Yes, it is," I replied, and immediately wondered if someone from Rex's family was calling to tell me to stay away from the family.

"Hi. I am Rex's daughter, your half-sister."

Nervously, I responded, "Hi."

"Where are you? Dad told us about you, and we all want to meet you."

I was completely shocked.

"Oh. Really?" I responded.

"How far away are you Bev?" She asked. "I am in Glovertown with my boyfriend and if you have the time, I would love to meet you and Jessica as you drive through."

Once I got over the initial shock, we decided to meet at a ranch not far from the highway. The ranch was easy to find, and she thought Jessica might like to see the horses.

Jess held my hand as we walked toward the picnic tables at the ranch. There was my sister, sitting with her boyfriend on the top of one of the tables. She waved as soon as she saw us.

She had dark curly shoulder-length brown hair and brown eyes. She was gorgeous. I looked for signs of possible resemblance as she stood, but noticed she was much shorter in stature and with an athletic build.

She smiled and appeared happy to see us. I was surprised, given the fact that I was a half-sister she did not know about until today. We chatted for over an hour before she asked if she could take Jessica for a ride on one of the horses. Jessica was excited and anxious to go. After the horse ride, I was told that the family had been disappointed we had left so soon. "They all wanted to meet you," she said.

I was astonished. I told her that I hadn't expected the family to be so receptive. She couldn't imagine why they wouldn't have been. We chatted some more before taking a few photos and then we said our goodbyes. I left happy and was glad we had made time to connect.

When I arrived home, Rex called to invite us back. Realizing it was a long drive, he suggested that we come when time allowed and reiterated how anxious the family was to meet us. "We have lots of room, so you are welcome to stay with us when you visit," he offered.

Almost a month later, Jess and I returned to South Brook. Rex, his wife, and two younger girls were waiting for us when we arrived. It was a little awkward at first, but everyone did their best to make us feel at home.

Rex had three daughters, and now a fourth. The eldest lived in St. John's and was a student at Memorial University. The youngest was only a few years older than Jess. She had straight strawberry blonde hair, and everyone thought she and Jess looked alike. The girls became fast friends and were inseparable for the entire visit.

The middle daughter was shy and more reserved than her sisters. There was no question that of all the sisters, she looked the most like her mom, with long wavy auburn hair. Her physique, however, resembled mine. We were both tall and slim with lanky limbs.

A couple of Rex's brothers dropped into his house while we were there. I assumed they already knew the situation because when I was introduced as Rex's daughter, no one stopped to question it.

In the evenings, we sat around and chatted over a glass of wine. I observed the interactions and felt proud to be related to this family. Rex's wife told me that he didn't sit still very long. "When he's not travelling for work, he's usually working on a project or two around here, or he's busy helping one of his brothers, or a friend," she said.

After three days I decided it was time to go home. Jess was upset and wanted to stay. It was the first time we really felt part of an extended family and Jess did not want the visit to end. Although we made a plan to come back again, she cried as we boarded the car to head home and quietly sobbed as we headed east on the highway.

At home, I worked day and night trying to catch up on my sewing projects. Early one afternoon when I was working away at the sewing machine, I received what would be, the first of many disturbing phone calls.

"Hello?"

The voice on the other end responded, "Hi!"

"Hi. Who are you looking for?" I asked.

"I am looking for you, Bev," the man's voice said, softly dragging out the sound of every word. He was clearly disguising his voice and I could hardly make out what he was saying.

After a brief pause, he asked "What are you doing today?"

With a lump in my throat, I nervously asked "What do you want?"

"I want you!" the strange voice whispered.

Scared and upset, I quickly hung up the phone.

The calls continued for a long time. They were always short, and the number was always blocked. Some days, I received multiple calls and then days or weeks would pass without any. The calls were disturbing and frightening. If I hung up, he often called back. When I dared to ask, "What do you want?" he replied, "You." I was petrified and I trembled each time I hung up the phone.

Chris and I had been dating for a couple of months and when a full weekend went by without hearing from him, I was annoyed. It was noon on a Monday, and I had an appointment in Bay Roberts. While driving through the main street, Chris passed me in the outside lane, driving his Z28 and waving. The T-bar rooftop was open as he took advantage of the rare warm day. I didn't return the smile or wave. As I pulled onto a clinic parking lot, Chris drove in behind me. He was wearing a pair of funky John Lennon sunglasses with round lenses. He smiled as he walked toward me.

"Hi," he said, in a cheerful upbeat tone.

From outside the car, I reached to grab something from the back seat, then proceeded to walk around him without responding.

Chris lifted both hands with a questioning gesture.

"What?"

I stopped, turned, and walked back. "Do you really have to ask? I haven't heard from you since last Thursday. Couples do not go four days without speaking and you're only here now because you saw me driving."

"Oh! Well, I have been busy," he offered.

Looking through the sunglasses, I stared into his eyes. "I see! Well, I am busy, too. Goodbye."

I walked around him and into the clinic without looking back.

From inside the building, I heard screeching tires as Chris

aggressively left the parking lot. He wasn't happy and I didn't care. I deserved better I told myself, as I questioned his maturity and ability to handle a long-term relationship.

As the week progressed, I still didn't hear from Chris. Instead of contacting him, I made weekend plans to go to the Top Hat Dance Bar in Manuals with a few friends. Featuring the best dance music, the Top Hat had become a popular hangout. This was evident by the long lineups of people waiting to get in every weekend.

As I walked into the club with a group of old friends, I spotted Chris.

Chris looked surprised to see me and even more so to see me walking in with a group of people he didn't know. He walked straight toward us and stopped directly in front of me as he kept his back to my friend Brad.

"Can we talk?" he asked.

"Not right now," I replied, without showing any emotion.

He pleaded that it wouldn't take long.

"Sorry, not right now," I firmly repeated, "I am here with friends."

As he walked away, I could tell he was miffed, but I chose not to let it bother me. We were no longer a couple and I was here to have fun with my friends.

That Monday, I was working on a sewing project when I heard the sound of Chris's car as it pulled into my driveway. His Z28 had a dual exhaust and that distinctive sports car sound. I always heard the car on my street before I saw it.

Chris quietly walked into the house and sat down across from me, "You said we could talk later, and now it's later."

He pushed for a second chance while assuring me that he was committed to our relationship. A lengthy conversation ended with us deciding to give it another chance.

Just outside my back door, were two, bright, strategically placed lights. One lit up the path from the driveway to the house and the other illuminated the deck behind. Whenever I left, I turned the lights on to ensure we never came home to darkness.

One particular evening, Jess and I returned home to a dark entrance. Knowing the lights had been left on, I realized there was a reason for concern.

My heart raced as I looked to the neighbouring houses to confirm we were not experiencing a power outage. I hoped it was an issue with the light fixture or that both light bulbs blew at the same time, but I knew that was unlikely. Jess squeezed my hand tightly as we walked toward the house. I felt helpless knowing she was scared. I was scared too.

Walking quickly in the dark, I placed the keys between my fingers with the point sticking out. I told myself I would use them as a weapon, if necessary. Once inside, I quickly locked the door and turned on the lights. As a distraction for Jess, I turned on the television while I walked around the house looking in each room and closet.

I took replacement bulbs out to the back door and began to replace one when I realized it was loose. As I twisted the bulb, a bright light shone directly on the back deck. With a lump in my throat, I twisted the second bulb and my driveway completely lit up. Horror-stricken, I realized both bulbs had been intentionally adjusted just enough to turn out the lights.

I sat and talked with Jess as she ate a bedtime snack, then prepared her for bed. We normally read a book together every night before she slept, but tonight we read three. I stayed with her a little longer, waiting for her to drift off to sleep. Jessica was intuitive; I knew she was picking up on my nervous vibes. I decided to leave the outside lights on all night and once Jess had gone to school in the morning, I would call the police.

Constable Edwards, from the RCMP detachment, took notes as he asked for specifics about the neighbour's ladder, the phone calls, and the most recent incident with the light fixture.

He asked the obvious questions, "Do you have any jealous or angry ex-boyfriends?"

I shook my head as I told him, "I don't know anyone that would be trying to scare us. Everyone knows I have a little girl here with me."

During the conversation, we were focused on the fact that everything had happened since we had moved into the new house in Georgetown. Then, I suddenly remembered the lug nuts being loosened from Chris's Jeep while I was living in our last house.

"Was this the first unusual thing that you noticed?" he asked. I answered yes.

"So, someone has either taken an interest or has been trying to scare you since the new boyfriend?"

"Yes," I said as I went through the timeline in my head, hoping it was just a coincidence.

I remained in the house as Constable Edwards walked around the property and thoroughly checked the exterior. Upon returning, he informed me that there was an area in the grass behind a few trees with a worn-down patch of ground, presumably from someone sitting and possibly watching the house.

"Ms. Moore, I believe you have a stalker."

His words echoed in my head as the meaning sunk in.

114

"I would like you to keep your lights on, both inside and outside the house, even if you are not home. Watch people around you and look for any familiar faces that seem to keep showing up. When driving, take notice of the vehicle behind you. I will speak to the other patrolling officers, and whenever we're in the area, we will drive by your house and keep an eye out for anything suspicious. Record the dates and times of the phone calls as well as anything else you notice. Call us anytime."

I tried to hide my fears from Jess and made sure that anyone who knew what was going on did not talk about it in front of her. Jess did not ask about it but looked for reasons to keep me in her bedroom at night.

"One more story, mommy."

"Can I have a drink of water?"

"Can you sleep with me?"

Now, when I worked in the evenings, Jess refused to go to sleep until I returned home. Sometimes she would sit and watch for me from her bedroom window. The sitter mentioned Jess would stall for as long as possible before her bedtime.

Although I didn't realize it at the time, Jess was paying attention and knew there was a reason for concern. I would learn later in life that this fear manifested into a childhood trauma that would stay with her for years to come.

Jess loved to spend time with her cousin Melinda and since moving back to Georgetown, we were now just a short drive from her house. They spent so much time together that it sometimes seemed like I had two children, or none, as Jess also spent a lot of time at Melinda's house. Marie and her husband were home during the weekends, and she offered to take Jess one night as I planned on attending a house party with Chris.

I only knew a few people at the party but was pleased to see Colleen, an old high school acquaintance. We chatted about high school and old friends until, in mid-sentence, she stopped to ask, "Have you ever modelled?"

I was surprised by the question but more so because Colleen had asked. People, including some strangers, had asked me the same question in the past. However, Colleen had belonged to an elite group of popular girls in high school; I liked and respected her. I was surprised that she would think of me as a potential model.

"No, I have not," I replied.

"Have you ever thought about it? You have great bone structure plus you're tall and thin. You could definitely be a model," she said. "In fact, my Aunt Linda has a modelling agency in town. If you're interested, I'll give you her number. You can always meet with her and decide for yourself." I took Linda's number and agreed to check into it.

We were late leaving the party and even later getting back to Georgetown. Jess was sleeping at Aunt Marie's, so I wasn't concerned that it was late, or that Chris was spending the night.

Tracey had recently given birth to a new baby boy, Adam, and he was being Christened the next morning. When morning came, I was a little rushed and asked Chris to lock up on his way out.

While walking towards my car, I noticed something looked off. A few steps later, I noticed a flat tire, a few more steps, another flat tire. What are the chances of getting two flat tires? I walked around the car and I was startled to see all four deflated.

"Someone let the air out of my four tires," I declared after storming back to the house. "Chris do you have a tire pump?"

At this point, I was upset and paced around the kitchen. Who would do this? I wondered. And why?

Chris told me he had a pump and said he would take care of it. He put on his sneakers before heading outside to inspect the tires for himself. I followed behind. Chris knelt on one knee to take a closer look. I watched him feel around the tire while waiting for a response.

"Bev, the air wasn't let out of this tire." He quickly stood and walked to the second tire. He examined it and then turned to face me. "Bev, my love, your tires have been slashed."

"What are you talking about?" I anxiously asked.

Chris walked around to the other side of the car to look. "All four of your tires have been slashed," he said, confirming my fear.

Without another word, Chris walked over and wrapped his arms completely around me. After a minute of silence, I spoke. "I need to call the police and report this. What the frig is going on? I am glad Jess is not here to see this."

I called the police but because it was Sunday morning, the call was forwarded to the Harbour Grace detachment. I was told that there was no one available to speak with me but someone would get back to me later that day. After hanging up, I cried.

"Bev, they are only tires, they can be replaced," Chris comforted.

"It's not that. I have no idea who is doing these things to me, or why. I just want it to stop. Constable Edwards told me to leave the lights on all the time, even overnight. With you being here, I assumed that was not necessary. I guess I was wrong."

Suddenly, I realized a possible motive. "Chris, this was the first time you slept at my house. The first time another car has been parked in my driveway overnight. Do you think someone is watching and is upset because you slept here?"

Chris paused before responding, "It sure looks that way."

I paced the kitchen floor. "We have a problem here. And now, I am scared."

"I'll stay here. I can't leave you two alone. God knows who this sicko is or what they're capable of... I have to go now but I'll be back later this evening. Are you okay with that?" he asked. I nodded in agreement.

As I noticed the time, I realized the church service was about to begin. Even if I went straight to the church without Jess, I would probably still miss the christening. Chris gave me a ride to Marie's house to pick up Jess, then dropped us off at April's. April was hosting a family get-together after the service and Jess and I had been invited. I was disappointed to have missed Adam's christening service but at the very least, I wanted to attend the gathering.

The next day, Rex called to check-in. I hadn't told him anything about the stalker and because I was still upset about the tires, I blurted it all out. I told him everything. He was both surprised and worried but relieved Chris would be staying with us.

"Don't stress about the tires," he said, "I'll take care of it for you."

I was comforted by the offer but told him not to worry about it. Rex, however, not only insisted but proceeded to make plans to have the tires replaced.

From Runaway to Runway

My high-school acquaintance, Colleen had planted a seed. I didn't think I looked like a model and I certainly didn't feel like one, but if Colleen thought I had a shot, maybe I should at least look into it. I had nothing to lose, I reminded myself, before calling to schedule an appointment.

I was nervous when Linda opened the door to greet me. She was tall, slim, and dressed completely in black wearing a long tunic, leggings, and matching high heel boots. Her jet-black hair draped halfway down her back and her complexion was fair. Linda had a beautiful petite face and as I observed her features, I suspected she was a model herself.

"Hello, you must be Bev," she said, smiling at the entrance.

The agency, Classique Models, operated from her home. Linda led me through the living area and upstairs to a studio. The entire wall leading up the stairs was covered with various size photos of models. The collection included headshots and magazine covers. I thought these girls were gorgeous and wondered if I was wasting her time.

Linda was sophisticated and professional. In a soft-spoken voice, she described the agency and some of her recent success stories. I learned she represented a diverse group of models and actors of all ages, including her young son. The agency offered evening and weekend classes in photography, personal development, and runway etiquette.

As I searched for the right words to inquire about my potential, Linda cut to the chase, "Your legs and your eyes are your greatest assets; though, the permed hair will have to go."

"With your height of five foot nine, you could do well on the runway, with training," she added.

I was surprised to hear that at age 23, I was considered a mature model. I signed up for a runway course and booked my first photoshoot with the agency's in-house photographer. Models need a portfolio or a "look book" with a spread of photographs that would represent diversity. Linda emphasized that without pictures, she couldn't promote me.

She explained the process. The photoshoot would include three different 'looks' with completely different hair, make-up, and clothes. From each look, they would hope to get two photos or six shots in total, just enough to get a beginner book started. Linda would also need a photo or two for her agency book.

To book talent (a model or an actor) clients could come into the office and select directly from the agency's portfolio, or they could contact the agency and provide specific details of the person they wanted to hire. The agent would then review their database and schedule auditions for those that met the criteria, based on availability.

Auditions were more time-consuming, but the client had the advantage of meeting all applicants in person before making the selection. I was excited and anxious to get started.

Soon after my first photoshoot, I heard a big-name professional photographer was travelling from Toronto to work with the agency. His work had been featured in top Canadian magazines and after speaking with several of the other models, I heard the shoots would be significantly better as our in-house photographer only dabbled in photography as a hobby.

For several days, I contemplated participation then went ahead and paid the deposit. I was excited and looked forward to the photoshoot.

As time passed, I became good friends with many of Chris's buddies. Some of us regularly met up at the Top Hat Dance Bar on Saturday nights and we often gathered as a group for coffee. Depending on the time of day, I sometimes took Jess along with me to the coffee dates.

At six years old, Jess was full of life and often the center of attention. Her stories were unpredictable, and she enjoyed making people laugh. The guys loved her, and she knew them all by name.

Through a mutual friend, I met Eddie, who was working on a psychology degree at Memorial University. Eddie spent most of his time studying, hanging out with his girlfriend, or helping his father with their vegetable gardens.

I had no idea where he found the time, but on top of everything else, he managed to foster friendships and volunteer with a local charity. We became fast friends and Jess looked forward to any opportunity to see him.

Eddie and his girlfriend lived with his elderly parents, who I was pleased to meet. Mr. Pardy, of Metis descent, was originally from Cartwright in Labrador and was one of seven boys. His wife, Mrs. Pardy, was a white-haired, petite lady from Western Bay,

Newfoundland.

They had been married for over 40 years and were still very much in love. The Pardys had a huge property and grew most of their own vegetables. Eddie arrived later in life for them, and he was the youngest of their four children.

Eddie had lost an older brother in a tragic car accident years ago and his remaining two siblings were married and lived in neighbouring communities.

While spending time together, Eddie and I developed a sibling-type of relationship. Whenever I introduced him to others, I would often joke that he was more like my big brother than a friend. Over time we began to refer to each other as family. The Pardys had no grandchildren and treated Jess as if she was their granddaughter. The feelings were reciprocal, and we enjoyed family time.

Meanwhile, at my retail job, my hours were reduced, and I had to find something else. So, resume in hand, I went to Wescal, a large department store in Bay Roberts, and met the manager. "I'm applying to work in the fabric department, but I would be willing to work wherever there is a need," I explained.

I was hired on the spot to work in the women's department. Within weeks, I was offered a full-time position as supervisor and buyer for the women's and lingerie departments. As a buyer, I would travel to Montreal where I met with vendors. I had a budget and was free to order styles for the coming season at my discretion.

My first buying trip was less than two months after the promotion and I travelled with my manager, Doreen, who trained me for the position. With the increased responsibilities, I received my first pay raise from the company.

Wescal was a family-owned business with over 40 employees. It was the only department store of its kind in the area, and they had been in business for 25 years. Customers travelled from all over the region to shop there, and every weekend there was an influx of customers coming from as far away as St. John's.

Doreen was middle-aged with a petite frame and ginger red hair. She was sharp, witty, and didn't miss a beat. The staff never wasted time on her watch and as the manager, she knew everything that happened in the store. There were no back doors with Doreen, she called it as she saw it and was confident in doing so.

As I planned my first week-long buying trip to Montreal, Eddie offered to help.

"Jess can stay with us while you're away," he said.

Before I had time to respond, Jess was jumping up and down with excitement and ready to pack. I didn't have a lot of options and I knew she would be in good hands. My mind was at ease knowing

Jess would be quite content staying with Eddie and his family.

While in Montreal, the workdays were long. We usually started at 9:00 a.m. but if an extra appointment had to be squeezed into our already tight schedule, vendors would see us as early as 8:00 a.m. We grabbed lunch while on the run and hoped to finish work by 5:00 pm.

If one appointment ran late, that theme continued throughout the day and we would arrive back at the hotel late in the evening. I was impressed with how Doreen bought merchandise. I made notes at all the meetings with vendors, watching as she confidently remembered everything, including style numbers from previous seasons. The days were long and by the end of the week, I was exhausted but pleased with how much I had learned.

Jess enjoyed her week with the Pardys; so much in fact, that she was surprised to see me back so soon.

"I am staying here next time too," she informed me when I arrived to pick her up. Mr. Pardy told me stories from the week-long visit, and it seemed clear that they had enjoyed having Jess as much as she enjoyed being with them.

I was back to work on Monday morning and met with the company president to discuss my first buying trip. As he sat behind his desk, he cleared his throat and adjusted his reading glasses.

"Doreen does not impress easily," he began while briefly glancing up from his papers. "She has high standards, and she expects the same from those around her. You have obviously impressed her. The only somewhat negative feedback was that you need to be more rested in preparation for the long workdays." I smiled in agreement. "We are both impressed; you have a good work ethic, Bev. Well done," he added.

I enjoyed the supervisory role and got along well with the rest of the staff. The women in my department all became good friends. I was still teaching evening classes at the college; however, I decided to cut down on the number of sewing projects I had at home. My income had stabilized, and I no longer needed to work as much to support Jess and me.

My first professional photoshoot with the photographer from Toronto was an incredible experience. The process started with outfits being selected for me for each look. In turn, the make-up artist had me sit in a chair facing a mirror surrounded by bright lights and a wide array of make-up and hair products.

It seemed like it took forever to get ready, but it was worth it. The make-up application was what I had imagined a movie star might go through and not something I could even attempt myself.

Once my hair had been styled, make-up applied, and wardrobe

assigned, I sat and waited for my turn with the photographer. A driver was ready to take the photographer, equipment, and model out to a location that had been previously scouted. These locations could be anywhere from an abandoned graffiti-painted building to a scenic coastline or someone's front porch.

When proofs or 'contact sheets' arrived at the agency several weeks later, I drove out to meet with Linda. Together we reviewed the shots and selected the most ideal photos for my book. Shades of brown eyeshadow were used to make my blue eyes stand out and the chosen outfits made me look taller than I actually was.

I looked at the photos and stared in disbelief. "I can't believe this is me," I told Linda. With my hair styled and make-up applied, I hardly recognized myself.

Once Linda added my photos to her agency book, I began to get calls for auditions. One of my first jobs was for a television commercial for a local college. This was followed by a booking for a couple of fashion shows; a marketing company hired me and another model to act as mannequins for an event they were hosting in St. John's. For that job, we had to stand in a comfortable pose and hold still for 20 minutes at a time.

As guests passed through, they questioned if we were real or not. After my first rotation, I asked if I could wear sunglasses. They were a game-changer as guests were no longer standing around waiting for me to blink. Some people even poked me to see if I was real.

I was excited when Linda called to ask if I would like to audition for a West Side Charlie's television commercial and ecstatic when I was selected for the job. The commercial was recorded as I repeatedly leaned over a pool table, lined up a pool cue, and broke the balls.

I thoroughly enjoyed the day of filming and the opportunity to meet new people from the industry. The pay was a bonus, as I would have been happy to do the work for free.

When the commercial aired on television, customers at the store and others I would randomly meet, asked if I was a pool shark or if I was really 'that good' at pool.

"I am not," I freely confessed. Jess was fascinated every time she saw me appear on television.

I recall on one of my days off, I was relaxing on the sofa when suddenly, I became extremely nauseous, and my eyesight went cloudy. Rubbing my eyes, I tried to clear my vision, but it remained blurred. I tried to relax, closed my eyes, and lay still. After 20 minutes my vision returned to normal.

I tried to get up but was stopped in my tracks by a severe

throbbing pain in the side of my head. The pain was intense and debilitating. It seemed that light made it worse and the brightness from the window hurt my eyes. This lasted the entire day.

When the excruciating pain finally subsided to a dull headache, I called the hospital emergency department and was told that I had likely experienced a migraine. The pain lasted for another two days. It was the first of what would be many severe migraines.

In a group email from the modelling agency, Linda told us about the upcoming Canadian Model and Talent Convention (CMTC) in Toronto. Agents came from all over the world to scout new talent. In advertisements for the annual event, previously discovered famous models and actors who had been at the convention were highlighted. Many returned as guest speakers to talk about their careers and how they were discovered at this event.

It was the opportunity of a lifetime. Models from all over the country participated and competed in various categories, hoping for their big break.

Linda invited me, and the others in the agency, to participate in an information session on the convention, "For those that are serious about a career in modelling, or who would like to model or act outside of the province or country, this convention is a must," she said.

I wanted to go, of course, but worried about how I would afford the trip. Linda proposed we pay a deposit and fundraise as a group to cover the balance. The more money we raised, the cheaper it would be for all of us. As a group, we would also train together to ensure we were in the best possible shape for any category in which we chose to compete. By the end of the night, there were a dozen people signed up, including me.

I was excited and I remembered an earlier conversation I had with Lulu. It turns out, I wasn't the only model in the family. Natasha, Lulu's granddaughter, was discovered at age 14 when she placed first runner up in a Casablanca 'look of the year' contest. Her beauty was internationally showcased at age 15 when she graced the cover of French Cosmopolitan for the first time.

During a visit to South Brook, Lulu proudly showed me Natasha's most recent work. Flipping through the latest magazines, we found pictures of her modelling for Oil of Olay, Lady Stetson, Old Spice, and more. We also found plenty of pictures in bridal magazines. Lulu had created her own collector's album of Natasha's pictures.

At 19, Natasha was cast in the lead role of the science-fiction feature film, Species. I was proud to hear about Natasha and even more proud to be related to her. I excitedly told Linda about my cousin while visiting the agency. "Natasha Henstridge, the Canadian Actress; she was born in central Newfoundland and she starred in Species with Forest Whitaker and Ben Kingsley... we haven't met yet though." I felt inspired as we talked about Natasha's success.

Linda had already recorded my weight, height, and body measurements for her files but now, in preparation for the convention, they needed to be updated regularly. I held my breath as she wrapped a measuring tape around my bust, waist, and thighs. She pointed to the widest part of my thigh and commented, "Maybe we can tighten up a little around here?" I agreed without hesitation.

At first, I hadn't grasped the significance of my conversation with Linda or the impact it would have on my body, but I immediately began weighing myself every day. I started the day by stepping on a weight scale and I finished the day by doing the same thing.

To exercise with workout videos, I moved the coffee table from the center of our family room. Some days, Jess changed into her 'exercise clothes' and joined me. When I saw no difference on the scale, I began to cut back on the amount of food I ate and stopped snacking between meals. When the scale flashed 120 pounds instead of the usual 121, I was tickled pink.

"It's about freaking time," I grumbled at the scale. That excitement lasted through to my next meal; the weight loss only motivated my desire to shed more pounds from my already small frame. On workdays, I avoided the staff room so my colleagues wouldn't know I hadn't eaten. I had grapes, an apple, or a few leaves of lettuce stuffed in my lunch bag, just in case the hunger became intolerable.

At home, I was careful to hide my reduced diet from Jess. Chris was now living with us but went directly to the garage most days after work. He dabbled in auto-body as a hobby and I usually didn't see him until late at night. He wasn't around enough to notice the changes in my eating habits. Although I was bothered by how little time we spent together, I was too busy preparing for the convention to make a big deal of it.

The Christmas holidays were pretty special that year. Jess and I spent time with Chris and his family before visiting the Pardys. Jess was thrilled as everyone showered her with gifts and special attention. Chris's mom cooked a large turkey dinner and her mom, Chris's Nan, joined us.

After dinner, we moved to the family room for the gift exchange. Christmas programs lit up the television screen in the background while Jess delivered each gift to its recipient before sitting next to the tree to open her batch. She leisurely unwrapped and showed me every surprise before moving on to the next. Chris's mom and I talked for hours, I enjoyed spending time with her. She was such a gentle, compassionate woman. I thought Chris was lucky. She was the ideal mother.

Early in the new year, a local newspaper called *The Compass* ran a story about me. They praised my talent and announced that I was headed to Toronto to compete nationally at the Canadian Model and Talent Convention.

My photo was included with the article and immediately people began visiting me at work or stopping me in public to ask questions about modelling and the convention. The attention was a little overwhelming at first as my self-esteem had yet to catch up with my public profile.

The closer we got to the convention, the more pressure I placed on myself to be thinner. I had become totally obsessed with food. The more weight I lost, or when people noticed and commented, the more infatuated I was with controlling every morsel that went into my mouth.

I was totally surprised and caught off guard when Chris proposed to me. He offered a beautiful high-set diamond solitaire ring and I accepted. We were excited and happy to share the news with his parents and closest friends.

The excitement, however, was short-lived. I soon returned the ring to him. I loved Chris, but I couldn't shake the feeling that something was missing from our relationship. We didn't spend much time together as a couple, and even less time as a family of three. I worried this would carry over into marriage, and I didn't want to live that way. Chris wanted to give it time, so we continued as a couple, but I wasn't convinced it would last.

Initially, Jess had been spending every second weekend with her dad, but eventually, she didn't want to visit as often. At first, I encouraged her to continue the visits but when her resistance turned to tears, I decided to let her make her own decision.

It was around that same time when I approached Joey for permission to change Jessica's last name to match mine. Joey immediately became angry and hostile. I tried to explain that it would be more convenient as she spent most of her time with me, but he disagreed. A heated argument escalated, and threats were made. I contacted the police and followed their advice to file a peace bond through court.

Joey and I were divorced and both dating other people. I was 27 years old, and he was 32. I was tired of the bickering and the peace bond was the last straw. After four years in our house in Georgetown, I decided to move to Bay Roberts, the community where I worked. I was ready to leave the community to put distance between Joey and me. This time, I asserted, I was ready to leave my hometown for good.

On my next day off, I went to Bay Roberts to look at rental properties. There was a 'For Sale' sign on my house only a few days before I received a call of interest. The caller, Michelle, asked if I would consider a 'rent-to-own' agreement with her and her fiancée. I asked for time to consider the proposal and after a couple of weeks and no potential buyers, I called and invited her over to discuss the option.

After walking through the house and looking at the rooms, Michelle looked at her fiancée and said, "I love it. It's perfect for us." He agreed.

We sat at the kitchen table to talk terms. We agreed on the numbers and a protection clause. If they missed three consecutive months' rent, they would forfeit all monies paid to date.

"I will have my lawyer draw up a contract with the specifics. I do have two requests. I'll need you to give me advance notice if your rent payment is going to be late because I too will have rent to pay." Michelle confidently agreed.

"I'll also ask you to notify me in writing and I will respond in writing if you want to make structural changes to the house," I said. "We can do that too," Michelle confirmed. "Perfect. I will include those specifics in the contract."

I wasn't sure who was happier, the couple about to move into the house or me moving out. I loved our home, but I was ready for the move.

As we packed everything, Chris and I decided to continue living together. We chose a basement apartment in a new house. The two-bedroom apartment was spacious. It had a private driveway and entrance, and it was close to both our work locations.

Jess wasn't happy about the move, and I couldn't blame her. We had built a life in Georgetown, and she had especially loved being close to Melinda, Aunt Marie, and her friends on the street. I knew the move was for the best and I promised to make it up to her, somehow.

As we walked into Jess' new school at Amalgamated Academy in Bay Roberts, we were directed toward the fourth-grade classroom. Mrs. Sheppard took Jess by her hand and welcomed her to the class. I could tell by the look on Jess's face that she was scared, but Mrs. Sheppard told me to "go ahead," that she would be fine.

Tears filled my eyes as I walked away from the classroom. I was sad that I had disappointed my little girl.

Mr. and Mrs. Pardy, Eddie and Jess

Sad Eyes

Before heading to Toronto for the convention, I spoke with Lulu on the telephone who had been talking to Natasha's mom, Helen. I was told that Natasha was in Toronto shooting a film with Jean-Claude Van Damme.

Although I had already met both of her parents, I had yet to meet Natasha herself. Lulu told me that Helen was currently on location with Natasha and planned to be there for some of the filming.

I arrived in Toronto a day early and while meeting a friend for coffee, talked about Natasha's movie. My friend told me he already knew about the film production. He had read about it in the morning newspaper; the article had revealed the set location and it wasn't far from my hotel. My friend knew his way around Toronto and offered to take me to the set.

I assumed Natasha's family had told her about me by now and I wondered if she would be interested in meeting me. I had no idea how busy she was or if I could even get close to her on set but I decided to give it a try.

As we got out of the taxi, we could see trailers, crew members, and film equipment on site. We walked around for a minute or two before asking for directions. I noticed a muscular guy with folded arms stationed next to a lineup of trailers. "He looks like a security guard and probably knows everyone around here," I commented to my friend. "Excuse me, sir, I am looking for my cousin, Natasha Henstridge." I politely stated.

"Yeah," he said, as he was clearly studying my face. "You look like her. Follow me, I'll take you to her." My friend and I smiled at each other. I expected it to be much more difficult and although I hadn't seen the resemblance, I appreciated the compliment.

"Natasha's grandmother and a few other members of the family have told me that I look like Helen, Natasha's mom," I told my friend.

Having stayed a few steps ahead of us, the security guard stopped to knock on a trailer door. I was happy to see Helen on the other side as the door swung open. "Hi, Bev! What are you doing here? Come on in," she said as she pushed the door open.

"I'm in Toronto for a convention, and I heard from your mom that you were in the area. I thought it would be a good time to stop by. I was also hoping to finally meet Natasha," I explained.

I had just uttered her name when Natasha appeared from a back room. She walked directly toward us with a smile on her face and an extended hand.

"Hi! I'm Natasha!"

Natasha was a sight to be seen. She was camera-ready for the next scene with her hair, clothing, and make-up all in perfect order. As she spoke with confidence, I stood there and figured she was probably the most beautiful woman I had ever seen. I couldn't help but feel a little star-struck.

Helen spoke up. "Bev is Marie's daughter. Do you remember Marie? She worked for mom."

"Yes, I remember," Natasha confirmed.

We sat and talked about family connections back in Central Newfoundland. Helen was pleased to learn that I had met my father and she was even happier to hear that his family had accepted me. We were still talking about family when the door opened and a man in full make-up, walked in and joined us on the sofas.

"This is my cousin from Newfoundland," Natasha announced.

"More of those good-looking genes," he said with a smile.

He was extremely handsome. His dark wavy hair was slicked back, and he was wearing small framed glasses. I couldn't believe my eyes. It was Jean-Claude Van Damme! A patch of heavy make-up above his right eye was shaded in just the right colours to mimic a bruise. Although I could see that the make-up had produced the fake injury, I suspected it would appear very real on camera.

He was dressed in black jeans, layered tops, a long dangling black scarf, and a brown jacket. Having seen some of his movies, I was surprised to see that he looked smaller in person than I would have thought.

As Jean-Claude Van Damme stood next to me, I observed that he was about my height and less bulky than he appeared on TV. I was pleasantly surprised by the casual laid-back conversation we were all able to share.

The entire encounter felt surreal. I could not believe my luck. Not only did I meet my cousin, but I also met Jean-Claude Van Damme on the set for the movie Maximum Risk. Before leaving, we snapped a few photos and exchanged hugs. I couldn't wipe the smile from my face for the remainder of the day.

Back at the hotel reception area, I ran into some of the other models from the agency. I was told Linda had requested we all meet in her room later that evening to run through a few things. As the group gathered, Linda reminded us that it was important we get enough sleep, eat healthily, and stay hydrated.

The next morning began with the photography competition. Along with the other participants in my division, I fell in line toward the back of the room. A single line formed around the room's perimeter, starting near the stage.

Every competition followed the same format. The competition was organized by age category, with the young children competing first and the mature models appearing as the last category. As the line slowly moved, I watched the models ahead of me.

For photography, I wore a short-sleeve black *Classique Models* t-shirt, black jeans and as Linda had recommended, I kept my hair up and away from my face. As I walked the length of the runway, two of my photos were being shown on large screens behind me.

For this particular competition, Linda had selected two photos: a headshot of me wearing a brown turtleneck sweater with matching eye make-up, and one of me and Jess, a black and white photo with our hair styled in ringlet curls. The picture looked like it could have been used to promote hair care products. I was especially proud when telling the others that the little girl in the photo was my daughter.

As each model from our agency walked the runway, the rest of us enthusiastically showed support with loud applause and cheers. The other agencies did the same.

The acting category was intimidating. I wasn't as comfortable as I had hoped to be as I read my lines, but Linda reminded me that it was another opportunity to be seen by scouting agents, and I was happy with that. The others from my division were probably more talented actors. I was relieved to see this competition took place in a smaller conference room and not on stage in the main ballroom in front of everyone.

Meals were served buffet style in the hotel restaurant. I watched my calories and went for the lighter fare. I chose salads for lunch and dinner, and I purposely didn't snack between or after meals. Scouting agents were everywhere, and as contestants, we felt like we were under a microscope with them watching our every move.

We were conscious about the people we passed in hallways and always quick to flash a smile. Without knowing it, we could have been sharing an elevator with an elite VIP. Most agents wore identifying name tags, but like us, they too probably felt as though they were being watched and some removed their lanyards once outside the ballroom.

Walking the lengthy runway in the main ballroom was nerve-wracking on its own. A quivering lip would make it that much harder so I tried to conceal the tension from my face.

Linda had taught me facial exercises to do just before stepping on the stage. The movements loosened my facial muscles and allowed me to smile more comfortably. I shared the tip with the other girls in my division and we practiced every time before hitting the runway.

From the stage, I looked out to see rows of banquet tables covered with white cloth, wrapping the perimeter of the runway. They were full of scouting agents who watched attentively. Most didn't return our smile from the runway but a select few always did.

Members of the agency met in Linda's hotel room every evening as a way of checking in. Together, we reviewed the day's activities before Linda prepared us for the following day's line-up of competitions. Before dismissing the group, Linda called several names, including mine. She asked those named to remain with her so she could talk to them privately. I stayed seated and waited for my turn as she spoke to models individually in the hallway.

When it was my turn, Linda revealed that she had been contacted by a South Korean agency and they were interested in me. I was speechless.

I asked, "What does that mean?"

"Well, assuming you're interested, they will offer you a contract for 90 days," she told me.

My brain was in overdrive as I spewed questions faster than I could process Linda's answers. I knew very little about South Korea. "Was it safe? Where would I stay?"

Linda interrupted. "They will provide travel and living arrangements, but we are getting a little ahead of ourselves. Before anything, we need to apply for a work visa. That can be challenging and might take some time. Let's get through the convention, and I will follow up as soon as we get home."

I was thrilled. If I didn't win anything at the convention, I was satisfied to have received interest from an agency. Excitement kept me awake as I thought about the potential of professionally modelling in a different county and South Korea of all places. Wow!

During registration, all contestants had received a three-digit ID number for the event. The number was boldly imprinted on a lanyard and we were advised to always wear it. The model's number (along with age, height, and representing agency) was published in a show guide, under the various categories. Everyone, including the agents, had a copy of the show guide. Throughout the week, agents referred to it for information on any model of interest to them.

At the end of the week, agents submitted a list of model numbers for those they wished to follow up with; basically, a call-back list. Event organizers summarized a list for each model and delivered it to their representing agencies. Linda told me that the South Korean agency would not request a call-back for me as they had already expressed their interest through her.

The competitions wrapped up on Saturday and an award ceremony took place that evening. Dressed in our best formal wear, we received a tasty three-course meal before the awards were handed out.

I became anxious when I saw a multitude of models from our agency being identified as winners. I listened attentively when the speaker reached my division for each award category.

Not surprisingly, my name was not called for the swimsuit or photography competition. My division had a lot of great talent and I hadn't expected to place in either of those categories.

However, I was hopeful for the runway category and listened attentively as winners were announced one by one. Third runner-up, second runner-up, first runner-up... and the winner - not me. I was discouraged. This was the category I had felt most confident in. I smiled through the disappointment.

Next were the acting awards. The recipients were named for each category starting with the youngest group. I sat a little taller when the speaker reached my division, not because I expected to win, but because I wanted to see who the potential actors were from my group.

I spent hours in the line-up with these girls and I wanted to show my support for them. They proceeded to announce the third-place winner, second place, and the first runner-up: "Bev Moore from Classique Models!"

I looked at Linda in total shock. While clapping with the crowd, she smiled and motioned for me to go to the stage.

My heart raced as I approached the podium. Was this for real? Of all the categories, this was not one I expected to be recognized for. I accepted the award and shook the presenter's hand before posing for a photograph. When I got back to the table, Linda proudly smiled and walked toward me for a hug.

As the evening came to a close, we proceeded to the lobby for an agency group photo. Linda beamed with pride as she talked about our accomplishments and gave out the call-back lists for the next morning.

Linda reiterated, "Many models do not get call-backs. I still encourage you to attend the networking forum. It's another chance to impress them as they look through your book and offer valuable feedback."

She continued, "Remember, you are not permitted to wear make-up. So ensure you are well-rested. Now go back to your rooms and get some sleep!"

Morning came too soon. I grabbed my portfolio and followed the others downstairs to a smaller ballroom. Inside, the space appeared less congested with a small quantity of round, white cloth-covered tables placed on the burgundy carpet.

There was an agent or two at each table and groups of networking people standing around them. The models stood next to the tables anxiously awaiting feedback as the agents looked through their books.

We had three minutes with an agent before a bell rang that signalled it was time to move on to the next table. As the first agent scanned through my book, I glanced back over my shoulder to see Nikki, one of the girls from my agency, crying. She had clearly been subjected to someone's harsh criticism. Linda had tried to prepare us for networking, but when you were face-to-face with a critical agent, it was challenging.

I moved from one agent to another, recording their feedback in a small notebook. One agent told me I was too commercial, while another told me I was too editorial. Several complimented me on my runway performance, and one said I had a very 60's look. I wasn't sure what that meant but thanked him just the same.

At the next table, an agent accepted my book and quickly browsed through it. His speed and limited conversation seemed to communicate a lack of interest. However, once he got to the last page, he surprisingly flipped the book back to the beginning and took another full pass through. At one point, he stopped and glanced up at me before returning his gaze to a black and white photo. He turned to the next page and looked up at me again. There was a brief pause before he spoke.

"Your pictures are beautiful," he commented.

"Thank you!"

There was another lengthy stare at the open book. I prepared myself for constructive feedback and hoped the comments would not be too harsh. There was another lengthy gaze. It felt like he was staring into my soul. I was starting to feel a little uncomfortable.

"Your pictures are beautiful," he repeated, before taking a pensive pause, "But your eyes are sad. You have sad eyes." I summoned an awkward smile and nodded in agreement.

Back in my room, I lay on the bed and scanned through my notebook of comments. The feedback was diverse, and fortunately, nothing negative. I reflected on the comment about my eyes. Could the agent be right? Did I have sad eyes? No one had ever said that to me before. I pulled the book toward me and began studying every photo. With an open page, I placed my hand over my face to entirely cover the bottom half; I wanted to observe just my eyes.

To my disbelief, I saw my eyes as the agent had. I moved from one photo to another, covering the bottom portion of my face with my hand. I was shocked! There was sadness in my eyes. I wondered if others had ever noticed this, or maybe he was the first person to ever really look into my eyes.

When I arrived home, I was exhausted. When the energy didn't return, and my breathing seemed to be shallow, I went to the doctor for a checkup. Dr. Power took my vitals before inviting me up onto the weigh scale. "Your blood pressure is low, and 110 pounds is not a healthy weight for your height," he said.

I knew he was right. I could feel the looseness of my clothes and my rib cage was much more pronounced than usual. Friends had started to notice and comment on my sunken cheeks. "I will put the weight back on," I told him, acknowledging that he was right –

I was too thin.

Seven years had passed since I had run away from home, still, nighttime was a challenge. The last thing I did before going to bed at night was check and recheck that the door leading into our apartment was secure. Yet I found myself waking up almost every night and walking to the door to confirm it was indeed locked. Many nights, I was still half asleep when I found myself at the door vigorously shaking the knob to ensure no one could enter.

Some nights, I slept through the nightmares, while other nights, I would wake up shaking. I often screamed for help in my dreams, but no sound would come out. Each time, I woke up terrified. On one particular night, Chris was startled when I woke up fiercely screaming. I struggled with blankets as I attempted to get out of the bed while crying for help. Chris tried to calm me, but I continued to intensely fight him off until I was fully awake. By then, I was in tears.

We remained close to the Pardys and visited them as much as we could. On one occasion, Eddie invited us over to see a surprise that he had built for Jess. With excitement in his voice, he led us through his property, past the vegetable gardens, through a winding path and dense trees to a wide-open space with a gazebo, horseshoe pit, and hammock.

We had been there before and enjoyed the beautiful setting with an assortment of amenities, all handmade by Eddie. Wooden chairs were strategically placed throughout the park-like space and to our right, we noticed something new. It looked like a small cabin! As Eddie handed Jess a set of keys, he announced, "Here are the keys to your new house."

It was approximately eight by ten feet in size and had a small window and door in the front. The inside was one big room with a small table attached to the back wall. Jess was excited as she ran around the inside, and then the outside, of her new house. Her little home was hidden in what looked like a magical garden behind Eddie's house. She loved it! Jess spent a great deal of time with Eddie and his family. I was thankful for the stability they brought to our lives.

My relationship with Chris was a bit of a roller coaster ride with plenty of on-again and off-again cycles. The break-ups usually went the same: I gathered the courage to end the relationship and explain, in my opinion, that something was missing. After a short break, he talked me into giving it another chance.

I maintained a limited relationship with my adopted parents. They had moved from Brigus to a new house in Bay Roberts. I dropped in for occasional short visits. Father appeared to be constantly medicated, and in a zombie-like state, at all times.

Memories of my childhood came back when I saw Mother controlling his every move. She told him when to get up and when to go to bed. She managed his every step throughout the day. Father watched television constantly and said very little. Being in their house was uncomfortable for me. However, I continued to visit and tried to maintain a relationship with the people who had raised me.

Surprisingly, Mother found herself a younger boyfriend. At first, he visited only at night when Father was in bed, but over time, his visits became less restricted. It was awkward to hear Mother talk about her boyfriend and I wondered what he thought of her situation. I decided not to judge, comment, or get involved. I also chose to avoid visits when she had company.

Chris and I were still living together. I begrudgingly paid rent every month as I mentally struggled with the notion of paying someone else's mortgage, instead of my own. Chris felt the same way, but I wasn't ready to share the responsibility of a home with anyone else. He was understandably upset when I told him that I had decided to buy a house without him.

I reached out to Lloyd, a well-known reputable real estate agent from our area and the husband of one of my co-workers. We talked about location, the type of house I wanted, and most importantly, budget. He listened attentively and made notes before he pulled out his book of listings. I had a modest budget but was hopeful about finding something affordable in the Bay Roberts area.

Although I lived on a fairly tight budget, I had investments, relatively untouched, from my insurance settlement. Occasional flare-ups with my back created instability and I was sometimes forced to take a week or two off work. During those times, I had no choice but to withdraw the equivalent of my regular paycheque from the investments. Fear of a significant flare-up prevented me from using the money for frivolous reasons, but a down payment on a house did not fall into that category.

Lloyd and I set out to visit houses and I was pleased with the location and price of a bungalow on Mission Lane in the same town. The house was older, but with the selling price, I could afford renovations to modernize. It was also within walking distance of Jess's school and minutes from my work.

We discussed the selling price, and I proposed a fair offer. I asked Lloyd to explain to the homeowners that I was interested in purchasing the home, but not in negotiating. I felt the initial offer was fair and hoped they would accept but had no plans to counter-offer. I didn't want to sound arrogant, that wasn't my nature, I just never liked haggling. Lloyd agreed to follow my instructions.

When he called with an update from the homeowners, his voice was calm and lacking enthusiasm. I immediately concluded that they had declined my offer. He continued to provide details of the meeting, but then he surprised me with a change in the tone of his voice as he declared, "They accepted your offer!"

We moved into the house and I immediately hired a contractor friend to start renovations. The exterior was the first to be updated with new windows, doors, siding and a large wrap-around deck. From the outside, the house looked brand new.

Next, I enlisted the help of a few more friends and contractors for the inside. Eddie quickly worked on the landscaping. In no time, he cleaned up the property, planted a chestnut tree and a rose bush, and built a rock wall.

Living in the house during renovations was awful. There was dust on my clothes, furniture, and even inside the cupboards. We decided to grin and bear it, hoping the result would be worth the anguish. I worked at Wescal all day and came home at night to help with plastering and painting.

The master bedroom closet was smaller than the one I left behind at the apartment. With a pencil and paper, I sketched a design that maximized the new storage space. I purchased materials, borrowed tools and in the end, I was proud to have a one-of-a-kind closet that I designed and built entirely by myself.

We were ecstatic when the renovations were finally completed. The house looked nothing like its original state. Jess loved her new bedroom and was happy to have helped with its design.

Just when I thought the stalker had given up or moved on, I would receive another phone call or some reminder that he was still out there. Once when I stopped for gas, I opened my gas tank cover to find a handful of maple leaves stuffed inside, most likely from the mature trees on my property. Another night, I left work late and found my car windshield had been covered in what looked like spit.

Each incident was more bothersome than the last. I arrived home one Sunday afternoon to a message that had been left on my answering machine. The recording started with a brief silence followed by the sound of running water. It sounded like the caller had placed the phone next to a tap. I thought it must be a bathtub faucet as the sound seemed to have an echo. I listened and waited for a voice. There was no voice, just the sound of running water.

I have had a life-long fear of water, though few people knew about it. I wondered if the running water was a coincidence or if someone knew about my fear and was taunting me. I was scared and made notes to have added to my file at the police department.

During one of our "off-again" phases, Chris moved back to his family home. Not long after, I received a phone call from Mother asking if she could stay with us for a while. She had purchased a new house and it wouldn't be ready for another few weeks.

April agreed to let Father stay with her, so it was just Mother who needed accommodations. I told myself that time had passed, and things were different now, and I agreed to her request.

She arrived with the bare essentials and told me everything else was in storage. She was content and enjoyed her time with Jess while I was at work. Tracey and her husband, both nurses, had been working in Alberta for several years and recently returned to the province to accept positions at the Health Sciences Center. Mother was happy to have Tracey back home.

One day at work, I received an unexpected call from Tracey. She was distraught and had trouble getting her words out. Once she calmed down, she explained that Mother had been at her house a couple of days earlier and saw Tracey lightly tap her son on the forehead to get his attention. Later, when Tracey and Mother had a disagreement, Mother decided to call the Department of Child Youth and Family Services claiming that Tracey was abusing her children.

As with any child abuse complaint, the protocol had to be followed. An investigation was opened, and a social worker visited Tracey's eldest son at his new school. Tracey was mortified when she received a call from a school official who informed her of the visit.

Tracey called Ms. Rose, the social worker that used to oversee our foster home years ago, and explained the situation. Ms. Rose told Tracey that the department took every complaint seriously because that was a requirement, and they would need to complete the investigation. However, she added that staff were quite familiar with Mrs. Moore and were accustomed to her accusations. My sister was heartbroken that Mother would do that to her; up until now, Mother and Tracey had a good relationship.

I had endured a lifetime of hurt from Mother and dealt with every problem as it arose. At the end of the day, I always forgave her, and I didn't harbour animosity. However, when she hurt my sister, I was affected on a different level. Lunchtime was 30 minutes away and by the time I left work to drive home, I was shaking. I calmly walked from my car into the house. Once inside, I couldn't hold my silence any longer. Mother was standing in the kitchen when I closed the door behind me.

In a trembling voice, I asked, "Did you call the child protective services on Tracey?"

"What if I did? What's it to you?" she responded with arrogance.

"Tracey is my sister... I won't let you hurt her," I said.

Mother placed her hands on her hips and mocked me, "She's your sister, is she?"

"She does not abuse her children, and you know that. If you want to talk about abuse, you know, I can tell you about abuse," I impulsively shot back.

Never one to back down, Mother asked, "Really, and who the fuck do you think you are?"

I could never go up against Mother, I quickly realized. My knees were already weak from speaking up to her.

"If you are hurting Tracey, you cannot stay here in my house. I won't allow it. I am going back to work and I want you to leave. I want you to be gone before I get home this evening," I said, as I turned and walked out the door.

My hands trembled as I shifted the car into gear and drove back to work. I could not believe I actually stood up to Mother. I had been to hell and back and never before had the courage to speak up for myself, or anyone else for that matter.

I felt numb when I pulled into the parking lot at work. I hadn't eaten lunch and had no appetite. For the remainder of my break, I sat in the car and replayed the conversation over and over in my head.

I was overwhelmed with relief and gratitude when I walked into the house at the end of the day and Mother wasn't there. When I spoke to Tracey on the phone, she disclosed that she and her husband had accepted nursing positions in Maine.

Tracey said she was done with Mother. She would leave with her family in a week, and they wouldn't be returning to Newfoundland. I was sad and disappointed but supportive of her decision. I decided then that I too would end my relationship with Mother for good.

About a month later, April called to chat. She told me that Father had been on a waitlist for an opening at a local senior citizens' home, which had become available two weeks earlier. Mother had quickly paid the fees and moved him in.

Despite the horrible things he had done to me as a child, I felt terrible for him. He didn't have a good life with Mother—no one did. I decided to visit him, and I took Jess with me.

It was early in the evening when we checked in at the nurses' station and asked for Father's room number. Jess and I swung arms while holding hands as we walked toward his room. As I turned left to enter, Jess followed. My eyes were immediately drawn to him lying there on a twin-sized bed.

He was completely dressed but had his penis out in his hands. I quickly pulled Jess's arm and jolted her back into the hallway. From outside, I bent down to talk to her as I anxiously listened to see if she had seen what I had. Fortunately, she hadn't.

I told Jess to wait in the hallway as I checked in on Father before we visited. I walked into his room and in a firm voice, ordered him to "Put that away!" I was disgusted. He laughed and zipped up his pants. "That's not funny. I have a child with me. What's wrong with you?" I snapped. There was no reply, only a burst of childish laughter. "If you ever do that again, it will be the last time you get a visit from either of us. Do you hear me?"

With a stupid grin, and without speaking, he acknowledged that he understood.

I led Jess back into the room for a very brief visit during which we remained standing the entire time. I was upset, though I successfully concealed my emotions from Jess. Father seemed more energetic and talkative, and certainly less medicated than I had seen him in a long time.

At home, I waited until Jess was settled in bed before calling Tracey to talk about the nursing home incident. Tracey told me that Mother took him to a psychiatrist after I ran away and asked that he prescribe a drug to kill his sex drive. "The street name is Salt-Peter, but I can't remember the actual name of the drug," she shared.

As the call ended, I thought about the conversation. Tracey didn't know Father had sexually abused me, and I wasn't ready to disclose it to her. Mother obviously had a problem with his sex drive.

I wondered why she had taken the issue to a doctor after I left home and not before. I couldn't help but think that she may have known what he was doing to me. Those thoughts haunted me.

Cal, the owner of Wescal, also owned a couple of other businesses including a building supplies company and the local gym. Employees of both companies had free access to the gym, though very few took advantage of the facility. The gym was within walking distance of my house and had the amenities to please any fitness enthusiast. With my own key to the gym, I could visit anytime, day or night. It didn't take long to make friends there and I looked forward to each visit.

My workouts were regimented; I started with 20 minutes of cardio, then moved on to resistance training. If time was limited, I skipped cardio and went straight to the weights. Going to the gym became somewhat compulsive as I challenged myself to go five days a week. Over time issues with food became less of a focus as I became more consumed with working out.

I needed extra energy for the gym, and I began eating more regularly. I now cared less about the types of food that I was consuming. Unbeknownst to me, I replaced my unhealthy addiction to monitoring food with a healthier obsession for working out. The more time I spent at the gym, the more I was focused on a healthier body image.

On and off, Chris and I had spent seven years together. When he took the last of his belongings from my house, I realized it was over. As Jess attended junior high, I began thinking about university. I was no longer content at Wescal and began considering other career choices. For years, I had thought about studying psychology. It seemed my timing, as well as finances, had never aligned.

When the timing was right, I walked into Cal's office and told him that I was ready to move on to the next stage of my career. I had worked at Wescal for seven years and had seen consistent growth in my departments. I had learned a lot from the team and felt good about my accomplishments. Now, I was ready to go back to school and work on a career. Cal was disappointed but supportive of my decision to further my education.

I enjoyed having a full summer off before starting the Fall semester of general studies at the Carbonear Campus, which was the closest to my home in Bay Roberts. I registered for Biology, Physics, Chemistry, English, and Calculus Math, all courses that were transferable to Memorial University programs in St. John's.

It was a couple of weeks into the school year when Chris walked into my physics class. He sat down in the seat directly in front of me.

I leaned forward and whispered, "What are you doing here?"

"I am going to school."

"Seriously. What are you doing?"

He reclined back, "I registered for an engineering program. I registered late and therefore had to challenge the program by writing a test."

With a wink, he smiled and nodded his head, "I obviously did well, so here I am."

Bev - Sad Eyes (photo credit Robert Collins)

Bev with Jean-Claude Van Damme

A New Life

That first semester was a major adjustment. As Jess left for junior high in the morning, I drove with my new school friends towards the Carbonear campus for my first year of general studies. My regimented workdays had been replaced with hours of sitting in a classroom and evenings of study.

Within the first couple of weeks, I realized I was in over my head with one particular subject. I hadn't taken chemistry in high school and without that foundation, I didn't have the background needed for university level. After speaking with an academic adviser, we decided it was best to complete the prerequisite course before advancing to this current university-level program.

I joined a study group for physics and calculus, and I carried biology and psychology notes everywhere I went. Whenever there was quiet time, I studied. The first semester was challenging, but in the end, I passed all five of my courses.

Jess and I enjoyed the Christmas holidays without work or studies cutting into our quality time. In January, Jess started preparing for her grade nine prom as I looked forward to completing another semester and getting the first year of general studies under my belt. The second semester hadn't been quite as challenging as the first and I was able to take some time for a social life.

On St. Patrick's Day weekend, Christine, a friend of mine, called to tell me about her holiday plans. She had reserved a room at the Battery Hotel in St. John's with her two sons and wanted to invite Jess and me to join them for the weekend.

Jess had already planned a weekend with her friend, Stephanie, and pleaded with me to allow her to sleep at Steph's house on Friday night. As a compromise, she proposed we take Steph with us when meeting Christine and her boys at the hotel on Saturday night. I agreed to the proposal, then drove her to Steph's house before I drove to the city to meet with Christine at the Sundance Dance Bar.

The Sundance was a multi-level dance bar located on George Street in downtown St. John's. George Street was a prime attraction for locals and tourists alike. It had two blocks of dance bars, pubs, and restaurants, and regardless of the time of year, it was always busy.

The popular nightclubs usually had a line-up outside their entrances as patrons braved the elements while waiting to get inside. The Sundance happened to be one such club with a regular line. Once inside, Christine and I separated as she stopped to talk to a few of her friends and I joined a group on my own.

While I chatted with Dave, a friend of his stopped to say hello. Dave introduced me to Tom, and I recalled that I had met him once before through a different mutual friend. I remembered thinking that he looked young.

Tom was tall and slim with dark curly hair. He was attractive with a pale, youthful complexion, and he wore a blue turtleneck sweater and jeans. The three of us talked for a few minutes before I went back to Christine and my friends.

A little later in the evening, I walked past the dance floor and noticed Tom was dancing. He looked at me and did a double-take when his eyes unexpectedly caught mine. I smiled and waved as I continued on my way.

The dance floor and main level were tightly crowded so I went upstairs for a cold drink and some breathing room. José, another friend, was standing next to the bar and turned to chat when I leaned in to order a bottle of water. José was doing his residency at the Health Science Center and I had met him through a mutual friend. We talked for a few minutes before I noticed Tom walking toward us. He immediately smiled as we made eye contact again. I returned the smile and made room for him to join us.

There was a brief conversation after I introduced the two guys. Tom then apologized for the interruption and proceeded to walk away. I gave him a puzzled look as I suspected he thought he may have interrupted something more than a casual conversation.

"You are not interrupting anything," I reassured him.

Tom smiled but continued to walk away. Then he stopped, turned around, and came back. "José, I don't normally do this, but would you mind if I asked Bev to dance? José stepped aside, "No, I don't mind."

I followed Tom as he walked toward the music. The popular song Amazed by Lonestar was playing. It was a slow song and one of my favourites at the time.

Weaving in and around groups of people, Tom led me to the dance floor. He somehow found just enough room and pulled me toward him.

When the song ended, we remained on the floor and danced to another song, and then another. At the end of the night, the lights

144

were turned on and Tom led me back to his group of friends. After meeting them all, I announced that it was time for me to leave. "I am driving a friend home before heading back to Bay Roberts," I explained.

"Can I get your number?" Tom asked.

"I'm sorry. I don't give out my number... but I'm sure you will see me again," I offered in an upbeat voice while trying to downplay my rejection.

It was a rule I had. I felt bad, but I just didn't like to give out that information. Especially after my experience with the stalker. It's not that I didn't trust him or like him, I just usually followed that rule. I gave him one last smile before I turned and walked away.

I picked Jess and her friend up the following afternoon. "Are you staying for a while Steph?" I asked when I saw her dragging an overnight bag, a backpack, and a pillow into the back of the car. She laughed.

Steph was four months younger than Jess but a full head over her in height. Jess was petite for her age, and I thought Steph was like a big sister in their relationship.

The girls spent most of their time together in and out of school. They had been friends since the fourth grade when we first moved to Bay Roberts. They did girly things together like manicures, pedicures, and facials. I loved Steph; she was friendly, polite, helpful, always upbeat, and smiling. She was a pleasure to have around.

From the back seat of the car, the girls talked and entertained themselves for the entire drive to St. John's. Christine's boys were just back from swimming when we arrived at the hotel but agreed to go back down to the pool with the girls. They spent an hour or more swimming before they returned to the room to make sleeping-bag style beds in front of the television, as they prepared for a highly anticipated movie night.

Christine and I chatted over a drink before heading out to meet friends at the Sundance. I was not a regular drinker, but tonight I decided to leave my car at the hotel and have a drink with the girls. I drank so infrequently that whenever I did, I usually limited myself to just two, and for good reason.

When we had celebrated a friend's birthday the year before, we drank tequila before heading out to a dance bar. I was fine until I walked into the men's washroom. The men squirmed to keep their backs turned as I placed my hands on my hips and asked what they were doing.

Fortunately, a male friend happened to be in the washroom at the same time and offered to walk me back to my friends. It was my only experience with tequila and I earned a hangover that lasted for two full days. My inexperience with alcohol usually left me feeling the effects before I even finished a single drink.

After entering the club, I left Christine to do my usual 'bathroom check'. I joked that my T.B. (tiny bladder) was acting up. As I walked out of the washroom, I glanced over at the bar and saw Tom waiting to be served. I wasn't surprised.

On Friday night, one of his friends asked if he was coming back to the Sundance on Saturday night. He had responded that, although he didn't normally go downtown often, he would likely be back after a Paddy's Day party. The same applied for me; it was uncommon for me to go out two nights in a row.

I had already consumed a full drink and was in a playful mood. I leaned in on the bar and waved, as I tried to get his attention. He didn't notice. I headed back to the group. The girls were in an equally playful mood as we all went to the dance floor together. One song spilled into the next as we continued to dance and enjoy the music.

When Tom walked by, I caught sight of him and flirtatiously pulled him into our circle. The girls and I continued to dance around him as he blushed from the attention.

Tom danced even as he tried to conceal his obvious shyness. I was intrigued and even attracted to his bashfulness. When the song ended, we were left standing together as the girls scattered.

"I told you that you would see me again," I teased, before walking off the dance floor.

Tom followed me back to a less populated area. As we nursed our drinks, we chatted and found connections through friends we had in common. We talked about the coincidence of us both being at the Sundance two nights in a row. The conversation was light and flirty.

When I realized Tom was attracted to me, I told him that I wasn't interested in dating younger men. I had no idea how old he was but suspected he was probably close to ten years my junior— much too young for me. After all, I had a daughter in junior high. In a surprising move, Tom pulled out his wallet and handed me his driver's license.

"Bev, I am not as young as you think," he revealed.

I was shocked to see he was only seven months younger. I acknowledged the ID as a game-changer, "Wow, you look incredibly young for your age."

Tom stated that he was hungry and invited me to join him at Classic Cafe for food. Given his obvious attraction towards me and without the age difference as a deterrent, I saw him through a different lens. Tom seemed like a nice guy. I had nothing to lose.

Maybe it would lead to a new friendship, I thought as we walked to the cafe.

Once we were comfortably settled at a table, I learned that Tom was from St. John's, divorced with two small children, and owned a local business. I did not see that coming. I reminded myself that he was 32, not 22 as I tried to visualize him with children.

Tom's ex-wife was in medical school and they shared custody of the children - a five-year-old boy and a two-year-old girl. While in university, Tom had started his own business and now had a business partner. Surprisingly, I recognized the business name and in fact, had been in his building within the past year.

I told Tom about my 14-year-old daughter and unlike him, I had worked for someone else up until last year when I left my job to go back to school.

I enjoyed Tom's company and the conversation made the hours evaporate. "It's 4:00 am, I have to get back to the hotel," I realized, glancing at my watch.

Outside the cafe, Tom hailed a cab and we drove towards the Battery Hotel. The cab driver waited outside as Tom walked me to the room. From outside the hotel room, we exchanged telephone numbers and programmed them into our cell phones. I thanked him for a fun evening and we both leaned in for a hug.

He was poised without being arrogant or presumptuous and with a slight head turn, our lips met. The embrace was romantic with a kiss so gentle, our lips were barely touching.

Tom called Monday evening. He had his kids this week and said he would wait until they were settled in bed before calling me back. I was happy to hear from him and looked forward to the next call. It was 10:30 p.m. when he called back and by that time, both our children were settled in bed. We talked for over three hours. I fumbled through my textbooks, somewhat studying, as the conversation led into the early morning hours.

The calls continued with a similar pattern every night and after a week, it felt like I knew everything about him. As usual, I was more of a listener than a talker, so consequently, he knew less about me.

Our relationship strengthened with every call and when time allowed, we met in person. Tom's family had cabins halfway between St. John's and Bay Roberts and we sometimes met there for an afternoon or evening.

When Tom had his kids on the weekend, I stayed home, and we chatted on the telephone. On other weekends, we took turns making the one-hour commute. Several weeks into the relationship, Tom invited me to his apartment. He was a gentleman in every sense. I loved being with him and felt no pressure to take our relationship to the next level.

When we slept at his apartment for the first time, I insisted on sleeping on the sofa while Tom pushed for me to take the bed. When I firmly declined, he announced that he would sleep on the sofa regardless of where I chose to sleep.

The sofa couldn't comfortably accommodate two people and after an hour of being cramped and restricted, I agreed to sleep 'on' his bed with him. We moved to the bedroom and although we were more comfortable, neither of us got much sleep. We spent most of the night twisting and turning.

Tom confessed that although he was thrilled to have me sleep over, he was totally intimidated by me. I was equally excited but for different reasons. I was enamoured with his gentle, kind demeanour and by the respect he showed - not only to me but everyone around him. He was a gentleman and quite possibly a prince charming.

When the time felt right, we met each other's children. 14-year old Jess was not fooled when I introduced her to my *friend*, Tom. She had a dry sense of humor and told Tom, "Don't get too comfortable, mom will probably go back to her ex-boyfriend."

I was flabbergasted, though I shouldn't have been. Jess had witnessed Chris and I separate many times in our seven-year relationship. And after all, she was a teenager and quite comfortable speaking her mind.

I met Tom's kids for the first time during a weekend visit. Sarah had brown eyes and curly hair. She was shy and very much her daddy's girl. She held on to her dad's arm as she sat in his lap and sucked on her thumb for most of the visit. When Tom left the room, Sarah followed him.

With a little perseverance, she warmed up to me and I was able to hold her in my arms. Jacob was a lot more rambunctious. He was excited when he led me into his bedroom to show me his toys. I sat on the bed and held figurines as he passed them to me one by one.

A couple of weeks later, Tom had tickets to the Juno awards and invited me to attend. We dropped by his apartment to check on the kids on our way to the show and I met his mom for the first time. She was friendly, but once she revealed that she grew up near Georgetown and knew of both my adopted parents, I became uncomfortable. As the conversation progressed, I wondered how much she actually knew about them.

I completed my second semester at the Carbonear campus and despite the lengthy telephone conversations cutting into study time, I did well in all my courses. I could transfer my first year of college courses to Memorial University, but if I wanted to continue my studies, I had to register at the St. John's campus for the next semester.

When an unforeseen work situation arose, Tom was forced to let go of several employees. Instead of registering for Spring Intersession courses, I agreed to help him out until he could replace the employees.

The business, Fairways Golf, was a large organization with over 20 staff members. It had both indoor and outdoor golf ranges, four professional golf instructors, three golf simulators, a pro-shop, a sports bar, and a paintball business. Without a true understanding of what I was getting myself into, I jumped in completely.

I would wait until Jess left for school in the morning before driving to town to work during the day. During that first week, I got to know the staff and some of the regular customers. As I set up a golf simulator for an early morning booking, a few gentlemen pulled me into their conversation.

"I heard a rumour," one elderly gentleman confided.

"What's that?" I asked.

The gentleman leaned in, "I heard the owner of this place is fooling around with Bev Moore."

With surprise, I asked, "Bev Moore?"

A second gentleman piped up, "Yes. She's a local businesswoman. Together with her husband, they own a bunch of properties and businesses in town."

"Oh, I see. Well yes sir, that is true. Tom is dating Bev Moore."

All three men looked at each other and exchanged affirming nods.

"I am Bev Moore. And I am dating Tom," I announced.

There was a brief pause before these men looked at me in a confused state. One of them spoke up and asked, "You're Bev Moore?"

"Yes! I guess there must be a few of us out there."

Before I had ever met Tom, I had recognized that I would need to move to St. John's eventually if I was to continue with my studies. Travelling from Bay Roberts, the round trip to and from Memorial University would add two hours to an already long school day. For five days a week, I would spend most of my time away from Jess. Then there was the added risk of driving on the highway in unpredictable winter weather.

Jess and I had talked about options, noting that she only had three years of high school left and after graduation also planned to attend university. Although there was no definitive decision, I didn't want to commute.

After completing her residency in St. John's over the summer, Tom's ex-wife decided she would move back to her home province of New Brunswick to set up a private practice. Tom then planned on moving back into his home, and he invited Jess and me to move in with him.

The custody arrangement allowed the kids to spend the school year with their mom in New Brunswick and fly to Newfoundland and Labrador for March break, summer, and Christmas holidays.

Although I was conflicted, Tom eased my worries as he promised to help us move into our own house or apartment, if we decided to part ways. With a leap of faith, I decided to rent my house in Bay Roberts and move with Tom, into his house in St. John's. The decision was out of character for me. After seven years in my previous relationship, I hadn't been ready to commit. I believed Tom was different from any other guy I had ever dated.

During spring and early summer, I met members of Tom's family and in July, we moved into the house together. A chain-link fence with three openings wrapped completely around the large property. The first opening in the fence was to Tom's house, the second was to his brother's and the last was to their parents.

The property was beautiful. The homes were set back off the road, with mature trees that shielded much of the houses from view during the summer and fall seasons.

Tom's place was approximately five years old. He and his brother had built their houses on the family property around the same time. Tom disclosed that he had financed the home through his parents instead of borrowing from a bank and paying interest. When I moved in, no payments had been paid toward the house loan.

We immediately met with Tom's parents and established a repayment plan. Our monthly payment was more than fair, and the entire loan would be repaid by 2021. Once the agreement was in place, no payments were ever missed. As a single mom, I had learned the importance of paying your bills first, before splurging on other things. I didn't think much about it, but Mr. and Mrs. Davis talked about how they appreciated these values.

Moving into the 'Davis compound,' as family friends called it, was a very different experience for Jess and me. Tom had three siblings, his parents and one aunt on the Davis side, so there was always family around.

Aunt Susan, or Tuse, as the family called her, lived a full and interesting life. She was a laboratory technologist, a pilot, and a flight instructor earlier in life, and then in her 40's, she went back to school to get a Bachelor of Nursing degree.

When I met Aunt Tuse she was working as a nurse, volunteering with several charities, and was more active than most people I knew. Among her other activities, she regularly hiked, swam, skied, and kayaked all over the world. Aunt Tuse biked to work when the weather was favourable. Like Tom, she was slim and had energy to burn.

Tom's family all got along well. There was no bickering, name-calling, or vulgar language and if there was a disagreement, they worked it out. They were respectful and spent time together participating in family activities like weekly meals at their parents' house. The Davis family life was very different from the family life I knew growing up.

I had been excited about moving to the city and I blended well into my surroundings. The stalker's phone calls and the suspicious activity was immediately cut off, and I no longer worried about running into Mother around town.

There was something secure and comforting about moving into Tom's house and being surrounded by his family. There was always someone looking out for us and for the first time, I truly felt safe.

As I prepared to register for the Fall semester at Memorial University, I helped Jess choose a high school close to our new home. One of Jess's friends had moved to the city with her family about two years earlier and she now attended a high school in Mount Pearl. This was Jess's only city friend, so she chose to go to the same school.

The school was six kilometres from our house but was not the designated school for our area. Tom and I committed to driving her back and forth plus anything else she needed to help her adjust to the changes.

During the summer months, Jess continued to spend most of her time in Bay Roberts with Steph and some of her other friends. I realized the move had been challenging for her, so I didn't mind driving her back and forth.

As Jess spent the summer commuting, I spent a lot of the summer with Sarah and Jacob. Sarah was pleasant and easy to care for, though Jacob was a handful. Aunt Tuse and I took the kids to the Provincial Experimental Farm's Open House to see farm animals.

Sarah stayed close to my side and held my hand. Jacob, instead of holding the other hand, ran away and hid from us. Aunt Tuse and I were terrified. The minutes seemed like hours as we searched everywhere on the farm, enlisting the help of a few concerned bystanders. By the time we finally found him, I was upset and visibly shaken. Jacob was amused.

By the end of the summer, the kids had joined their mom in New Brunswick, Jess began grade ten at O'Donel High School in

Mount Pearl, and I had enrolled in several university courses and continued to work at Fairways with Tom. My house in Bay Roberts was rented and Eddie had agreed to oversee any issues that arose with the tenants.

Although Jess settled into the new school, she was unhappy and missed her friends from Bay Roberts. At her old school, Jess had been an honour roll student, involved with student council, cheerleading, and various sports teams. Maybe more importantly for a 15-year-old, she was one of the popular girls.

At her new school, Jess made friends and earned a spot on the girls' hockey team. However, it seemed she had stopped caring about her grades, activities, and almost everything else associated with school. The harder we tried to help with the adjustments, the harder she pushed back. Tom was patient and spent hours talking to her as he tried to help with the situation.

Tom and I continued to work together and my obsession with the gym and fitness had now been replaced with an obsession for work. When I wasn't in classes, studying, or driving Jess around, I was working at Fairways. Tom appeared to have a similar work pattern.

While working through the financial challenges of running Fairways, a potential buyer came along and made an offer to purchase the business and property. We talked to Tom's dad about the options, then decided to sell.

Initially, the new owners were only interested in the property. However, once they reviewed the financials, they decided to include the golf portion of the business in their proposal. Their offer was accepted and the entire business and property, minus the paintball portion, was sold.

Within weeks, we began getting calls from paintball customers and Tom realized there was increasing demand. We immediately began working together to open a stand-alone paintball business.

As we started the new business venture together, a couple of business acquaintances expressed interest in talking to Tom about their own company. The couple owned a trade show business and were interested in selling half of the company. They asked Tom if he was interested in forming a partnership. Tom saw potential in the business and suggested I consider the proposal as well.

We set a time to meet with the owners, Sandra and her husband, to learn more about their business. Through the existing company, they organized several trade shows, including a five-day show that ran in the Fall. The event, which happened in October at the Glacier Arena in Mount Pearl, was called Christmas at the Glacier and featured vendors from all over Canada.

It was an annual, sold-out show, with a long waitlist of vendors who wanted to participate. The other shows were one-day events and although they were well attended, Christmas at the Glacier was by far the main event.

I had no experience in organizing a trade show, but Sandra told me not to worry. She intended to teach me everything I needed to know. We talked it through and decided to accept their offer, purchasing half of the company. The paperwork was drawn up and we presented a cheque for our portion of the business.

In less than one year, Tom and I had worked together on selling a large business, started a new business from the ground up, and invested in an existing company. Life was suddenly busier than ever.

One of Tom's good friends, Derek, was getting married in Montreal in April. I had been booked for a Spring photoshoot in the same city. When I reached out to the photographer, she was able to adjust her schedule and work with me during the week of the wedding. So, Tom and I decided to turn the trip into a mini-vacation, and we stayed at his parents' condo in old Montreal for ten days.

Tom and I thoroughly enjoyed the time travelling together. Montreal was a busy city with no shortage of places to go or things to see. Once Derek's wedding and the photoshoot were over, we made plans for the remainder of the trip. Walking hand in hand, we explored the oldest parts of the city.

During my previous buying trips, there had been two restaurants that I liked to visit in Montreal. Beauty's Restaurant on Mont-Royal and Nickels, which happened to be owned by Céline Dion, on Saint-Laurent. Tom took me to both.

Sadly, our plans came to a screeching halt when I developed a migraine. I retreated to a dark bedroom as Tom lounged around. The migraine continued for several days and just as I felt I was getting over it, another one started. To add to my discomfort, I developed a gastrointestinal issue that seemed to linger for the remainder of the trip.

I was not much better by the time we got back to St. John's, so I visited a doctor. After listing my symptoms, she confidently told me I had Irritable Bowel Syndrome (IBS). There was no test to confirm IBS, but she suggested I keep a journal of all the foods I ate to determine which ones were making me sick; then, I should eliminate them from my diet. The most common culprits were usually gluten and dairy.

The process was anything but simple and my condition worsened. While following my doctor's suggestions, I began to lose weight and was suddenly plagued with painful, swollen joints and days with barely enough energy to get out of bed. I enlisted the help of a naturopathic and medical doctor and I was sent for a multitude of tests.

With routine blood work, I tested positive for Antinuclear Antibodies (ANA) and I was given a referral to Dr. Trahey, a doctor of internal medicine. I was forewarned that a positive ANA test by itself didn't mean anything, but along with other symptoms, it could indicate an autoimmune disease.

After several visits to Dr. Trahey, I pushed for answers and asked for her opinion on what was happening. She was careful with her answer when admitting that she suspected I was in the early stages of lupus, an autoimmune disease that affects your tissues and organs.

I was conflicted about the best treatment plan. Tom's recommended approach involved dietary and lifestyle changes, rather than medications. He firmly believed those changes would fix most issues. And on some level, I agreed. I removed gluten, dairy, and all processed foods from my diet, and while the changes helped, I continued to experience flare-ups from time to time.

Bev (photo credit Scott Bowring)

The Wedding

We had been living in the city for over a year and Jess was in her senior year of high school. Sarah and Jacob had settled in New Brunswick and returned home for Christmas, March breaks, and summer vacations. I was sleeping better, and my nightmares were occurring a lot less. Tom and I continued to work on the businesses, and as a couple, we were blissfully happy.

We enrolled in a two-year Nutritional Wellness Program offered through the Edison Institute in Ontario. We weren't looking for accreditation, we simply wanted the education. Although I had tested negative for celiac disease, I definitely had gluten sensitivities. I had removed most traces of gluten from my diet and surprisingly still experienced the same uncomfortable symptoms.

From the nutritional program, I learned that our bodies view any foods that cause a negative reaction (bloating, headache, brain fog, painful joints, etc.) as poison. A small amount of poison is still poison.

As long as I continued to consume any gluten at all, even in the smallest amounts, I was putting poison into my system and causing my body undue stress as it worked overtime to get rid of the substance. It was a painful but valuable lesson and once I removed gluten entirely from my diet, most of the symptoms subsided. As weeks and months passed, my energy levels returned.

My house in Bay Roberts was now being rented by a second tenant. Lloyd, my real estate agent and friend, called to let me know he had seen the house recently. He told me it no longer looked like the property I left two years ago. Lloyd had originally sold me the house and he had been impressed with the work I had done on it. I called the tenant to give advance notice that I would be dropping by later in the week to check on things.

Eddie agreed to tag along with me for the visit. When we pulled into the driveway, I spotted old tires, broken toys, and other debris laying around outside of what had been a well-groomed property when we left.

As I walked into the house, I was met with a foul smell and

clutter. The house was untidy. There were carpet stains in the family room, holes in the walls, and the kitchen counter was missing its end-cap. I promptly gave the tenant an eviction notice before leaving the house.

I was noticeably upset at the state of my house. Being sensitive to my distress, Eddie offered to help fix it up. He tried to make me feel better by downplaying the damage and the amount of time needed for repairs. I saw right through him, and he knew it.

"I am going to sell it," I said, after a lengthy silence. "Once the repairs are done, I will call Lloyd and ask him to list the house."

"Are you sure you want to do that?" Eddie asked, with doubt in his voice.

"Yes! I don't need the hassle. And it's not like we are going to move back. It would be best for me to sell it now and get the money back that I've invested, while I still can."

Always true to his word, Eddie did help. He spent countless hours cleaning and overseeing repairs. In the end, the house looked good, not as good as it did when I had left it, but much better. Lloyd added my house to his listings and came back with a buyer fairly quickly. I accepted the offer and hoped the new owners would take care of the house as I had.

Things were going well with Tom and me, and we always looked forward to date night. One particular evening, we had a little time to kill before a dinner reservation, so we wandered into a nearby jewelry store.

We were dressed in formal wear and stood out from the everyday shoppers. Tom's dark curly hair was slicked back, and he was wearing a shirt and tie. I was wearing my favourite dress jacket. I made the jacket a few years earlier and received compliments whenever I wore it.

I was suspicious when Tom started asking for my opinions on yellow versus white gold and I suspected he was trying to get a sense of my style for wedding rings. I wasn't sure how I felt but pushed wedding thoughts out of my head while trying on a couple of rings for size and style. A friendly sales agent handed me her business card and offered to help with any of our future needs.

The ambiance of The Cellar restaurant created the perfect atmosphere for an intimate dinner. It was a weeknight, so the restaurant wasn't busy. The lights were dimmed just enough to create a romantic setting. We enjoyed the main course and waited for dessert as Tom began talking about our relationship.

"Bev, we've been together for a year and a half, and it has been the best year and a half of my life."

I knew where the conversation was headed. Tom continued

explaining his thoughts on our relationship and there was no doubt he was happy. The entire evening had led to this and although I saw it coming, I didn't have an answer when he reached for my hand and asked, "Bev, will you marry me?"

"I... well..." I stalled. "I think we need to talk... I'm not sure if... maybe? Did you think about this?" I fumbled with my fingers while trying to articulate an answer to his question. "Marriage is a big step. We would have to talk about it and we would have to make plans. I love you, but marriage...? Okay... I will marry you."

Tom smiled and leaned in for a kiss. "If we hurry, we can rush back to the jewelry store and pick up that ring you liked."

Tom paid for the meal and we drove back to the jewelry store. The attendant acknowledged our return and met us on the staff side of a showcase displaying engagement rings.

"You came back," she commented.

"Yes, and now we need a ring," Tom said, as he beamed with pride.

The jewelry store had an extensive selection of rings. I leaned in for a closer look and found the one that had caught my eye earlier in the evening. "This one," I said pointing through the glass.

"That's a gorgeous ring," the salesclerk said as she carefully picked it up and handed it to me. I glanced at Tom before trying it on.

"Wait! That's my job!" he announced, with an extended open palm.

Tom carefully slid the ring onto my finger. It was one size too big.

"We can have it sized for you," the clerk offered.

As Tom paid for the ring, I posed my hand in various positions and watched the diamonds as they reflected the display lights in the store. It was a beautiful ring and now I was officially engaged.

When inside the car, Tom asked, "Should we go tell my parents?"

"Sure. I think they'll be happy," I agreed.

Mr. Davis was watching the news and Mrs. Davis was folding laundry when we walked into their house. As Tom announced he had news to share, they both walked toward us. Without wasting any time, Tom told them we had gotten engaged. Both of their faces expressed happiness.

Mr. Davis was the first to congratulate us and he shook his son's hand. Then he opened his arms and offered me a congratulatory hug. Mrs. Davis was also smiling as she hugged us both. "You were already a part of the family... you know that, right?" Mr. Davis asked rhetorically. Mrs. Davis chimed in, "And, you sure do fit in with our crowd."

I could tell they were both genuinely happy with the news. When we returned to the car, Tom reached for his mobile phone. "Now we have to call your father."

We were still parked in his parent's driveway when Tom made the call. From my seat, I heard Rex's voice as he answered the phone. After a brief check-in, Tom asked in a somewhat traditional, yet romantic way: "Rex, I would like to ask for permission to marry your daughter."

Rex was quick and to the point. "Well now Tom, you're going to have to ask for her permission, not mine."

"I already have hers, but I would like yours too."

"If she says yes, then there's your answer," Rex replied.

Rex had met Tom only a couple of times. There was mutual respect between them and although they were very different, they also shared similarities. They were both honest, hardworking, and as stubborn as the day was long. They also spoke their minds. There was no tiptoeing around any subject. If they had an opinion, good or bad, we were sure to hear it.

It was December, and while I pushed for as much time as possible to plan, Tom voted for a summer wedding to ensure his kids were home to attend. We settled on September 3rd, which gave us exactly nine months to arrange everything.

I was told that selecting a wedding dress, sooner rather than later, would remove a lot of stress from the planning. I promptly moved 'wedding dress' to the top of my priority list.

There were three local bridal boutiques and I planned to visit all of them, but by the time I got to the second, I was already feeling deflated. Most of the in-store dresses were in larger sizes, or if I found a dress that actually fit in size, it was too short in length.

As the day progressed, I found an elegant wedding dress that fit in size and length. The dress was a simple style with spaghetti straps, a sequined front, and a low cut back. It was definitely my style.

My eyes widened when I caught a glimpse of the $3,999 price tag. It was beautiful, elegant, and yet unpretentious. As much as I loved it and tried to rationalize these benefits, the miser in me could not justify paying over $4,000 for it.

Watching myself in the mirror, I examined the dress from every angle. I thought I could probably make this dress and it wouldn't cost anywhere near $4,000. I allowed myself a little more time to examine the pattern and structure of the dress.

When I operated my own seamstress business, I had a talent for replicating styles that I saw in catalogue or magazines. Surely, I could do the same with this wedding dress, I confidently told myself. I thanked the salesclerk as I handed back the wedding dress, already zipped up and back on the clothes hanger.

On the drive across town to the local fabric store, I remembered specific graduation and wedding dresses that I had designed and constructed for other people. Thoughts of the $4,000 price tag continued to motivate me to want to make my own dress.

I spent several hours at Fabricville, the local textile store, looking through patterns. I finally narrowed my choices to three different ones that included most of the features I wanted in my wedding dress. When I got home, I would amalgamate the patterns to create the ideal one.

I handed a bolt of ivory satin-backed crepe to the clerk and requested more than enough yardage to complete my dress, plus enough to make a long, flower girl dress for Sarah out of the same fabric. I also bought 25 meters of the same fabric in the navy colour, for the five women who were standing in my bridal party.

The girls all had different body shapes and very different styles. With five meters each, they could choose a specific design, one that reflected their individual style, and have someone make the dress for them.

Before starting my dress, I helped Jess choose a style for her bridesmaid dress and then made it for her. Next, I made Sarah's flower girl dress leaving room for alterations as I knew she would likely grow over the summer months. Then, I could barely wait to get started on my own dress.

In a cheaper fabric, I created the dress three times and made modifications to it each time before I felt my precise style was perfected. Once preparations had begun, I used a form-fitting mannequin to display the dress. I covered it with a white sheet anytime I wasn't working on it, as I didn't want Tom to accidentally walk in and see my wedding dress.

The dress had a completely open, low-cut back. Spaghetti straps were attached to the front and crossed over in the back, holding everything in place. There was a small train in the back that would be pinned in place after the church ceremony.

I hand sewed tiny clear beads across the front of the dress and down the sides. The line of beads tapered and followed the cut of the dress. I spent hours on it and Tom teased that it may have been cheaper for me to invest the $4,000 in the store's dress as I had probably spent the equivalent in time to make my own.

As summer approached, my health conditions flared up. My joints were swollen and painful, I had reduced energy and very little appetite. Consequently, I began losing weight. The wedding dress had been 'completed' several times, but every time I tried it on, it no longer fit.

In August, a month before the wedding, I tried to persuade Tom to postpone the wedding. I had lost more weight than I was comfortable showing in the dress I had made. My cheeks were hollow, my breasts had almost disappeared, and my bones were overly exposed. I didn't like the reflection in the mirror. Tom assured me I didn't look as bad as I thought, so I altered the dress for what I hoped was the last time.

I loved to bake and although I didn't have any professional baking experience, I decided to make our wedding cake and enlist a professional to decorate it. Tom was open to the idea and we agreed on a three-layer cherry cake. I set out to find a decorator willing to do the job.

While experimenting, I baked every cherry cake recipe that I could find and after each tasting, I donated the balance of the cakes to delighted family members. The consensus was that Mrs. Lester, a family friend, had the best cherry cake recipe. I was pleased that there was agreement and decided to add the recipe to our wedding favour for guests - a cookbook that contained a collection of recipes from family and friends.

The wedding day was only weeks away when Mrs. Davis wanted to talk about the upcoming event. She was concerned that I might be a 'runaway bride,' and if that was the case, she encouraged me to cancel beforehand rather than running on the actual wedding day.

Tom regularly talked about me getting 'cold feet' and I suspected that might have been playing on her mind. I assured her we were fine and if I did decide to run, I would take Tom with me. She appeared relieved.

Cathy McDonald, a longtime friend, dropped by for a pre-wedding visit. I was excited to see her and decided to show her my wedding dress. Cathy sat and faced the cloaked dress on the mannequin as I pulled the sheet off from behind, for a dramatic reveal. Her mouth dropped at the sight of the dress; I smiled in response.

Without speaking, she pointed to the lower half of the dress with one hand and she covered her mouth, almost horrified, with the other hand. I was confused. As I walked around to the front of the dress, my confusion turned to panic when I saw a large 'A' drawn on the bottom half of the dress, in a yellow marker. I couldn't believe my eyes.

Cathy comforted me and suggested I bring the dress to a dry cleaner. She told me a story about a friend with a similar experience and assured me the marker stain would likely come out.

I barely slept that night as I considered my options if the stain didn't come out. Tom tried to rationalize the predicament. "It will make an interesting story," he said, as we assumed one of the children had left the mark. With little time left before our special day, I was stressed at the thought of shopping for a second wedding dress. I certainly didn't have the time, or the heart, to make another.

The dry cleaner promised they would try their best to remove the stain. They also committed to rushing the job for us. I drove back a couple of days later and became emotional at the sight of my dress as it was displayed - without the yellow mark!

A week before the wedding, my dress was once again in need of an alteration. I expressed concerns to Beth and Heather, my soon-to-be sisters-in-law. I wasn't sure I could make the dress bodice any smaller without affecting the integrity of the dress. We called a professional seamstress and asked for advice. She made a home visit and after I tried on the dress for her, she offered a solution. I followed her advice as I altered the dress one last time. Thankfully, that was the last alteration.

The big day arrived. The sun shone and it was a perfect day for a wedding. I sipped champagne with the girls from the bridal party as our hair was styled. One of the girls delivered a gift from Tom. It was an elegant tennis bracelet with a handwritten note, saying that he couldn't wait to see me at the church. I was touched by his romantic gesture.

Tom's family and friends filled the right side of the chapel, and my friends, along with several family members, sat on the left. I had only a few family members to attend but I was honoured to have Rex walk me down the aisle. We had organized a conventional service and my friend Glenda was now poised to sing.

Sarah walked down the aisle hand in hand with my nephew, Spencer, Tracey's son. The awkward look on her face gave away her displeasure of walking with a boy, especially one she didn't know. Sarah stood with Jess for the duration of the service. As we held hands, Tom and I whispered and communicated with our eyes like high school sweethearts.

Outside the church, Tom and I spoke with our guests. Tom told his brother Ted how impressed he was by Jacob's good behaviour. Ted laughed, "Yeah, your groomsmen are all inside now compensating him for it." He described a scene where the groomsmen, one by one, were placing money in Jacob's open hand.

Mr. Davis drove Tom and me to Bowring Park in his prized Jaguar for our wedding photos. The temperature had dropped, and the girls cuddled up in blankets between shots. Once the photos had been taken, we went back to the reception for a sit-down meal and entertainment.

Tom's longtime friend, Mike, was the emcee and entertained the guests with his hysterical commentary about each of our wedding party members.

"Eddie is Bev's best friend and sat on her side of the wedding party with the girls. Alex and Beth, Tom's sisters, are on his side with the guys. Katrina started as Tom's good friend but now is Bev's. She's with the girls but split between both parties!"

Mike's explanation was accompanied by an organized flowchart which he drew as he spoke. He used a marker to direct our attention, hopping from one side of the chart to the other as guests laughed hysterically. We were impressed with his clever commentary and agreed he was the best emcee we had ever heard.

Tom left the reception after the bridal party dances to bring Sarah and Jacob home to a sitter. The kids were flying back to New Brunswick in the morning to be with their mom and he wanted to tuck them in one last time before they left.

I talked and danced with family and friends and hoped no one noticed his absence. An hour later, Tom reappeared. The kids were settled in bed and he was happy to be back. We joined friends on the dance floor and partied until a little after midnight.

Tom had prearranged our entire honeymoon. He took great pleasure in planning every aspect of the trip and kept all the details a surprise. Aside from regular trips to visit Tracey and her family in Maine, and a few trips to Montreal and Toronto, I hadn't travelled much before now. I didn't care where we were going, I was simply looking forward to the time away with my husband.

At the airport, Tom handed me a boarding pass and I deliberately avoided looking at the destination. I wanted to prolong the surprise, along with the pleasure I knew he was receiving from his efforts, for as long as possible. At some point, the blinders came off and I realized we were boarding a flight headed for Cancun, Mexico.

My excitement couldn't be contained; I was like a child visiting Disney World for the first time. Our honeymoon started at an all-inclusive resort. I saw palm trees for the first time and was fascinated to see and touch bananas hanging from a tree. There were small lizards on the ground around the resort.

The delicious food and drinks were unlimited. Alcoholic drinks didn't normally appeal to me, but piña coladas were quickly established as my favourite. It was an incredible experience.

Through the resort, we booked an excursion and prepared to travel to the famous Chichén Itzá. I was initially nervous to travel outside the resort, though Tom reassured me that we would be fine with our local tour guide and the group from the resort.

We had arrived a few days earlier by plane and travelled from the airport to the resort by a luxurious chartered bus. It had been dark, and we were tired. Through tinted windows, we saw very little of Mexico from the first drive. I looked forward to seeing communities, local houses, and landscapes.

I hadn't experienced tropical heat before now and welcomed the cool air as we boarded the air-conditioned chartered bus. As the bus drove through the tall resort gates, I prepared for my first glimpse of Mexico. The posh resort was like a private paradise, but I was curious to see what was outside the gates. The drive to the famous Mayan ruins was mind-blowing.

We had been on the highway for a while before seeing any communities. I was appalled with the sight of dilapidated, run-down homes. The houses looked more like ones that my brother and his friends built as children with bits and pieces of gathered wood.

"Do people actually live in these?" I asked Tom, pointing out the window.

My naïveté was on display and Tom squeezed my hand.

As the bus slowed to pass through a shopping area, I saw a woman and a young girl, who I assumed was her daughter, knelt down cleaning the floor of a store. They waved to us as the bus passed. I was surprised to see the big smiles on their faces.

A little further down the road, I watched a teenage boy stand with his mom on the shoulder of the gravel road and wave. The boy wore shorts, a graphic t-shirt, and no footwear. They were both smiling. I didn't know what to think, but Tom commented that all the local people seemed happy.

"Their wants are much less; they lead a simpler life than people do in North America. The people here aren't consumed with commercialism," he said.

The Chichén Itzá ruins, one of the seven new world wonders, was a popular tourist destination located about 125 kilometres west of Cancun. The focal point was a towering pyramid that boasted 365 narrow steps on each of its four sides. The number of steps represented the days within a solar year.

A tour guide explained the games that had been played on the very field where we stood, as well as the sacrifices that were made to the gods. Once the educational element had been delivered, we were free to climb the pyramid.

Sweat beaded down our backs, chests, and foreheads, and our straw hats offered little protection from the unrelenting sun. There were a lot of tourists and most climbed the pyramid in pairs. We noticed a lot of people creeping down the pyramid by sitting on a step and moving down one at a time. The temperature was extremely high, and I suspected balance was an issue for a lot of them.

Tom and I were up for the challenge and climbed all the way to the top. From there, we admired the view before taking photos and resting in a shaded area for relief from the sun. Our climb down was slow and the steps were extremely narrow.

I could now understand why many people chose to go down the pyramid in a seated position. Tom and I kept close together and carefully made our way back to the ground.

Back at the resort, Tom encouraged me to swim with him in the ocean. He was a strong swimmer and enjoyed swimming in pools and ponds, but he especially loved to swim in the ocean. I didn't mind swimming, as long as I was able to reach the bottom. I regularly stopped to check for the bottom with my toes and if I couldn't feel anything, I panicked.

The fear was debilitating, and I couldn't get to shallow water fast enough. Tom knew about my apprehension when he asked if I would join him, but he never fully understood my fear of water and how it was connected to negative childhood experiences.

I declined the offer to swim but settled for running into the waves. Tom held my hand and said he wouldn't let go. No matter how strong the waves, he would be next to me holding my hand. He was trying to encourage me to feel more comfortable in the ocean and I did my best to embrace it.

Tom slowly edged us further out into the water. The water was deep enough to cover the bottom half of my bikini and Tom stood behind me with both his hands firmly gripping my waist. He hoisted me up into the air just as each wave was about to strike. We laughed and had fun playing in the water. When we left the beach, I felt the ocean was just a little less intimidating than when I had arrived.

As the week came to an end, Tom reminded me that we still had another week before returning home. From Mexico, we flew to Toronto for four days. We spent time with Derek, Tom's longtime friend and best man at our wedding, and his family.

We attended Mamma Mia, the Broadway musical. After the show, Tom took me backstage and introduced me to one of the lead actors. Being introduced as his wife, to an old high school girlfriend of his, felt a little awkward. I was even a little intimidated, given she was totally beautiful and incredibly talented. Nonetheless, it had been nice to meet her, and I congratulated her on the fantastic performance. With one last surprise up his sleeve, Tom and I flew to Montreal to attend a Phil Collins concert.

Tom definitely outdid himself with the honeymoon and I was

extremely thankful for all of it. The time away was just what the doctor ordered, and we came back feeling refreshed, totally connected, and - as a bonus for me - I had regained a few pounds.

The honeymoon trip had been such a hit that Tom took on the challenge of organizing an annual surprise vacation. Once he chose the destination, he would spend months researching the location and its amenities. He would look for a suitable hotel and ensure it was close to a grocery store and public transit. If we rented a car, then we had more flexibility with accommodations.

Tom took immense pleasure in organizing every detail and keeping all the specifics secret. We continued to work, usually six or seven days a week, for most of the year. We then looked forward to a month of travel during the beginning of each year, which was our least busy time.

Jess graduated from high school and decided to work for a year before starting a university program. I took time off work or worked from home whenever the kids visited. The rest of the year, Tom called me a workaholic. On vacation, he would joke that the only way to get me to 'turn it off' was to take me out of the country.

He didn't see it in himself, but I thought he was the same when it came to working. Vacations served as a great time for us to see the world and reconnect. Every vacation was an adventure and another honeymoon.

***

Linda, from Classique Models, sent a group email to announce she was closing the agency. She recommended I contact Alma, from X-Posure International, to continue modelling or acting with a new agent.

Like the others, I was disappointed to lose Linda as an agent. I trusted her judgment and respected her professionalism. Her decisions had been unselfishly made and always in the best interest of the talent. As sad as we were, we knew Linda had no choice. She was going through a divorce and needed time to focus on her son, herself, and her work.

I met with Alma and her boyfriend, Scott, to discuss representation. They were impressed with my existing portfolio but recommended I do a test photoshoot with Scott for a book update.

We arranged the session and I immediately got involved with the agency by working in their seasonal fashion shows. Alma and I were the same age and quickly became friends. I was pleased when she asked for my opinion on work-related issues.

When Alma and Scott organized a weekend event to promote the agency, they offered me an opportunity to showcase my clothing line in a fashion show. Although I was no longer sewing as a business, I was still creating the occasional piece and Alma had noticed me wearing some of those designs.

I went through the process of formalizing my label. I called it *bevie* and ensured the label was attached to every new piece I designed. I had no desire to sell my clothes but thought it would be fun to showcase them in a fashion show.

Before I fully committed to Alma's offer, I rushed home to take an inventory of the *bevie* pieces hanging in my closet. I was pleased to see I had many styles that could be worn in the show.

The next couple of months were mapped out as I committed to sewing several new designs to add to the collection. As the show date approached, models from the agency contacted me to arrange fittings and I was surprised when some of the women requested specific pieces that they had seen me wear. The jacket I wore the night Tom and I were engaged was the most popular request.

It was extra-long in length and the fitted waistline was double-breasted with eight nautical style gold buttons. The sleeves had two gold stripes, similar to those found on jackets worn by pilots.

Most of the models were close to my size and I had no trouble matching them with items they liked, except my wedding dress. I had worn that dress when I was at my smallest and I was challenged to find someone else to fit into it.

With only a couple of models left for fittings, I contemplated removing the dress from the collection, but was delighted when one of the last models to arrive was able to fit into it. The dress was too long but she suggested pinching and holding up the sides of the dress while walking the runway. She had walked in other fashion shows and confidently said she would make it work.

The show was a success and I beamed with pride as my designs were paraded in a fashion show. As the show came to a close all the models walked back on stage, clapping their hands, falling in place along the length of the runway. I nervously walked through the tunnel of applauding models to take a bow.

As we celebrated the success of the fashion show, Alma suggested I participate in the upcoming American Model and Talent Convention, which was taking place in Orlando, Florida, early in the new year. Tom and I discussed the competition and with his support, I decided to attend.

I joined the other participants in the weekly runway and acting practices and booked a few more photoshoots to ensure my book was totally up to date. The other models from X-Posure were attending an earlier show than me but we still practiced together.

The flights were booked well in advance. I would fly solo and

Tom planned to join me on the second day of the convention. When flying to or from our home in Newfoundland during the winter months, there was always a risk of interrupted travel due to unpredictable winter weather. Unfortunately, I was subjected to one such delayed flight and did not arrive in Orlando until a day later, just as the convention was getting started.

The luggage took forever to dump onto the carousel and as I patiently waited, I learned that my luggage did not make it. I headed to the baggage claim department and pleaded with them to track my luggage and have it delivered to the hotel as soon as possible.

Without clothes, shoes, and make-up, attending a modelling convention would be pointless. I contacted Alma to explain my predicament. She gave me contact information for an agent friend of hers from Atlanta and offered to call ahead to give her a heads up. At the very least, I could borrow clothes from some of the other models, Alma reasoned.

Tom arrived in the morning and I was discouraged that my luggage still hadn't shown up. It was day two and I was wearing a black t-shirt with the convention logo, and the same black jeans that I had worn the day before. Consequently, I felt less prepared and less confident for the day's lineup of competitions. Tom picked up a rental car and committed to taking me to the mall in the evening.

During mid-afternoon, I noticed hotel staff and an event organizer walking toward me. With excitement, I also noticed my suitcase was being wheeled along beside them. I had never been so happy to see a piece of luggage in my life. Tom thanked the staff members before taking the suitcase for me.

He led the way to the elevator and back to our room, where I flirtatiously shed my clothes and threw them at him. The convention wouldn't be ruined by the missing luggage, but it had certainly dampened my spirits for the first few days.

During that week, Tom and I met many models from the United States. Other Canadians were attending but not many and organizers confirmed I was the only talent competing from Newfoundland and Labrador. The competition was stiff and I didn't expect to be taking home any awards. I was completely shocked when my name was called as a winner in the runway category.

At the networking session, I received interest from several agencies, but there had been significant inquiries from two. One was based in Los Angeles and the other was in New York City. The agency in New York City represented mature models. The agent took pictures of me with my hair pulled back as well as other angles. She also took out a measuring tape and recorded my measurements.

As the convention concluded, Tom and I celebrated. He was

proud of my award and the agency interest, but confessed he had no interest in me working so far away, without him. Fortunately for him, I had no desire to be away from him either.

Wedding Day

Wedding dress, designed and sewn by Bev

Revelations

Whenever we visited Rex and his family on the west coast of the island, we usually tried to squeeze in a visit with my cousin Helen and her husband, Brian. It was usually hit or miss whether they would be in the province, based on his work schedule.

One particular summer, we visited when everyone was home, including Natasha. Natasha lived in Sherman Oakes, California, where she tried to avoid the paparazzi as she raised her two boys and worked on her acting career.

Since I first met her on the set of the film she was shooting with Jean Claude Van Damme in Toronto, she had starred in many movies and shows. Her career had really taken off and I was thrilled for her.

It was a beautiful evening when we dropped by for a visit. The temperature was cooling off as the sun was setting, but it was the perfect evening to sit on the deck with Helen, Brian, and the rest of the family. That's where they were when we arrived, laughing and enjoying drinks together.

Helen played host as Tom told the family about our latest travelling adventure. Natasha was intrigued by the effort he had put into organizing the annual surprise vacations. When Tom hinted that we may be in California the following year, she immediately invited us to stay at her house.

As January approached, we prepared for our vacation. Tom normally kept the travel plans top secret, but he let it slip that he had been chatting with Natasha about our upcoming trip. Although he wouldn't say where we were headed, he revealed there was a short stopover in Los Angeles and that we would be staying with Natasha and her boyfriend, Darius. I could barely contain my excitement.

Driving on Natasha's street, we noticed most of the houses were hidden behind security gates. I imagined the properties were quite luxurious. We were captivated when Natasha listed the names of the neighbouring celebrities. Natasha and Darius showed us around the house as they talked about the evening plans.

Along with several other celebrities, Natasha had been asked to host one of President Barack Obama's inauguration parties at a Hollywood nightclub. Tom and I enthusiastically accepted an invitation to join them. A couple of Darius' cousins accompanied us as well. Natasha's two sons were spending time with their dad during our stay, so, unfortunately, we didn't get to visit with them.

Natasha went to her bedroom to get ready, and I went to the guest room to do the same. The guys, clearly not in a rush, relaxed and chatted over a beer. Foraging through my suitcase, I decided on a simple black dress as I rushed to get ready.

It didn't take long and when I heard Natasha's voice from the kitchen, I joined the group. Natasha looked stunning; I swear she could wear a potato sack and would still look like a supermodel.

I had my first introduction to the paparazzi when we arrived at the nightclub. Darius handed the car keys to a parking attendant and we entered through the back entrance. There was a red carpet for Natasha to walk on, as the rest of us - Tom, Darius, the cousins, and I - stood back to watch.

As Natasha stepped onto the carpet and posed, a group of photographers immediately snapped photos and called out her name. Natasha looked confident and appeared to be comfortable with all the attention.

Once inside, Darius led the way to a less congested area of spacious table booths away from the main dance floor. I felt a little nervous, although Tom seemed to fit right in. The music was inviting, and the guys periodically stood and danced without leaving the booth. Natasha and I remained seated and chatted for hours.

The entire evening was a little surreal as we partied with a couple of celebrities. Fortunately, there were no paparazzi permitted inside and Natasha and Darius could relax and enjoy the evening. To catch a glimpse into the lives of the rich and famous for a day was such a cool experience, one that Tom and I thoroughly enjoyed.

It was around midnight when we walked through the back entrance and waited for our vehicle to return. The private conversation was abruptly interrupted when paparazzi caught a glimpse of Natasha standing on the curb.

Photographers raced towards us and were just a few feet away when the vehicle pulled up. Camera lights flashed in our faces as photographers frantically called her name and asked random questions. Natasha was calm and answered a few before getting into the car.

The next day, as Natasha and Darius prepared for an early morning hike, we said our goodbyes before heading off to visit the Hollywood Walk of Fame and do a little sightseeing. While strolling hand-in-hand, window shopping on Rodeo Drive we noticed a group of people that looked a lot like family friends from back home. As we walked closer, we were flabbergasted to realize that it was actually the people we knew.

As we approached, Tom called out to them, "What are the chances of running into a couple of Newfoundlanders on Rodeo Drive?"

"Apparently pretty good," one of them replied, with a chuckle.

For the next leg of our trip, we drove to San Diego where we dropped off the rental car and took a taxi to a pier. I was skeptical when I noticed cruise ships lining the full length of the dock.

"Bev, we are going on a cruise," Tom proudly announced.

With a lump in my throat, I looked for clarification, "On a boat... you want me to get on a boat? Tom, you know how I feel about the ocean."

He pleaded, "Bevie, it's a very short cruise, only five days. I have booked an inside cabin, so you don't have to see the ocean if you don't want to. Being on a cruise ship is like being at a resort. The ship is huge, and you won't even notice we are sailing. You will love it, I promise."

There was a hint of desperation in his voice. I could see he was concerned and somewhat worried while he stood outside the open door of the taxi as I did not attempt to get out.

I inhaled deeply and tried to reassure myself, "Okay, we can do this," as I stepped out of the taxi. I was doing this more for Tom than myself. He put a lot of time and energy into booking our vacations, and as much as I feared the ocean, a bigger part of me didn't want to disappoint him.

The cruise ship set sail and stopped at two Mexican ports before returning to San Diego. Thankfully, Tom was right - I barely noticed we were on a ship in the middle of the ocean. Tom enjoyed the cruise and hinted that we ought to do it again.

Following the cruise, we spent time in San Francisco and Las Vegas. It was our first time visiting both these cities and Tom had a list of must-see attractions. It was a wonderful trip.

Once we arrived home, Tom was energized and ready to return to work. I arrived completely exhausted. It wasn't a normal kind of tiredness but more of sickly exhaustion. I didn't think it was a result of our adventures but decided to see my doctor. She ordered some routine blood work, just to check on things.

The results showed that my iron was low, something I dealt with my entire adult life. However, this time, the numbers were low enough that Dr. Trahey prescribed a series of iron injections. The twelve injections were scheduled two weeks apart and had to be administered intravenously at the Health Sciences Center.

When I chatted with a friend about the prescribed treatment, she recommended that I see a blood specialist. The cost was $80 and if it revealed something that I didn't already know, it would be worth it. I immediately called and made an appointment.

The technician pricked my finger, extracted a drop of blood, and prepared a computer monitor to display the results. It took only seconds for the monitor to display a microscopic view of my live blood cells. As plump cells of different shapes and sizes swam around, she immediately pointed to certain shapes and stated there were toxins in my blood. We determined it may be from the hair colour that was applied just a few days ago.

I noticed the tiny cells were different sizes and shapes and some even looked like they had bites taken out of them. The technician explained that the shapes of the cells were indicating liver-related stress. I was told that an influx of hormones and a buildup of heavy metals, such as mercury fillings, could be causing strain on my liver and prevented my blood from being efficiently cleansed. Additionally, the shapes of the cells indicated an issue with protein assimilation or absorption.

As the technician studied the monitor, she observed, "You've had emotional trauma."

The comment was surprising, and I wasn't sure if she was asking a question or simply stating the obvious.

With a puzzled look, I asked, "How do you know that?"

"I can see it in your blood," she replied, as she pointed to the screen.

"I'm confused. I'm watching the same thing you are, and I don't know how you can see that. You have to explain how you can see trauma in my blood cells."

The technician, clearly not understanding my need for that information, began to justify her findings by explaining the science behind the test being performed.

"No, that's not what I mean, I want you to explain how you see trauma in blood cells. You're right, I have had extreme trauma in my childhood, but I want to understand how you - a stranger with no knowledge of my background - can see this by looking at a blood sample."

The technician's words were clear. "Your white blood cells are stagnant. They aren't moving around and fighting as they should be. If you specifically watch them, they are barely moving. This can be a strong indicator of deep emotional grief."

The technician continued by explaining that trauma is felt throughout the body and on a cellular level. It affects the heart, brain, and every other part of us. She explained that if it is not altered or changed, it could possibly turn to cancer or some other life-threatening disease.

I was speechless! A complete stranger just saw my deepest and darkest secrets by examining a sample of my blood. I realized I wasn't ready for the conversation, but I also realized that if I didn't deal with it, I may have more than lupus to worry about. I had been given a lot to think about.

Jess and I drove out around the bay regularly to visit Eddie and his family. On the way back from a visit, we dropped in to see one of Mother's relatives. The results of the blood analysis were still on my mind and I couldn't shake the thought that the technician was able to identify my trauma. The conversation turned to Mother and Father, I decided to ask some questions about her past.

"Your mother was treated no different than her siblings," Jess and I were told.

This family member knew of my abusive past - at least some of it. She knew of the physical and emotional abuse and I wondered if she knew more when she unexpectedly added, "He, (referring to Father) was no better than her," she said.

Among family members, Father was known for being a hardworking man. He was also known as an alcoholic. I never heard them say anything else about him. I was puzzled.

Jess interrupted, "I don't understand how she could be so evil. She has done some pretty crazy things to my mom. How did she get away with that?"

"She knew what she was doing," my relative said, then added in a mocking voice. "Your mother used to say, 'I wouldn't be convicted, I am a mental patient.'"

Jess and I looked at each other in disbelief. Was she a sick woman, or an evil one? On the drive home, we continued the conversation. Shockingly, it appeared as though Mother knew exactly what she was doing. "I am nothing like her, and I am thankful for that," I told Jess.

One day while I was working from my home office, Tom interrupted to tell me I had a phone call. "There is a guy on the phone, his name is Adam, and he is asking if you're the Bev Moore from Georgetown. He also asked if you still talk to your mother."

There could only be one Adam that would link me to Georgetown. It had to be my little brother Adam, the one that was taken, along with three other foster siblings, a year after I ran away from home. I gave Tom a puzzled look before picking up the office extension.

Adam identified himself with his full name. This included his biological name, the only name I would recognize, plus he gave his adopted name. He told me he had been living in Mount Pearl, a nearby city, with his girlfriend for several years.

I had questions, but I noticed he was hesitant with his answers. Adam asked if I ever saw 'our foster mother'. I had not. In fact, I had not seen or spoken to her in over ten years. Adam and I decided to meet for coffee and continue the conversation in person.

I was excited and wondered if I would recognize him. Adam had been a beautiful little boy with blonde curly hair and big blue eyes. Tracey adored him. She was devastated when he, and the other children, were taken from the home.

When Tracey's first son was born, she named him after Adam. I believe it was Tracey's love for Adam that protected him from most of Mother's abuse. Mother loved Tracey and wouldn't do anything that would hurt her, physically or mentally.

Some part of me still expected to see a youthful-looking Adam, and as I walked in and looked around the coffee shop, I was surprised I didn't recognize anyone. When a couple began waving, I soon realized it was Adam and his girlfriend. I gave the 'one-minute' finger before ordering a green tea, then joined them at a window seat.

Adam was now a larger man with short, light brown hair. He wore a plaid jacket and was slightly hunched, leaning over the table as he held his coffee cup with both hands. There was an obvious shyness as he leaned back to greet me with a slight smile.

Sitting across from him at the table, I observed Adam's face in search of a shred of evidence to confirm he was the same Adam from my past. It was not there. I saw no resemblance to the childhood Adam that I remembered. I would have never identified him if he didn't say who he was.

When I asked, Adam briefly told me about the family that had adopted him, as well as his new family with his girlfriend. In turn, I told them about my life in St John's. The mood changed when Adam asked about Mother.

"You said you don't see or speak with her."

His comment sounded more like a question and echoed our earlier conversation.

"No, I don't. Why do you ask?"

"I visited her a few months ago. I don't remember anything about my life with her and I wanted to see if the visit would help me remember. I heard she was a mean woman, and I guess I wanted to see for myself. And I wanted to get some of my baby pictures."

"Well, how was the visit?" I asked.

Adam paused, in an obvious attempt to gather his thoughts.

"Not good. I had a bad feeling when I was around her. I can't explain it, but I felt like I needed to get away from her as soon as possible. When I asked for my baby pictures, she said I would have to come back for them. Even though she told me on the phone that the pictures would be ready for me to take."

"Well, I can identify with that feeling of wanting to get away from her," I said.

"When I asked about you guys, she told me that she didn't see Tracey. She said Tracey is divorced and living in Maine with her four boys. She said April was still living in the bay and she said she spoke to you recently."

"She said she spoke with me recently?" I repeated.

"Yes, that's what she said to me."

"Well, I can assure you, she didn't speak to me recently."

I went on to tell him about the last time I spoke with Mother. It was ten years ago after she sold her house and asked to stay with me for a few days. I told him about the argument she had with Tracey and how Mother called child protective services on her.

"Tracey was crying when she called to tell me that her eldest son was being interviewed by a police officer," I said. "My heart hurt for Tracey."

Up until that point, Tracey had a good relationship with Mother and was completely shocked that Mother would hurt her that way. While growing up, Mother made false accusations about other foster parents or people in the community, but I never imagined she would do it to Tracey, I told him.

"That's a pretty mean thing to do to your daughter," Adam said.

His girlfriend echoed, "Yeah, that was pretty mean."

"Yes, it was," I continued. I told him that when I asked Mother about the incident, she didn't admit, or deny, reporting Tracey; instead, she stood in my kitchen and mocked me.

"I stood up to her and asked her to leave my house," I said. "That was the last time we spoke."

"Bev, I'm so sorry. I am sorry for Tracey too," he said in a quiet, reflective voice.

"It is sad Adam, but I think we're better off removing toxic people from our lives," I told him. "I went back a couple of times and attempted to have a normal mother/daughter relationship. In the end, I realized it was not worth the stress that it brought to my life."

While staring into his coffee, Adam took a deep breath and released it. I didn't want to interrupt, so I accepted the silence and waited for him to speak. He began by telling me about his life. This time, he talked openly and was more forthcoming with details. I listened attentively and paid attention to his body language. Adam talked for a while and painted a very detailed picture of his life both

175

before and after adoption.

When he seemed to have communicated all that he was comfortable disclosing, I asked, "Adam did you ever talk to anyone about the abuse?"

Adam looked me in the eye as he shook his head from side to side, "No. I did not."

I explained the health challenges that I had struggled with for the past eight years.

"I'm not sure if you ever thought about it, but as survivors, we are more susceptible to many health problems and life-threatening diseases. We live with anxiety, depression, PTSD, and a host of other issues. Yet perpetrators seem to live normal, seemingly unaffected lives. Adam, I don't know about you, but I think there is something wrong with that picture."

Adam agreed. "Yeah, definitely something wrong with that picture."

I noticed our empty cups and the fact that two hours had passed. We parted ways and committed to another visit.

With tears in my eyes, I sat in my car and watched Adam drive away. I remembered him as an adorable little boy, energetic and full of life. Today, after I watched and listened, I realized he was not the same person. In my careful observations, I could see how he had been impacted by child abuse.

Adam was over medicated for the first five years of his life - while living in our house. It was likely that the medication had negatively affected his learning ability in school.

As I sat quietly in my car, long after Adam left, I experienced a "eureka" moment. I realized how wrong it had been for me - and maybe other victims - to remain silent. I struggled with nightmares, migraines, eating disorders, and an autoimmune condition.

I lived a lifetime suppressing "poison" as I lived with guilt and shame, thinking it would just go away. In the end, I had done more harm than good to myself. Ironically, I suffered through all of this while protecting my abusers with my silence.

I can't explain how, or why it hit me this way, but it did. I was suddenly motivated to use my experiences to help others. With more courage than ever, I drove home to tell Tom about my visit with Adam. I told him what I had observed and how I realized that it was time to break the silence.

I bravely announced that I was no longer allowing myself to be afraid of Mother. I decided then that I would start to talk about my past, and perhaps, if it could help others who were suffering in silence, I would write about it too. I felt like my purpose became clear. I would share my story of survival and hope.

Within days, I began writing about my past. Almost immediately, I started having nightmares, flashbacks, and migraines. My appetite disappeared and as I wrote, I experienced an uncomfortable tightness in my chest. With a draft of my story outlined, I reached out to a publisher friend for advice. To my surprise, she confessed to shedding tears when she read what I had drafted. She told me that I had an interesting story, one that people would want to read. She also cautioned me about the writing process and suggested I seek counseling while I wrote.

I took her advice and went to my family doctor for a referral. I had been with the same general practitioner for several years. Although she was shocked by my disclosure, she was sympathetic and suggested I meet with someone trained specifically in childhood trauma. To my surprise, she called a colleague and was able to get me an appointment for the following week.

The psychologist advised me that my inner child was reliving the memories as I wrote, and my brain couldn't distinguish between past and present. Given that my brain wasn't differentiating, my body went into 'fight or flight' mode causing panic and anxiety, just the same as when I was a child. I was given exercises to practice, and I was told to nurture the little girl inside of me. I agreed to both and began to push through these unpleasant side effects.

Once I got into the story, Tom and Jess read some of the details and were very upset. This was my life, and I couldn't look at it objectively. So much time had passed, and I was somewhat immune to the pain. I couldn't really grasp the reality of it when they told me the abuse was far worse than they had ever imagined.

We talked about the other children that lived in the house, and I wondered how they were doing. Like me, Clarence had endured horrific physical abuse and I couldn't help but wonder where he was today.

One by one, I began to track them down through Facebook. Through conversations with them, I realized the depth of pain and the sheer volume of crimes that had been concealed within the walls of that house. I realized my silence only added to the problem - I had protected the perpetrators.

After some deliberation, I made the difficult decision to report the crimes to the police. Not because I wanted the perpetrators punished, but because I believed there should be some kind of accountability. I needed to speak up; for myself and the other children from the house.

Before going to the police, Tom and I decided to tell our family and closest friends. We had no idea how this story would unfold and preferred they hear details directly from me.

Next, I tracked down one of the social workers from my past. A lot of time had passed but I believe decision-makers, including social workers, could still learn from my experience. I was surprised to hear Mrs. Manning, who was now retired, still needed permission from a past supervisor before she could agree to talk with me. Permission was granted and over lunch, I shared the details of my childhood.

"There is always that one case that stays with you," she confided. "Even years later, you still think about it."

"Were we that case?"

"Yes," she confirmed.

Mrs. Manning apologized for my childhood suffering. I assured her that I understood the limitations on how she could help back then. Mother could beat me black and blue and if a social worker knocked on the door, I was warned not to speak as she switched modes and became sickeningly sweet to the visiting social worker. I dared not disobey her.

I was in my teens when Mrs. Manning was assigned to our foster home and I always thought she was suspicious of what was really happening there. I believed Mother sensed it too and didn't like her because of it.

When evidence finally presented itself and the children were taken, it was too late for Mrs. Manning, or anyone else, to undo the damage that had been done in the Moore house. I appreciated the apology and while it didn't change what had happened, it did offer some comfort.

Weeks went by and I worked on building up the courage to go to the police. When the day arrived and I was finally able to go, Tom got called away for work. I called Eddie to explain, and he immediately offered to accompany me.

The abusive crimes happened in Georgetown and that community fell under the jurisdiction of the Bay Roberts RCMP. The quiet drive from St. John's to Bay Roberts allowed me time to mentally prepare.

Feeling nauseous, I refused Eddie's food offerings and insisted we continue immediately to the police department before I lost my nerve. Once inside, we were greeted by a sergeant who told me he couldn't take my statement as he was a supervisor.

"I have to give a statement today, because if not today, I can't guarantee that I will come back," I pleaded.

The officer showed us to a room then excused himself. Minutes later, he returned to let us know a constable, who could take my statement, was on the way to the station.

Eddie was permitted to sit in on the interview, though I wasn't sure that was a good idea. He was one of my closest friends and although he knew about the physical and emotional abuse, I didn't particularly want him to hear the intimate details of the sexual abuse. He assured me he was fine, that he had been subjected to this scenario many times already through his day-to-day work.

Eddie was one of the strongest people I knew. I accepted his offer to sit in a corner away from me, though he was close enough if I needed him.

The interview itself was painful and lasted over two hours. I crossed my arms, sat back, and tightly grasped my ribcage as my hands reached almost completely around my body. With forced efforts, I released horrific details of a childhood plagued with severe physical, mental, and sexual abuse.

On my first birthday, I was delivered to the Moore house and adopted by them two years later. I was approximately five when I remembered my first sexual encounter with my adopted father and around the same time, my mother began to physically and mentally torture me.

I relayed details of unprovoked beatings, some so brutal that I thought I would die. My body had been battered with extension cords, broom handles, kitchen utensils, hairbrushes, and anything else within arm's reach.

I had been pushed, punched, choked, and dragged through the house by my hair. Sharp kitchen knives were held next to my throat as Mother threatened to "Just get it over with," And end my life.

There was no longer any physical evidence, but I described the anguish of a horrifying childhood growing up in the Moore house.

I was kept inside and controlled like a caged animal. I was told when to get up, when to go to bed, and everything in between. As the others helped themselves to snacks or meals of their choosing, I ate only foods given to me and was forced to eat regardless of whether I liked the food or not. My hair was cut short, and I was not permitted to wear fitted clothing. My sisters each had long beautiful hair and wore clothing of their choice. I was different.

I described debilitating lifelong fears of sharp knives and water. These fears were a direct result of Mother's sick forms of punishment. I was self-conscious when I described my fears and how they continue to haunt me as an adult today.

Through sweat and tears, I struggled with words and sometimes used gestures and non-verbal communication to describe my childhood, tainted by repetitive sexual abuse at the hands of Father.

As a small child, I learned to identify Father's sexual intentions through his facial gestures. It was his way of giving advance notice that he would be visiting my bedroom when everyone else was in bed. I never responded; instead, I pretended not to see his "warnings." My lack of response never stopped him.

He came to my bedroom and sexually violated me at every possible opportunity, as the rest of the family slept. At a very young age, I was introduced to a distinctive smell. It was an odour so offensive that decades later, I can still smell it. It was the smell of my father's manhood.

I cried myself to sleep most nights and I usually started my day doing the same as I left for school. As a teenager, I contemplated suicide, but thankfully I got scared and failed. Instead, I survived.

***

When I felt there was nothing more to add, the officer thanked me for my bravery in coming forward. I didn't feel brave and sadly, I didn't feel better for telling my story.

I felt depleted, unhappy, and totally exhausted. I now had a whole new appreciation about the reluctance of victims to come forward and tell their stories.

Police Investigation

The nightmares were terrifying. Mother was vindictive, malicious, and lacked any trace of empathy. She was on a mission and showed no mercy when administering lethal poison into my food. My face was bright red, and I was sweating profusely as my body laid motionless on the kitchen floor. Tom was terrified and desperately trying to conceal it while brushing his fingers through my hair.

"There's an ambulance on the way. Hang on Bevie, they're almost here," he repeated over and over while attempting to comfort me.

I was unable to communicate. I should have been freaking out, but I wasn't. I was fine. I felt nothing but a sense of calmness running through my veins in the form of radiating heat. The poison was making its way from my core and into my limbs. It wouldn't be long now.

My face and body were of my five-year-old self as it lay helpless on the floor, yet my husband was comforting me. I should have been confused, but I wasn't. I just didn't care.

Tom's voice became louder and more irritating as he insisted that I wake up. I lay comfortably with no desire to move. His persistence overpowered my subconscious while pulling me from a deep sleep dominated by yet another nightmare. It wasn't real, I reminded myself, as the nightmare continued to replay over and over in my mind for most of the day.

After giving a statement to the RCMP, the nightmares increased. I contacted April and Tracey to let them know about the investigation. Tracey wasn't surprised: we had already spoken about it several times since my initial meeting with Adam.

I was nervous when I shared the news with April. After all, I was pressing charges against her birth parents. April quietly nodded her head before she recounted a few of her own memories of my childhood. She wasn't angry like I imagined she might be. Instead, she was supportive. I was relieved and felt an overwhelming sense of gratitude for her.

Within a week of giving my statement to the police, I was

contacted by Victims Services and was pleasantly surprised to learn about their different types of support. A kind representative took the time to explain the investigation and court process. If my case made it to trial, she would prepare me for court and even attend the proceedings with me, if I needed that.

I was entitled to a predetermined amount of counseling at no cost to me; however, I would need to choose a therapist from their list of recommended professionals. I had paid for several therapy sessions already, so I knew the value of counseling.

In reviewing the Victim Services list of therapists, I requested the best one for dealing with childhood trauma. Karen was recommended and fortunately for me, she was taking new patients. After I had given my statement to the police, I began experiencing many symptoms - anxiety, nightmares, lack of appetite, nausea, and trouble sleeping. I needed help.

As we dug into my past, I become fairly comfortable talking to Karen about the physical and emotional abuse; however, the sexual abuse still remained difficult to discuss.

The police investigation was unpleasant. It was long and drawn out. It was a historical case and because no one was in imminent danger, the investigation seemed to sit on the back burner.

I called and sent letters to the investigating officers, their supervisors, and the supervisors' supervisors. Without the constant nudging, there seemed to be no updates.

Nevertheless, I persisted.

When investigators spoke with several people that had been in care at the house - all of them confirmed my story and some even added to the horrific details. Although nervous and uncomfortable, April was courageous and agreed to give a statement to the police.

My brother and I did not see each other often but after several months, I called to talk to him about the investigation. He wasn't home so I talked with his wife and was surprised to learn Mother hadn't yet been contacted by the police.

When my brother heard the news from his wife, he promptly called Mother and told her about the allegations. Mother in turn called April with questions and when she didn't provide answers, Mother threatened: "If I see Beverly first, she will not have to worry about court."

As April relayed the message, the words disturbed and further punished me.

"If I see Beverly first..."—it was as though her threat was personally delivered. I heard her voice echo in my head, and I felt a heaviness in my chest. I wished she still didn't have that control over me.

Most people called me Bev, but for the occasional person that called me Beverly, they usually got a 'deer in the headlights' look from me as I cringed at the sound of my full name. No matter who says it, I hear Mother's voice.

A distraction came in the form of opportunity. Tom was excited when he told me Wade, an acquaintance from Classique Models, was selling his high-end fashion boutique. The boutique was called August & Lotta Stockholm and was located in downtown St. John's.

Wade didn't have health insurance and when his daughter was born with a health issue, he was forced to take a job outside the boutique with a company that provided insurance. Tom thought the business was a great opportunity for me and a good investment for us.

Working full time, running the boutique, and caring for his family had become too much for Wade. With Carson, a mutual friend, Wade discussed selling the boutique for just the cost that would cover the outstanding bills and enable him to get out of the retail business. Carson called Tom to suggest that it would be a great business for me, and we readily agreed.

I hadn't worked retail for a long time, though I had a lot of experience in the fashion world and as a buyer. Tom and I made arrangements to meet Carson and Wade at the boutique that afternoon to discuss the business.

Both Wade and I had started our modelling careers with Linda at Classique Models.

Wade was the same age as me, he was very good-looking and always seemed busy. August & Lotta was his third business in downtown St. John's.

Wade didn't hide the fact that he was ready to get out of the retail business and jumped right to the point, trying to establish how much money he would need to comfortably walk away from it.

The price was more than reasonable for an established 10-year-old business and Wade offered to work with me for as long as I needed him. It was an incredible opportunity and the guys all thought it was a great fit for me.

The decision was made before we even left the meeting; Tom and I planned to purchase the boutique. It was a rushed decision and one I hoped not to regret. I was excited and nervous at the same time.

Tom started working on the legalities while Wade and I developed a transitional strategy. We set the beginning of July as the date for me to officially take over, which gave us less than two weeks to have everything in order.

I was so eager that I started working at the store early. Wade worked old-school without an electronic tracking system to record sales and inventory, so that was the first thing we changed. Tom came in and installed the same Point of Sale system that we had at Frontline Action, our other business. That worked out well as I was already familiar with it.

After meeting Della, an employee, I was pleased to have her continue with the company and work with me. Della was a professional who decided to stay home and raise her son while her husband continued to work in his field. Once her son was grown, she went back to work part-time. This got her out of the house, and she looked forward to it, but her primary focus was always her family. I appreciated those qualities.

Della was an attractive woman with shoulder-length brown hair and a youthful face. She had a great appreciation for nice clothes, and her wardrobe was quite trendy. I enjoyed working with Della and was proud when I watched her interact with customers.

Her approach was very similar to mine and it included being respectful to all customers through building relationships as opposed to selling them something they didn't need or want. Della and I became fast friends.

Business, I soon realized, was good but not great. Rent had significantly increased in Wade's initial location and he moved the boutique from a busy main stretch on Water Street to a more affordable location on the next street up just months before I purchased it.

Wade assumed customers would follow him to the new location. Some did but not everyone. In the new location, August & Lotta had fallen off the radar for many shoppers. To add to the challenge, many customers were now shopping online.

Wade worked with me through the transitional challenges. I started by decreasing the quantity of higher-priced items on hand and increasing inventory for a few lines that were more moderately priced. We also found several new European lines that were better priced and suited to August & Lotta.

With Tom and I now operating three businesses and Jess a full-time university student working on a nursing degree, our personal lives were almost nonexistent. We each committed to cooking at least one family meal a week and had leftovers or fend-for-yourself meals on the other days. Life was busy and some days we felt like ships passing in the night.

Tom's kids moved, with their mom, from New Brunswick to Ottawa a few years earlier and were still on the same schedule of spending Christmas, March break, and summers with us. Tom flew to Ottawa to spend time with them and was ecstatic when they told him they wanted to move home and live with us full time in St. John's.

Arrangements were made for both kids to move home after completing the school year in June. Tom's extended family - grandparents, aunts, uncles, and cousins were all excited and could barely wait. Living with us would be good for the kids. There would be two parents in the house and a large supportive family circle.

Although happy to be surrounded by the children and family, I was also nervous. The kids were now teenagers and bringing a whole new set of challenges to the table including Jacob's attitude. As he got older, he pushed the envelope with negative behaviors such as being disruptive and uncooperative in class.

The move was in their best interest, but I worried about being a primary caregiver. I worried about the structure of our home. I suspected having two teenagers living with workaholic parents was going to be challenging.

The school year ended, and the kids moved home. They travelled with most of their belongings stuffed into a cluster of suitcases, backpacks, and large boxes. It didn't take long for them to settle in and find space for their most prized possessions.

When September rolled around, Sarah registered for grade eight and Jacob for grade ten. Jake impressed us when he attended school in the fall and there were no issues, complaints, or negative feedback from any of his teachers. He was happy and had adjusted to the move nicely. We were extremely proud of his improved behaviour.

***

Fourteen months after I gave my statement to the RCMP, I finally received an update. Father was living in a locked-down unit within a psychiatric ward at the Waterford Hospital. He had symptoms of dementia and in his doctor's opinion, wouldn't be able to defend himself against sexual abuse charges.

Criminal laws that were in place at the time of my childhood abuse prevented Mother from being charged. The statute of limitations stated that perpetrators could not be charged more than six months after the date of the assault.

The exception was when the assaults occurred 'with a weapon.' I was given the option of returning to the police station to provide a second statement, this time outlining only assaults that included a weapon.

I was satisfied that the charges against Father would be dismissed. He was institutionalized and there was no danger of him sexually abusing another child. However, I was frustrated that I had to go back 14 months later to give a second statement - it prolonged the agony of possible charges against Mother. Our laws hadn't changed in the past year and a half; how did investigating officers not realize this before?

To make matters worse, Mother still hadn't been interviewed about the allegations. I was discouraged, though I realized I had to continue to push the case forward - If not for myself, then for the other children that had been brutalized by her.

With the follow-up interview scheduled, I began thinking about my childhood and recalled notable attacks with weapons. I linked precise attacks to specific school grades or other memorable events from my childhood and in the end, I was able to provide exact details for seven offences. There were many more, but these seven were the most savage attacks.

Although not in chronological order, I started by detailing an attack that occurred when I was in the third grade and ended the interview by giving details of the brutal pregnancy attack. Although details of the seven attacks were gruesome, the interview itself was faster and not as difficult as the first.

Three months later, I was working at the boutique when I received a telephone update from the police. Although witnesses - other children living in the home at the time - had confirmed the horrific abuse, they could not recall the exact details as I had. How could they? We were children and we all processed the attacks in our own different way.

I was mystified when told Mother had been asked to come into the station for an interview but had blatantly refused. Unbelievable! As the alleged perpetrator of such crimes, I didn't know she had a choice. That logic still escapes me. It wasn't just allegations to me - it was my life!

The investigating officer told me that the Crown prosecutor wouldn't waste time or money on a case unless they were confident they could, beyond the shadow of a doubt, prove that the accused was guilty. The case would be closed. However, it could be reopened at any time if one of the witnesses recalled something that could help move things forward. Although I had been unsuccessful in Mother being criminally charged, I was told I had the option of pursuing civil charges.

My brain struggled to understand the justice system. My foundation years - the most important years of a person's life - were irreversibly damaged by monsters. I was savagely beaten and mentally tormented daily by one parent, and the other violated my young, child size body for his own sick sexual pleasures. The damage was so great, I would spend the rest of my life recovering from it. I felt numb. For reasons beyond my grasp, the travesty did not matter. I did not matter.

At home, I talked to my family and delivered the devastating news. I had not wanted nor did I expect either of them to go to jail; I simply wanted them to be held accountable for their grotesque, immoral, and illegal actions.

For me, that meant acknowledging, if not to their victims, then to a court of law, their guilt in the wrongdoing. To say this entire process was disappointing would be a major understatement.

I didn't know where to turn next. Walking away didn't seem like an option. Several friends had recommended I seek legal advice or at least consider the option. With my limited knowledge of the justice system, I decided to meet with a well-known local lawyer who had worked on similar cases involving child abuse.

Mr. Andrews was an older gentleman. The multitude of framed certificates accessorizing his office walls validated his extensive training in the field. As he sat comfortably in a leather chair behind a rather large desk, he took notes as I explained the reason for my visit.

"On my first birthday I was placed in a foster home," I started to explain a condensed version of my life story. "I was the couple's first foster child. The father sexually abused me from an early age and instead of protecting me, the mother tortured me. I believe she knew the abuse was happening."

Without going into details, I skimmed through my experiences and highlighted some key focal points. I was still more at ease when I disclosed details of the physical and mental abuse rather than the sexual abuse.

Mr. Andrews paused briefly before clearing his throat to speak. "Victims often suppress details of abuse for as long as possible. Memories work their way from the subconscious to conscious and become increasingly more difficult to live with," he said.

"In my experience, victims come forward for one of three reasons: money, accountability, or for therapeutic reasons. Judging by your personality, the way you talk and carry yourself, I suspect you are looking for accountability."

"That is a fair judgment and an accurate one," I agreed.

The lawyer expressed surprise for the authoritative dynamics of the home in which Father, the sexual predator, was not the 'ruler of the house'.

The conversation continued as I revealed the traumatic details of my past.

I told him that at age 10, I spent time at the Janeway Children's Hospital for a persistent medical problem. When the doctor couldn't determine the cause, he sent a letter to the local Department of Social Services requesting an investigation into my home life. A social worker from the area followed up with a phone call to my mother, rather than visiting the home and speaking to me.

He continued taking notes as I explain that Mother told the social worker that everything was normal at home and there was no connection between my illness and home life.

Mr. Andrews agreed that the fact that the doctor requested a home investigation, was an obvious red flag, and that the social worker's decision to speak with Mother over the phone instead of seeing and speaking with me directly, was total incompetence.

Had she come to our home, she may have picked up on something. Unfortunately, the red flag was ignored, and the opportunity to end the abuse was missed.

The lawyer questioned the due diligence in the adoption process.

"Was there a thorough investigation before the adoption or was the couple able to adopt simply on the grounds of them already being your foster parents?"

"Good question. One we are unlikely to ever know the answer to."

As he concluded, he told me that if I chose to pursue civil action, I had two options. I could attempt to sue the provincial government and/or my parents for negligence. Or, based on the abuse inflicted on me and my foster siblings, we could collectively start a class action lawsuit.

I had no interest in soliciting for damages. I wanted accountability, not compensation. Money wouldn't undo, change, or fix my sadistic childhood. The police Investigation had absorbed almost two years and produced no results. There was no legal action or accountability. I had no desire to continue on the same path.

But what route to take now?

I searched for local support services online. I envisioned meeting people with similar backgrounds and everyone supporting one another. I thought it would be a great place to start.

As I looked for support, I was surprised to discover there were no local groups specifically for survivors of child abuse. I persisted in my research and discovered an organization in San Francisco, Adult Survivors of Child Abuse (ASCA), that not only offered support for adult survivors but also free online training for anyone interested in establishing a community support group. I immediately registered for the program.

The training took six weeks and once completed, I plastered posters in public places throughout the city. I received plenty of calls and emails with questions but at the first meeting there were just two survivors, and I was one of them. I shouldn't have been surprised, facing the monsters from the past is a hard thing to do. It took many years before I was ready to talk about the abuse I suffered.

During training, we were told that survivors, although interested, might take some time before they were ready to attend meetings. Many survivors don't tell family members or friends about their abuse, so attending a support meeting is a big step. I continued to offer meetings on the first and third Monday of every month and was pleased when participation increased.

With three kids in the house, what was once a quiet home was now full of activity. Jess spent more time studying at the library and less time at home. When the opportunity arose, she moved out and into an apartment with her boyfriend.

Tom insisted we continue taking our annual breaks. Vacation was the only real downtime we got during the year when we could truly turn work off.

Our marriage was the second one for both of us and the challenges that came with a blended family, stepchildren, and ex-partners, meant we had to work extra hard at making the relationship work. With time, we had found vacations were instrumental in keeping us connected as a couple. Now that the children were living with us for most of the year, we realized it was more important than ever to continue creating that time away for just the two of us.

That year, Tom divided our vacation time between Australia, Cambodia, and Hong Kong. I realized my life felt at times like a fairy tale and I would probably never see those places without him. There were times when I could barely contain my excitement, like when we saw exotic animals or special places. I often felt like a child in a candy store.

I worked long hours at August & Lotta. If I knew Tom was home with the kids in the evening, I would often work late into the night. While working at the boutique, I usually took the paperwork from the other businesses to work on during quiet times. The after-hours were peaceful and very productive.

While at work one evening, I went online to look for ideas on other ways to help child abuse survivors. I was happy to be facilitating the ASCA meeting and even though participation had increased, I was not satisfied. I was convinced there was something else that could be done.

I was intrigued to discover April was Child Abuse Prevention Month and began looking for ways to raise awareness. I found

189

organized walks for almost every known charity and even came across one for child abuse. I thought it would be an easy way to raise awareness and spent hours researching the idea. In the end, I decided to organize a walk in St. John's for the month of April.

That night, a picture frame on display in our house caught my eye. In an ivory-coloured, square frame were three photos. One of Tom and I at our wedding, one of him when he was five years old, and another of me at approximately the same age. I noticed Tom's smile, he looked happy and even a little mischievous. His smile was of a kid without a care in the world, as it should be.

My photo, however, had a different kind of smile. My mind went back to the model convention when the agent told me I had "sad eyes." While looking at my childhood photo, I covered my face area, leaving just the eyes exposed. It was very evident, shocking almost; my five-year-old self had very sad eyes.

Children are carefree and happy by nature, as was evident in Tom's childhood photo. When a child doesn't have a smile, a real smile that includes the eyes, it should be a red flag that something is wrong.

Why didn't anyone see it in my face? I was sad and scared. I had the same forced smile in all my childhood photos. Did others see the sadness and choose to ignore it? I have since learned that, generally, people might see it but choose to not "get involved."

The name for the walk ought to have something to do with smiles, or lack of them. While I was at work I doodled on paper and played with the words smiles, walk, and miles. When a friend dropped in to see me, I showed her my doodles and told her about the project. She took one look at the paper and observed, "it should be Miles For Smiles. You are encouraging people to walk the miles for smiles."

With an event name, I created a Facebook page that told people we were organizing the city's first child abuse awareness walk. The walk, I committed, would help us raise awareness and support people who have been affected by child abuse. When I talked to ASCA participants, they were thrilled with the concept and some even volunteered to help.

Weeks later, while participating in a fashion show for the Heart and Stroke Foundation, I was luckily positioned in the lineup next to the Mayor of St. John's, Dennis O'Keefe. During the event's intermission and between runway walks, I used the opportunities to explain the upcoming walk.

He was interested in the idea and where it came from as well as my plan to pull it off. We talked for a while and he suggested I submit a request to the city to have April proclaimed as Child Abuse

Prevention Month. I knew nothing about proclamation requests but was keen to pursue his suggestion.

Three weeks later, I attended the St. John's City Council meeting where the Mayor introduced me as his partner in crime from the catwalk. I was proud when the Child Abuse Prevention Month Proclamation was read out, and nervous when I spoke to Council on its importance.

Support for Miles for Smiles grew; we had accumulated 1,000 Facebook followers in a fairly short period. I was determined to provide free registration for participants and Tom agreed to help. Kerry Lynn and Kora Leigh, a couple of friends, and survivors agreed to help in whatever way they could.

Local businesses had also offered to help. Tom tried to keep me grounded by asking, "How many people do you expect to attend to consider this event a success?"

"There will be hundreds of people," I replied with excitement.

Tom shook his head.

"No Bevie. Lots of people will have the best intentions, but charity walks don't usually see a lot of participants. We need to be happy with... 40?"

I dismissed him. "But there will be hundreds and hundreds of people at this one."

We secured a location, musical entertainment, face-painters, entertainment for kids, two guest speakers, and refreshments - all at no cost - for the walk. Tony, from The Print Shop, took care of all our printing needs for our businesses and when I met with him to discuss printing event posters, he told me he would take care of everything we needed, and at no charge to us. I was delighted with his level of support.

As the walk approached, we only had two items that weren't donated - a technician with a sound system and the order of t-shirts. Sandra, my trade show business partner, and I agreed to cover the cost of the technician and sound system while Tom and I paid for the shirts. We planned to give a free shirt to every participant at the walk.

During the last Sunday of April, the kids travelled to Ottawa to visit their mom for Easter break as Tom, Jess, and I went to Bowring Park for the first-ever Miles for Smiles Walk. We arrived early and set up in the park bungalow. The sun was shining, and it was a perfect day for the event.

Jess was tasked with registration and giving out the t-shirts. Kerry Lynn and Kora Leigh handled refreshments, timekeeping, and the musical lineup of bands. Eddie helped Tom set up and supervise a bouncy castle and laser tag.

As registration started, the people poured in. I greeted and spoke with local politicians including Minister Paul Davis and his wife, Cheryl; Members of the House of Assembly Paul Lane, John Dinn, and Gerry Rogers; the Mayor of St. John's, Dennis O'Keefe, as well as a large collection of friends and supporters.

Local musicians performed for the first hour during registration. Then we had our opening ceremonies with two guest speakers. The speeches were short and when finished, we led the group on a walk through the park then back to our starting point for the featured band, refreshments, and entertainment for kids. With over 400 participants, we were pleased to have organized our first successful Miles For Smiles walk in St. John's.

It was an incredible year of growth. The ASCA group continued to offer support to adult survivors, and we raised awareness province-wide with our first proclamation and walk.

The year wound down with me accepting the NLOWE - Newfoundland and Labrador's Organization for Women Entrepreneurs - Community Impact Award.

In front of my peers and the business community, I disclosed a painful past as a survivor of child abuse who eventually became a runaway. I spoke from the heart when I accepted the award on behalf of all survivors, and I received support in the form of a standing ovation as I left the stage.

The second annual Miles for Smiles awareness walk in St. John's
(photo credit Gerry Carew)

Conversation with a Pedophile

After two years of therapy, I was comfortable talking to Karen about Mother's physical and mental abuse. She noticed how I often tightly folded my arms into my chest whenever I talked about my past.

Sometimes while sitting on the sofa, I took my shoes off, pulled my legs up into my chest, and wrapped my arms around both legs. Apparently, that was all quite normal and was body language that she had seen before.

I was making progress and I talked to her about most things, but when the discussion shifted to my childhood sexual abuse, I always locked up. I knew I would feel better once I released the horrid details, yet I couldn't seem to articulate what needed to be said.

I drove myself to Karen's office, prepared for difficult conversations but generally left frustrated when I inevitably failed to divulge details.

I was especially frustrated on one particular day and decided to take action. From Karen's parking lot, I called April and asked her to meet me as soon as she got off work. When she arrived, I surprised her by saying that I wanted to drive to the Waterford Hospital to visit Father, and I wanted her to come with me.

April was resistant and tried to talk me out of it, or at least postpone the visit to a later date. I was determined to go and although she had limited time, I managed to talk her into it.

Mother placed Father in a seniors' home when he showed signs of Alzheimer's disease. After an incident at the home, he was brought to the Waterford Hospital and admitted as a long-term patient.

He was now in his 70s. It had been 12 years since I last saw him and I had no idea what to expect, or if he would even remember me, but I knew I wanted to see him one last time before he passed.

Once we were inside the hospital, April led the way.

"Dad is on a lock-down unit and we need authorization to visit," she said.

April had visited Father regularly and was familiar with the process. As April rang a doorbell, I glanced in through a small window for my first view of the ward. A couple of minutes passed before the door was opened by a staff nurse.

I stood back and allowed April to do the talking. I was a little uncomfortable with us being referred to as 'his daughters' but realized it was necessary if I wanted to visit.

The nurse opened the door and allowed us enough space to pass through. I heard a loud bang as the door closed and locked behind us. I immediately noticed an older man in the hallway leaning over the side of a wheelchair. Further on, I saw another man who was walking around in a bathrobe. Both appeared to be heavily sedated, to my untrained eye.

April walked ahead and into the second room on the left. The room contained two twin beds with matching night tables and a corner shelf that contained personal pictures above each bed. Both patients were asleep.

April approached the bed closest to the window. The shelf of photos confirmed the sleeping man was Father. Although he had noticeably aged, he looked much the same. With a slight shake of her hand on his shoulder, April woke him. He was groggy and unconcerned.

"Do you know who I am?" she asked.

He sat up and responded. "Yes," then a pause. "April."

I noticed the unusual shape of his belly. Both sides were caved in and I assumed it represented the amount of time he spent laying down. His hair was gray with some black remaining, and his hands were cleaner than I had ever seen them.

As a child, I remembered the stains on his hands and dirty fingernails from his work as a mechanic. I also noticed that he appeared sedated. Not wanting to get too close, I stood back and observed.

Pointing to me, April asked, "Do you recognize this person?"

Father shook his head from side to side. "No."

"It's Beverly," she announced.

He didn't comment or show any emotion. He just nodded his head up and down.

April initiated a conversation. "Does mom visit?"

"She's dead," he responded, devoid of emotion.

"No, she's not," April refuted, before moving on to another topic of discussion.

Without saying a word, Father calmly stood and walked into the bathroom closing the door behind him. I noticed the time and realized I needed to come out of my shell if I wanted to get any of my questions answered.

Upon his return, he lay down on the bed and turned toward us. I walked to his bedside and sat on the edge of his night table. Father looked at me but didn't speak. I contemplated how to break the ice. After a couple of uncomfortable minutes, I moved to the side of Father's bed and crouched down in front of him.

"Do you remember me?"

"Yes."

"Do you remember when I was a little girl?"

"Yes."

"Do you remember Tracey?"

"Yes."

"Do you remember Katie?"

"Yes."

"Do you remember Clarence and Leonard?"

"Yes."

"Do you remember Christine and Guylaine?"

"Yes."

"Do you remember Lorraine?"

"No."

"Lorraine was older. She was very pretty with long brown hair."

"No, I don't remember."

"Do you remember the garage?"

"Yes."

"Remember you used to like beer?"

"Yes! I got picked up for impaired (driving) outside Clarenville and lost my license for 13 months," he said with a chuckle, showing the first sign of emotion since we arrived.

"I didn't know that," April said.

In an attempt to stay focused, I continued, "Do you remember when you used to come into my bedroom? When you were drinking?"

"Yes... but I gave that up."

I was completely caught off guard by his response. He could have told me that he didn't remember, but like his other answers, he wasn't putting any thought into his replies. He was just simply answering the questions.

So, there it was, the answer to one of my lifelong questions. Did he remember the abuse when sober? Yes, he most certainly did.

While growing up, I believed that he only came into my room when he was intoxicated and that he didn't remember the incidents once he was sober. I had given him the benefit of the doubt because I saw no signs of recollection when he had been sober. I truly believed he couldn't remember the sexual activity. Maybe I wanted to believe it or needed to believe it for survival.

I could have stood up and walked away. I had received the answer I was looking for. Instead, I chose to stay and continued the conversation.

"Do you remember the house? It was a horrible place."

"Yes."

"She was not very nice, was she?"

"No. She was bad to me," he said.

"Yes, you are right, she was bad to you. She was pretty mean. And do you remember how she hated me?"

"Yes."

"Do you remember how much you worked?"

"Yes, and she took all my money."

"Do you remember the bad stuff we did when you were drinking?"

"Yes."

"Did you - and anyone else?"

"Yes."

"Who?"

"The others."

"What are their names?"

"I don't remember."

"Do you miss Mother?"

Father sat up and positioned himself on the edge of the bed. I stepped back but remained close enough to hear his monotone voice.

"No, she's dead," he continued.

"What happened to her?"

"He shot her seven times."

"Who shot her?"

"The man she was seeing."

"Dad, she's not dead," April interjected.

I gave April a look and shook my head. I thought it was best not to argue or irritate him, and I communicated my position to her in a non-verbal manner. April understood and said nothing else.

"Who's the man?" I repeated.

"I don't know his name. He lives in Cupids in a two-story house."

Father got up to walk around and the conversation came to halt. April noticed the time.

"We have to leave now. I have to drive back out around the bay. Dad, I will come back another time."

She gave him a quick hug and I left the room. Outside the door,

I waited for April as she put on her jacket and walked towards me.

Although the visit was short and we were in no danger, I still felt uncomfortable being around him. It was, however, not the same anxiety or discomfort that I felt around Mother. If I knew she was in the same building, even one as large as a shopping mall or a hospital where the chances of seeing each other were slim, I still regressed to a frightened, childlike state and couldn't get out of the building fast enough.

Unlike Mother, Father didn't scare me. His presence, however, raised within me very uncomfortable emotions too difficult to describe. I felt a great deal of betrayal as he had infected my entire childhood with the vulgarity of his sexually abusive behaviour. Nonetheless, it was Mother who I intensely feared. It was a fear that governed my every move.

Father's abuse was a secret and never discussed. Due to the forced participation in activities outside my comprehension, I didn't understand the depth of violation to which my child-sized body was being subjected.

I was robbed of the pure essence of what it meant to be a little girl. My innocence was stolen as I was forced to do grownup things, in a little girl's bedroom. I should have hated Father - his actions damaged my soul.

I will forever be affected by what he did. However, it wasn't hatred or hostility that I felt for him. Rather, I felt pity.

Father was not the 'man of the house' and he rarely asserted any form of authority. When he did, Mother overruled him. She was a ruthless dictator and maintained constant control. Father was right when he said she was not nice to him. As a child, I witnessed it and felt sorry for him.

He was an alcoholic and that upset her. She may have been justified in her feelings towards him but during my childhood, he wasn't outright mean, angry, or cruel to me. He tried to intervene during a few of my harsh beatings and although he couldn't make her stop, I was grateful for his attempts.

It was probably some combination of pity, dependence, and appreciation for those attempted interventions, that enabled the sexual abuse to continue for as long as it had.

As we walked away from the Waterford Hospital, I thought about Father and my past. I was satisfied with the visit, and now - I never had to see him again.

I contemplated visiting Mother, though I doubted I would ever have the courage to be in the same room as her. I wished I could be brave and that she no longer had power over me. Just hearing her voice had always been enough to paralyze me with fear. It had been many years, but I could still hear her voice in my head as she sounded out every syllable of my name.

It was while sitting in a clinic and anticipating the dreaded sound of my name being called for a doctor's appointment that I decided to change it. People changed their legal names every day, so why couldn't I change mine?

A call to Vital Statistics confirmed that I could make the change, and within 24 hours, I was in their office completing the necessary paperwork.

I requested a copy of my birth certificate after Jess had been born and noticed that at the time of my birth, I had been baptized Beverly Rexine. That was a surprise as all my other legal documents identified me as Beverly Roxanne. My adoptive parents evidently changed my name during the adoption process.

The original documentation obtained from Vital Statistics had been useful in helping me find my biological parents. Most notably, the documents helped me make the connection between the name Rexine and my birth father.

On the application I requested Beverly be legally changed to Bev, and that my middle name go back to Rexine. When I returned to pick up the documents, I was told that my middle name had never been changed, so legally it was Rexine all along, even though my baptism and birth certificate identified me as Beverly Roxanne. I decided not to waste time on it. I was happy to have a new and official birth certificate with my chosen name, Bev Rexine.

After leaving Vital Statistics, I immediately contacted the health authority to have my name changed on my medical records. Now, I never had to hear a doctor or receptionist call me by that name again. It was a relief!

***

While stopped at a downtown traffic light, my attention wandered to a nearby billboard. My eyes widened as I was shocked to see a familiar face - mine! I had been hired over a year ago, along with several other models, for the print campaign of a national business. I had no idea billboards were part of their campaign.

Earlier that summer, a friend texted me to say that she had driven past the Avalon Mall and saw a billboard with my picture on it. That particular billboard promotion, for a different company, wasn't a surprise.

The new downtown billboard sparked reflection. At age 23 I had started modelling and according to the industry's standards, I was already too old to start a career in a normally short-lived profession. I was told I would already have habits—good and bad—

which put me past the "malleable" stage. Looking back, comments like that only motivated me to work harder.

My modelling career lasted more than two decades. In that time, I was lucky to be featured in TV commercials, print campaigns, posters, and billboards, and I even had a few acting gigs.

I had been selected for a magazine cover and although the chosen photo (without makeup) was one of my least favourites, I was proud to have been selected for the job. I had participated in many fashion shows and won several awards while competing at national and international levels.

Although I never did pursue the summer contract offer from South Korea or move to New York or Montreal when representation from larger agencies was offered, their interest alone was enough to improve my severely damaged ego and self-esteem.

My body paid a hefty price from years of battling eating disorders. However, I believe the lessons gained were greater than the loss. In the end, I felt I remained humble. I was still a small-town girl from Georgetown, a community that most still don't know even exists.

After the first Miles for Smiles Walk was organized, I was asked frequently to speak on issues related to child abuse and domestic violence. At first, it was difficult. I was nervous and occasionally emotional, depending on the circumstances.

I once read in an article, "Every time you push yourself outside your comfort zone, you grow as a person." Speaking to groups of people, from any type of platform or stage, was definitely outside my comfort zone.

I now regularly speak to college and university students as they prepare for careers in child protection. That has been especially gratifying. As I share my story, I provide insight as a survivor and as a result, they are better equipped to help other victims.

I tell students that, "As a child, I could have been recovering from a horrific beating –my body covered with black and blue bruises while broken ribs punctured my lungs with every breath I took. However, when interviewed by Child Protective Services, I would deny anything had happened to me. I was that afraid."

My advice to students or anyone responsible for the well-being of children:

"Truly listen as children talk or answer your questions; look for clues on the child and in their environment; look into their eyes, and most importantly, trust your instinct. If something feels wrong, it usually is. Never walk away leaving a child unprotected, unheard, or not believed."

One speaking event was an annual Foster Parents Symposium.

That opportunity enabled me to speak to a large group of foster parents, social workers, and front-line employees who worked with children in protective care. As I listened to their questions, I could tell they were engaged and wanting to learn from my experience. I talked about the many red flags that were missed in my home. I also had the opportunity to honour a special lady.

I told the audience about Mother's friend, Louise. As a foster parent, she enriched the lives of many children that came into her care. Sadly, Louise passed away a few years ago. By coincidence, I spoke at the symposium on her birthday and wanted to commemorate her as the kind, caring mother that she was to many children. We need more foster parents like Louise.

***

On a Sunday afternoon, April called to share some news.

"Not sure if you want to hear this but mom is at the Carbonear Hospital. Her doctor called to tell me she's not doing well. She is in stage five renal failure."

I had mixed emotions. The compassionate person inside me wanted to tell April that I was terribly sorry to hear the news, but because it was Mother, I was conflicted.

April had always been respectful of my feelings. She had wanted me to hear the news from her so I could decide if I wanted to see Mother before she passed. I appreciated her reaching out and giving me the option. After a brief conversation with Jess, we decided to drive out to the hospital together.

During the hour-long drive, Jess asked, "What will you say? What will you do when you see her?"

I was already nervous and anxious with knots in my stomach. I really didn't know how I would react. We waited outside the hospital for April, her daughter, and her young granddaughter. Then, we all walked in together. As we approached the room, April and the girls walked in ahead of me. I reached the door but was unable to bring myself past the entrance.

The head of the hospital bed was in line with the doorway. I noticed her body was much smaller and frailer than I remembered. Her hair was long and gray. I had never seen her with long hair. As the girls entered, Mother strained her neck to look back and see me in the doorway. My body froze. I turned my head to avoid looking at her.

April opened the conversation by asking Mother how she felt. She began to ask, as she pointed to me, "Do you know who...?"

I quickly shook my head and put my hand up to stop her. I didn't want Mother looking at me. I didn't want any attention drawn to me. I was still in the doorway and at that point, I didn't know if I would even enter the room. April quickly shifted the attention and her pointed finger, toward Jess. The last time Mother had seen Jess, she was a child. I didn't expect Mother to recognize her.

"Is it Beverly?" she asked.

Jess was quick to respond. "No. Mom is taller, thinner... and much nicer than me."

I gave Jess a stern look that, without words, communicated disapproval. As a child, Jess knew I had limited contact with my parents, though I had never disclosed reasons. Later in life, when I finally went to the police and began speaking publicly, Jess was an adult and ready to hear about my past. She had always been like a protective mamma-bear and unforgiving of anyone who hurt me. I was on edge as I worried about what she might now say to Mother.

The conversation was superficial, and Mother kept peering back at me. She didn't ask, but I believed she knew who I was. I resisted looking into her eyes and refused her the opportunity to look into mine. I didn't need a reminder of the evil within nor would I grant her the pleasure of extracting pity from me.

Being a little standoffish, Jess matter-of-factly told Mother she was now training to be a nurse. She talked about the different hospitals that she had worked in, including her time at the Waterford Hospital. Jess was looking for a reaction, hoping Mother would mention that her husband was a long-term patient there, but Mother didn't bite.

Jess warmed up and made her way to Mother's IV station. While reading the fluid package, she asked a few questions before explaining the IV solution and its purpose to Mother.

When it was time to leave, April and her girls hugged Mother and then joined Jess and me in the hallway. I was not ready to be close to Mother and I was satisfied with the visit from outside the hospital room door.

Mother's boyfriend met us in the hallway as we left the ward. As he chatted with April, he expressed concern for Mother.

On the drive home, Jess talked about Mother's condition. She educated me on kidney failure and told me she didn't expect her to live much longer. I told Jess that the visit had been difficult and painful. I did not plan on going back.

***

In my quest to promote awareness about child abuse, many people passed along valuable pieces of information to me. Through a mutual acquaintance in St John's, I met Andy Bhatti, a child abuse survivor from British Columbia.

Andy was sexually abused from age 10 to 14 by his sponsored 'big brother' from the Big Brothers/Big Sisters Association.

At 14, Andy ran away from home and became involved in a life of drugs, crime, gangs, and violence. Two years later he was addicted to heroin and cocaine while living on the streets of downtown Vancouver.

Andy was 27 and in prison when he learned that he was going to be a father. Not wanting his child to grow up without a father as he had, Andy was quickly motivated to turn his life around.

Andy raised his son as a single dad while working in the field of addictions and interventions. He also spent a considerable amount of time fundraising for various charitable organizations in British Columbia.

I admire Andy. He not only turned his life around but used his negative experiences to help others. He is a strong advocate for child sexual abuse prevention. Andy worked with high-profile sports celebrities to raise a lot of money for Sophie's Place, a Child Advocacy Center in Surrey, British Colombia.

Andy was both surprised and disappointed to hear that we did not already have a Child Advocacy Center in Newfoundland and Labrador. When I told him about my advocacy plans for the future, he offered to come to the island and help me bring my charitable work to the next level. I was impressed by his efforts in British Columbia and the amount of money he had already raised. With renewed excitement, I welcomed the opportunity to work with him.

Andy and I spent hours on the phone brainstorming. When he proposed bringing NHL hockey legend Johnny Bower to St. John's, I thought he was a little too ambitious. It was a great idea, but I really didn't think we could make it happen. It didn't take long to realize Andy was a man of action. If he committed to doing something, he would not rest until it happened.

It was the first week of December on a cool crisp day when Johnny and Debbie Sittler - sister of the famous NHL hockey player, Darryl Sittler - stepped off a plane at St. John's International Airport. Local reporters were already at the Ramada Hotel waiting to speak with the legend when he arrived.

Johnny was a Canadian Hockey Hall of Fame goaltender who won four Stanley Cups during his career with the Toronto Maple Leafs. I had never followed hockey but after a couple of conversations with Johnny, I developed a greater understanding and appreciation for the game.

Johnny was shorter than I expected. He wore a Toronto Maple Leaf jersey, dress pants, and a gray baseball cap. He was clean-shaven with short hair and glasses.

Without the signature jersey, he could have easily been mistaken for someone's grandfather. He shook my hand during our introduction, though I could tell he was rushed.

"I can wait," I told him, as I pointed to the reporters.

Once the interview ended, Johnny, Debbie, and Andy joined Tom and me for a fish-fry at Tom's parents' house. Weekly fish-frys were Mom Davis' way of keeping the family connected as she cooked the traditional codfish meal most Fridays. All of Tom's siblings and their families, except Alex, who lived in Ottawa, gathered around the table for the delicious meal and to catch up on the weekly family news.

We were delighted to have Johnny and his entourage join us for a family meal. I noticed every member of the family, grandchildren to grandparents, were immersed in conversation and completely charmed by our 90-year-old guest.

On Saturday, we had a scheduled meet-and-greet fundraiser event at The Big's — a sport's themed restaurant in St. John's, followed by a sit-down meal. First in line to meet Johnny was a young boy by the name of Bower. Bower came from a local hockey family and happened to be named after Johnny. It was a special moment for both of them.

Many visitors brought memorabilia for Johnny to sign. It was impressive how he didn't rush his fans. He listened attentively as he gave them time to tell their stories, then smiled graciously for each photo.

During the meal, I listened to Johnny recall stories from his hockey days. He told us how he met Jean Beliveau for the first time in Montreal. Johnny described seeing Jean across the street, but he was unsure about approaching him. It was Jean who then walked over to Johnny, stuck out his hand, and wished him luck on the ice.

"I should have been the one walking over to him," he said. "He was a gentleman both on and off the ice, maybe that's why I let him score so many times," he joked.

Every one of Johnny's stories was interesting. When fans asked questions about his locker room days, he smiled and said, "I would like to talk about that but there are ladies in the room."

We reserved Sunday morning for a drive. Tom offered to show our guests some of the local sights before they left for the airport. Whenever we travelled in a vehicle over the weekend, I noticed Johnny waiting to close my door for me.

If I carried any bags, my large handbag included, he insisted on carrying it for me. We thoroughly enjoyed the weekend, and I was pleased to have met the Canadian hockey legend and gentleman, Johnny Bower.

Planning for the third annual Miles for Smiles Walk started early in the new year. When Andy contemplated flying in to attend, I asked him to consider being a guest speaker. He immediately agreed and then offered to ask his friend Graham Wardle, from CBC's hit television show *Heartland,* to join us.

I knew better than to challenge Andy but bringing heartthrob Graham Wardle to our walk sounded too good to be true. Andy suggested that I send an official letter to personally invite Graham to attend.

The letter was sent, and Andy called the next day to confirm that Graham and his new wife, Ali, would travel to St John's to attend our walk. I was excited and could barely wait to start promoting the event and highlighting his attendance.

During the last week of April - the week of the walk - I was working at August & Lotta when Andy, Graham, and Ali walked into the boutique. Graham was exceptionally handsome. He was a little taller than me with dark hair and a show-stopping smile. Graham wore blue jeans, a basic t-shirt, and a backward baseball hat. Ali was petite, with blonde hair and blue eyes. Her hair was tied back in a loose ponytail, and she was also dressed casually. Ali seemed a little more reserved - maybe even shy.

Andy announced the happy couple was just married and the trip was serving as somewhat of a honeymoon. Although we would see them over the weekend, they planned on doing a little sightseeing beforehand on their own. Both Graham and Ali seemed to be down-to-earth, genuinely nice people. Within minutes, the guys drifted off into a conversation while Ali and I were wrapped up in our own.

Sunday brought traditional Newfoundland weather - rain, drizzle, and fog - for the Miles for Smiles event. While somewhat disappointing, it did not dampen our spirits. During his speech, Andy spoke off the cuff as he told the audience about his experiences as a survivor of childhood abuse.

The details were raw, but Andy had told the story so many times that he seemed unaffected. Graham also said a few words to the crowd before we cut the official walk ribbon together and then led the group on a stroll throughout the park.

Local bands performed when we got back from the walk and although the rain was light, we moved the remainder of the day's activities inside. The band played a great selection of music, including plenty of popular songs from the '80s and '90s. When most of the crowd left, Ali pulled the group of us together in a circle to dance in front of the band.

As the day's activities concluded, Tom and I prepared to take our guests out for dinner. Graham and Ali had an early morning flight, so we booked an early reservation. We all rushed in different directions, to our house and hotels for quick changes, and then met at a downtown restaurant. Andy spoke to the host and requested space in a quiet area. Everyone was tired but we appreciated the time to unwind over a social drink and delicious meal. Andy passed on the drink disclosing that he hadn't had a drink since becoming sober years earlier.

Our conversation was interesting and covered random topics about work, children, relationships - including how the couples at the table met - and our advocacy work. Before we left the restaurant, we said our goodbyes. Ali wasn't on Facebook, so we exchanged email addresses and committed to staying in touch.

With the busy month of April behind us, we turned our attention to Jacob's high school graduation. He insisted on keeping it low-key, even teasing that he wanted to wear a hoodie instead of a tux. On graduation day, he did indeed wear a tux and looked rather handsome in it. Along with his date, Tom and I accompanied him to the big event. I felt honoured to be there for the parents' dance and could not have been prouder of him.

Bev, Graham Wardle and Andy Bhatti

Drowning

Tom registered us for a Child Sexual Abuse Prevention Training program in Tucson, Arizona in February. He then booked our vacation around that location and time frame. The program was facilitated internationally and gave participants the tools needed to teach how to prevent sexual abuse of children. I had been looking for an educational program about prevention that was designed for adults and this one came highly recommended.

There were trained facilitators in several other provinces; however, Newfoundland and Labrador didn't have any. The training was informative and interesting. Once we completed the courses, we were presented with certificates and included in a group photo with the latest group of trained facilitators. I was committed to the program and looked forward to returning home with what we learned.

The weather was beautiful as we drove from Arizona to California in a rental car. Once we dropped off the car, a taxi took us to a pier where we boarded a cruise ship. Tom had prepared me for the cruise this time by telling me the number of sea days and the expected temperatures, though I had no idea where the ship would take us.

As we settled into our stateroom, an itinerary arrived listing the ship's scheduled ports of call. Tom scanned through each description and read them aloud. One of his favourite things to do when we travelled was to swim in the ocean. I tagged along for the adventure. I liked to walk on the beach and depending on the strength of the waves, I sometimes got in. I hadn't overcome my childhood fear, but thanks to Tom I was a lot more comfortable in the water.

"Puerto Vallarta has a public beach and it's close to the port. We should definitely swim there. With the beach so close to the ship, we could go for a swim and still have time to do some exploring," he suggested.

Tom continued to map out plans for each port and I didn't mind him taking the lead. For sea days, however, I had my own agenda, and he was always respectful of that. I started the day with a workout at the gym and spent the rest of it writing or studying, depending on my current project.

Meanwhile, he enjoyed swimming, reading, and talking to new friends that he made on the ship. We enjoyed starting our day together over breakfast and we would meet up for lunch, then later again in our room to prepare for dinner and date nights. On vacation, especially those that involved a cruise or all-inclusive resorts, every night was a date night.

The ship had already docked by the time we got up. It was a bright and beautiful day, and from the top deck of the ship, we caught our first glimpse of the scenic coastlines. As we talked to other cruisers over breakfast, we discussed our plans for the day. Back in our room, we slipped into swimsuits and covered ourselves in sunblock. Tom packed snacks, water, and a few essentials into a backpack as I fussed with pinning my hair up underneath a wide-brimmed hat.

When we arrived at the beach, I immediately noted the force and height of the waves.

"It's not that bad," Tom remarked, as he looked for an open spot on the beach for us to nestle into. On some level, I was comforted when he pointed out the number of swimmers already in the water.

When it came to getting in the water, my fear would inevitably get in the way. I realized that it was all in my head and I had to work on overcoming it. I reminded myself I was doing much better and that I wasn't nearly as fearful as I had been five years ago.

We chose a quiet area away from the concentration of sunbathers and groups of people. As Tom rolled out two large beach towels, I modestly removed a button-up shirt, denim shorts, my sunglasses, and hat.

Tom and I walked into the water together, and although I was content to stand in the waist-high area, he encouraged me to go further out. As long as I could still reach down and touch the bottom with my toes when swimming, I was fine. Otherwise, I panicked.

Since our honeymoon in Mexico, I had challenged myself to overcome my fear of the water. It wasn't an easy task, but Tom was vigilant anytime I was in the water with him. Tom was a strong swimmer and usually swam out into the ocean and then back to me. As he swam away, I was always satisfied to stay in the shallow area.

The waves were rough that day and although Tom held my hand, I was nervous about going deeper into the ocean. He suggested we swim out past the wave crash point where the water was a little calmer.

I initially wanted no part of that. After about 20 minutes of casually frolicking in the water with Tom and debating whether to take the plunge, I agreed to swim out a little further and face my fears head-on. After all, he was right, I could swim. It was just the fear in my head that held me back.

After several attempts, I failed to move from my safe space. One more pep talk from Tom and I was ready to go, or so I thought. After another series of waves, there was a brief pause. I held my breath and lunged forward with Tom against the current.

There was instant resistance and I immediately felt the powerful tide against me. I pushed past and waited for a break in the waves to raise my head and breathe. The break didn't come. The waves continued with one smack after another as they forcefully pulled me down and jostled me in different directions.

With my eyes tightly shut, I no longer felt Tom's presence. Seconds felt like minutes as I lost my sense of direction. I stretched my legs in search of the ocean floor, but there was nothing. No sand, rocks, or bottom. Panic set in. I was underwater; I couldn't breathe, and I couldn't see. What was most unnerving was that I couldn't tell if I was swimming to shore or away from it.

The ocean asserted its authority and showed no mercy. With every toss and turn, its firm grasp reminded me how little control I actually had. I felt powerless in this vicious body of water. I suspected I was being pulled out further from shore, and I imagined Tom was frantically looking for me. I knew he was panicked now too.

If I could only get my head above water, he would see me. I was scared and knew I was in trouble. Jess popped into my head as I struggled to focus. With every fiber of my being, I kept holding my breath.

I had to remain calm, I told myself. "Hang on... keep swimming... keep swimming."

I didn't know how much longer I could do this. "Don't stop... keep going... keep going..."

Once again, I felt the intense grip of the ocean's currents as it yanked me up and body-slammed me into the water. This time I felt a sudden jolt as my body smashed into the ocean floor. I realized I was closer to the beach.

"Stand up, stand up," a voice in my head commanded.

With the push of my foot, one after the other into the sand, my head broke through the surface. My legs were shaky. With a pronounced gasp, I pulled air deep into my lungs. My eyes were stinging when I tried to open them. I kept them tightly closed trying to rely on my other senses to guide me out. I felt the water level against my body drop as I got closer to shore. By the time I was completely out of the water, I was gasping for air.

Before proceeding up onto the beach, I wiped the water from my eyes. As my vision returned, I noticed my bikini top had twisted, exposing one full breast. I covered myself with my arms until I could fix the swimsuit.

Tom appeared, frantic and shaken. I was upset and couldn't speak. He guided me back to our spot and wrapped me in a towel. I was unnerved by the incident and insisted we move further back - away from the water.

A lifelong fear of the water had kept me away from it. My husband's love for the ocean continued to bring me back. Having faced one of my most paralyzing fears that day, I managed to mentally talk myself through a situation that could have ended tragically. The mind is a powerful thing. I couldn't explain it, but I felt lucky to be alive.

***

When our vacation ended, I began planning the next Child Abuse Prevention Month. Andy called to once again offer help. He had another idea; he suggested biking across the island of Newfoundland, as a fundraiser. He had done that already in British Columbia and raised money for charity. I wasn't sure he had thought the idea through. By vehicle, it took about nine hours to drive from one side of the island to the other and our terrain was anything but flat.

Andy said reassuringly, "I have thought it through. And, no, I'm not crazy."

It took several calls and in-depth conversations before the decision was cleared to proceed. Andy was prepared to pedal the full distance by bike and have me drive a pilot vehicle.

"That won't work, I will want to ride a bike as well," I told him.

We agreed to take turns and started preparing a schedule.

"The days will start early with one of us on the bike and the other driving just behind in a vehicle. We should finish before dusk, and every fourth day should be a rest day," Andy proposed.

With our unpredictable summer weather, we planned this for the height of summer and hoped for the best. Andy managed to secure hotels or B&B's for each night with many being offered to us for free in support of our effort. He also talked to the manager of Budget Rental Cars and we were given a white cube van to use as a pilot vehicle for the trip. While planning, I spoke with local organizations to acquire enough sponsors to cover our costs for the two-week trip. Tony, from The Print Shop, offered to print vehicle magnets of each sponsor's logo.

"Maybe I'm crazy," I mused, as I looked for a bike with Tom. "I did have a bike as a child, though I only rode it a few times. I have very little experience."

Tom tried to be supportive and suggested I start getting experience by riding his bike. It was a bike that he had acquired in a trade with his brother for golf clubs when they were younger. The bike was an older model. It was a custom Diamondback Topanga Mountain Bike. Ted was over six feet tall, and the bike had been custom-made for him. We agreed it might be a good bike to start with.

As Spring arrived and temperatures warmed, I began training on the bike by travelling to and from work every day. It didn't take long for me to get comfortable with it.

On Canada Day, just three weeks before we were due to leave, I spent the day in bed with a migraine. To make matters worse, the bike was stolen from our deck. I was devastated when I discovered it missing.

When a news story and social media campaign failed to bring the bike back, I was forced to look for another one. A couple of friends plus a Memorial University group offered to give me a bike. Another couple of people reached out through social media and offered to sell me their similar bikes. I was appreciative but declined the offers.

A man named Walter called and left several messages for me at work wherein he offered his bike. When I called him back, I learned the bike was brand new and due to a health issue, he could not use it. I was hesitant because he wanted to give me the bike. Walter suggested we come and look at it and if it was not perfect, I could leave it. We agreed to check it out.

Tom and Walter recognized each other from their younger years as soon as we arrived. While they chatted, I accepted Walter's invitation to take the bike for a spin. To my surprise and delight, the bike was a perfect fit in terms of height and comfort. When I refused to accept the bike as a gift, Walter suggested I borrow the bike for the trip and then return it. I was not interested in that idea either, I had one bike stolen and didn't want the responsibility of another one that was borrowed.

I agreed to take the bike but only if Walter would accept payment for it. He was resistant but I absolutely refused to take the bike without paying for it. In the end, he was pleased that I would use his bike for the tour. I was thankful to get a replacement bike and at a good price.

To get used to the new bike, Tom and I took bike rides in the evenings after work. With less than two weeks to go before the trip, my back suddenly flared up. I held off from telling Andy the news and reached out to my friend Clare for some emergency advice.

Clare and her sister, Estelle, co-owned a physiotherapy clinic in St. John's, where I had visited with previous back flare-ups. I had difficulty walking so Tom helped me into the clinic. In the waiting room, Estelle noticed my obvious discomfort and asked me to follow her inside. Estelle was an excellent physiotherapist.

She quickly and accurately assessed my back situation and prescribed ten days of treatment, including physio and laser therapy. As I checked out from the clinic, Clare told me they wanted to offer the treatment free of charge as a contribution to our cause. I was speechless and so appreciative of their kindness.

With each passing day and treatment, my back gradually healed. Over the phone, I explained the situation to Andy, though I confidently told him I would be in top shape for the bike ride.

When the departure day arrived, Tom helped Andy secure the overnight bags and bikes inside the van as I climbed into the passenger seat with refillable ice packs. At this point, I was still having pain and irritated by it.

I didn't want to let Andy down, nor did I want him to worry about it. When Andy and I began bickering over trip details, Tom advised us to be nice to each other. He also reminded Andy to stop regularly for ice pack refills.

It was a good day to start the 903-kilometre drive from St. John's to Port aux Basques. We stopped, usually at Tim Horton's, along the Trans-Canada Highway where I refilled my ice packs and Andy took time for a cigarette and a coffee refill. We talked about the steep hills, and I asked if he planned to get off the bike and walk them.

"No! I don't get off my bike," he replied.

We talked the entire length of the drive. I was interested in Andy's life and asked lots of questions about his past. Andy was open, honest, and forthcoming. His direct responses surprised me as I had asked about his childhood, the life of crime, living with drug addiction - nothing was off-limits. I listened and appreciated the brutal honesty. I felt sad for the low points in his life and proud of his accomplishments.

The drive across the province was long. We were exhausted when we finally arrived and checked into a hotel in Port aux Basques. The ice packs had done the trick, and thankfully, I arrived in top shape, ready for the big adventure.

I snapped photos of Andy as he officially started the early morning bike ride in Port aux Basques and posted them on social media. With flashing indicators and an emergency light attached to the top of the van, I slowly followed from behind. Andy paddled his bike for hours. I was excited when he finally pulled off to the side of the road and told me to take a turn.

Wow, what an incredibly amazing, exhilarating feeling.

After several hours, I noticed I wasn't tired; in fact, the opposite was true. I felt energized and was in no hurry to give up my bike time.

We drove for as long as we could to minimize stops. Depending on our overnight accommodations, we sometimes shared a room. Feeling almost like siblings, Andy gave me no reason to feel uncomfortable. As I suspected, he was a perfect gentleman.

As we passed through Green Bay, we spent the night at my father's house. The next day was a scheduled rest day. My cousin, Rocky, along with Brian (Helen's husband) took us out fishing in Brian's boat. I was thrilled when I caught my first fish. It was a fair size and Rocky helped me reel it in. Andy had no trouble catching a cod and told us he had plenty of experience fishing back home.

The bike ride between communities was the longest and we looked forward to provincial highway signs advertising the distance remaining to the next community. For most of the trip, we were lucky with good weather, however, as we approached Gander, we were greeted by dark rain clouds.

Andy took one for the team and offered to swap places just before the rain turned to a torrential downpour. The hotel was just a few kilometres away but by the time we arrived, Andy was drenched.

It was my turn on the bike as we approached one of the steepest hills on the island. I was feeling pessimistic when I remembered Andy's comment about not getting off the bike for the steep hills. So, I pushed myself through the mental and physical challenges. I lowered the gears on my bike and looked only in front of me. I persevered, keeping my eyes peeled to about ten feet in front of the bike, and didn't allow myself to look any further, especially not to the top of the hill.

Before long, my bike reached the apex – with me on it. I beamed with satisfaction knowing I had ridden the entire way up and conquered the hill. Andy, without knowing it, had motivated me to bike that hill. In doing so, he had also taught me a valuable life lesson about breaking major challenges down into smaller, more easily handled bite-size pieces.

I kept in contact with Tom, Jess, and Eddie throughout the entire trip. When we reached Goobies, approximately 162 kilometres from St John's, Eddie was there waiting to greet us. He brought fresh fruit and gluten-free treats. I had already lost a little weight on the trip and he joked that the baked treats would help me regain some of it. Andy and I were excited being so close to the capital city, and we stopped just long enough to fuel up with the food while visiting with Eddie.

The next stop was Whitbourne, approximately 90 kilometres from St John's. I was amazed and excited to see my friends Cathy and Terry waiting at the gas station. They too had brought a surprise: their bikes! They wanted to show support by riding with me for part of the journey. Andy agreed to drive the van and let me bike ride along with them.

Together, we travelled from Whitbourne to the Bay Roberts intersection, approximately 35 kilometres. I realized I had built up my endurance and speed, especially when Cathy commented how I kept pulling ahead of them. I was delighted to have them with me for some of the journey.

On the final day of our trek, a friend took over the pilot vehicle as Andy and I finished the last leg together on our bikes. At Frontline's Topsail Road location, we met an entourage of people waiting to ride with us. Rocky and his friend had travelled five hours on their motorcycles to accompany us for the ride, and Aunt Tuse, my friend Kerry Lynn, and Sara Tweed were all there waiting to travel with us on bicycles. Members of the RNC were also waiting and ready to lead us through Topsail Road, one of the city's busiest streets, to Bowring Park, our final destination. There was even a CBC journalist there travelling on roller blades.

At the main entrance to the park, there was a group of people waiting to congratulate and welcome us back. There were family members, friends, news reporters, federal and provincial elected officials, and Newfoundland-born actress Shannon Tweed Simmons, the wife of KISS musician, Gene Simmons.

Shannon's sister, Sara, had met us at Frontline and rode with us to the park. It was an incredible journey and now that we were back, we received a warm welcome. I was thrilled to have completed the journey and looked forward to going home and sleeping in my own bed.

Unwittingly, Mayor O'Keefe had started a thought process following his suggestion that the city could sign a proclamation for Child Abuse Prevention Month, if requested. With that successfully done, and in an attempt to increase support and awareness, I had also sent a letter to the Minister of Child, Youth and Family Services (CYFS) in 2014. I had requested they issue a similar proclamation at the provincial level, but I had not received a response.

In 2015, I sent a second letter to the Minister of CYFS with another proclamation request. At the same time, I reached out to all of the larger municipalities within Newfoundland and Labrador, as well as the capital cities of the other provinces in Canada.

I was pleased and impressed when proclamations were signed by many of them. They included the capital cities of British Columbia, Saskatchewan, New Brunswick, Nova Scotia, Northwest Territories and Nunavut.

I was disappointed when a response letter from the provincial Minister's office suggested we umbrella under February's Violence Prevention Month. I appreciated the response but was not interested in partnering with another mandate, organization, or charitable cause.

Child abuse is a global problem with alarming statistics and devastating consequences. It affects every family and community. In my opinion, it warranted its own stand-alone month.

For the third annual proclamation request to the provincial government, I enlisted the help of my friend Connie to research child abuse statistics. Connie was a retired member of the Royal Newfoundland Constabulary and the RCMP.

She had also worked extensively within the community, including a stint as the executive director for the Avalon East Violence Prevention Board, a role dedicated to preventing violence on the Avalon Peninsula in Newfoundland.

Connie was a guest speaker at the first Miles for Smiles walk and since then, a big supporter and volunteer to the Miles for Smiles Foundation. She also became a close friend.

I received correspondence from the Minister's office telling me the province normally recognized a day or week for such "causes," and they would be open to discussing a proclamation for those time frames.

This was good news - at least they were now open to the idea. I promptly requested a meeting with someone from the Minister's office to discuss the issue.

In a face-to-face meeting, I presented provincial statistics on the number of violent crimes that were reported involving children under the age of 18 in Newfoundland and Labrador over the past few years. To emphasize my point, the statistics were further broken down to reflect the number of reported incidents by month and by day.

"As disturbing as these numbers are, we need to remember over 90% of these crimes go unreported," I added.

Department staff listened attentively and waited until I finished to say that the department had reviewed the information and would sign a proclamation for April. I was ecstatic and could barely contain my excitement when I told Tom and Jess the news.

"April 2016 will be Child Abuse Prevention Month in Newfoundland and Labrador for the first time!"

There was a change in government after the November 2015 provincial election. The Progressive Conservative government was replaced by a Liberal majority. April was four months away when I reached out to the Minister of Children, Seniors and Social Development (CSSD), formerly known as Child Youth and Family Services.

I was told everything was still in place, and the proclamation would be signed. In early April, I emailed a follow-up letter and received a confirmation for the date for signing.

One week before the scheduled signing, I received a call from the Minister's office informing me that the Minister was unable to sign the proclamation. I was understandably upset when the Minister's assistant did not explain. I advised that I would contact other government officials, including relevant Ministers and Members of the House of Assembly (MHAs) for support.

Within minutes, I drafted and sent an email to three officials that I had met at Miles for Smiles events. The email included details of what had transpired and a request for assistance or advice. I knew they were all busy but was pleasantly surprised when all three responded.

Within the hour, I had also received two phone calls from different employees within the department of CSSD. Both employees offered to support us in other ways such as encouraging government officials to participate in the lineup of activities that were already organized by the foundation for April. I wanted nothing short of a signed proclamation and verbalized my position to both callers.

A few days later, MHA Paul Lane called to tell me he had spoken with someone from the CSSD Department. He was told that they had researched the Miles for Smiles Foundation and determined that our mandate did not align with theirs. More specifically, we advocated for prevention - and they did not. Paul was just as dumbfounded as I was.

By midafternoon, another email response came from Dale Kirby, the Minister of Education and Early Childhood Development. Minister Kirby offered to sign the proclamation along with his colleague, Andrew Parsons, the Minister of Justice.

I was thrilled that the proclamation goal had been achieved and made arrangements for it to be signed as soon as possible. Several Miles for Smiles volunteers accompanied me to Minister Kirby's office a few days later for the signing.

We were disappointed that CSSD, responsible for the welfare

of children, was strictly reactive. Welfare is literally defined as the health, happiness, and fortunes of a person, and the department responsible did not advocate for the prevention of child abuse.

I acknowledged that it would be a fight for another day. In the end, I was thankful that the proclamation was signed making Newfoundland and Labrador the first Canadian province to proclaim April as Child Abuse Prevention Month.

***

There was more good news and another reason to celebrate when Jess passed her National Council Licensure Examination (NCLEX) and received her designation as a Registered Nurse. Before her graduation, she had been offered a position with Eastern Health, and with her acceptance, she could now continue working in her chosen field. As a family, we were proud to have another nurse in our midst.

Jess had spent many hours with me at work. She regularly set up a study station at August & Lotta in a chair next to the large street-facing window. If we were busy in the boutique, she took to my office and closed the door. I was grateful for her presence and loved the company. When she needed a break from studying, we sat and talked, and these chats could go on for hours.

She was also my back-up staff. If I needed to run an errand or had an appointment and needed to come in late, Jess was my girl. Customers loved seeing and talking with her. Jess was personable and very approachable. When customers learned we were mother and daughter, many commented that we looked more like sisters. It was more of a compliment to me, but I think she liked hearing it too.

The nursing program had been challenging and Jess often teased that she would quit school and take over the boutique. In the back of my mind, I believed she might take it over someday, although I had always insisted that she finish her degree first.

After graduation, I expected to see less of Jess as she worked 12-hour shifts at the hospital. At the same time, I was also prepared to face difficult decisions related to the business. Tom and I had purchased August & Lotta five years ago. At that point, many of the regular customers expressed disappointment with the new location, and consequently, sales were down. We decided to look for another location back on the busy main stretch of Water Street.

On Water Street, we found the perfect spot and turned a previously operated jewelry store into a luxurious boutique. An exposed wall inside the location was from the original structure. It was a combination of red brick and rock. We completely removed everything else inside and designed the layout using that wall as a focal point.

The floors were dark hardwood, and an expansive white wooden desk was designed and constructed to sit in front of that striking brick wall. Directly behind the counter hung a large landscape mirror. Our contractor built three dressing rooms, a small storage room, an office, and a washroom.

I chose a black and white wallpaper with burgundy accent stools and curtains for each dressing room. An elegant chandelier also hung in each dressing room with another two over the front desk. Two elegant black and white chairs were placed in front of one of the windows, Jess's main study area.

Once it had been completed, the new location was absolutely stunning. Customers regularly complimented us on the elegant decor. To minimize operating costs, we installed mini-split heat pumps. These gave us a cost-efficient heat source during colder months and air conditioning during the summer. We were one of the few businesses on the street to offer air conditioning on hot summer days.

The renovations cost $60,000 and we worked out a deal with the landlord to offset costs by paying a reduced rent for the first three years. That was a big help, given that rent in the new location was significantly higher. I realized we were taking a chance with the rental cost increase but hoped sales at the new location would warrant the investment.

Online shopping had taken over and customers told us they could often find better prices online than in our store. That became even more apparent when a customer pointed to a French Connection dress in our store. She told me it was available directly on their website for $75. I checked our inventory and was surprised to see our cost on the dress was $79.

When I expressed frustration to the company representative, she told me there was nothing they could do as they reduced inventory at a specified time in their season. I immediately discontinued the line and grew increasingly frustrated when customers continued to tell me they shopped more online than in person. Jess and other staff told me they were hearing the same story from others.

Charitable work through the foundation was taking up more and more of my time and I struggled to stay on top of the boutique and trade show business. I also spent one day a week working at Frontline to reconcile sales, bank deposits, and to help with the accounting. As health challenges resurfaced, I experienced an overwhelming concern of becoming burnt out while usually working seven days a week.

Regular conversations with Jess brought home the realization that there were only so many hours in the day. My heart was with the charitable work, not the fashion boutique. As much as I loved the interactions with people at the store, I realized I had to choose.

Sandra and I shared the responsibility of the trade show business while Tom and I shared Frontline. As for the boutique, I was on my own. Letting go of the boutique seemed to be the obvious decision yet months passed, and I was unable to take the leap.

With five years in business, and only one year of actually taking a salary, the business continued to bleed as costs escalated and sales did not keep up. I had read that most businesses take five years to see a return on investment, but ironically, this timeline for us had become painful.

When I talked to the building owners, Mr. and Mrs. Dwyer, I was nervous because I was still under a lease agreement. They were sympathetic and open to the idea of breaking our lease agreement early.

I felt much better after talking to them and decided to call a real estate friend, Debbie, for advice. Together we talked about the business, reviewed numbers, and believed there was sales potential. A new owner, without the many distractions that I had, could immerse themselves into the business. With a renewed faith, we listed the business and in less than a month, Debbie had a buyer.

My accountant prepared financial reports and after two meetings with the potential buyer, I received an offer. The offer was reasonable, and I accepted it. Weeks turned into months, and when the potential buyer asked for more time - for the third time - I told Debbie to take the business off the market. I decided to close the shop.

It was September and I had already spent a considerable amount of money accepting fall orders based on the pending sale. Sadly, I now had a boutique full of new fashions and was forced to sell it below cost in order to close. I was devastated.

I mapped out a schedule of discounts, starting at 20% with increases bi-weekly. Della worked with me until the end of October. I think she was just as upset about the closure as I was. When the store was emptied, I felt a pang in my stomach as I handed my keys back to Mr. Dwyer.

The Dwyers were incredibly supportive, and they had even dropped in to check on me from time to time. They knew I struggled with the prospect of closing the business, and I valued their friendship.

There were mixed emotions when the store closed for the last time. I was relieved to bandage the financial bleed. In those challenging times, Tom and I had taken money from our savings to keep the business going longer than we should have. On the plus side, there was a certain redeeming satisfaction in closing the store. I knew this long overdue and much needed break would now allow me to focus on family and health. At the same time, I could try to recover from years of burning the candle at both ends.

April is proclaimed Child Abuse Prevention Month in Newfoundland and Labrador

Take It To The Grave

In April 2017, I received a call from Amy, the Communications Director with the Department of Justice and Public Safety. The Department was implementing a new program to help victims of sexual assault. We had met previously at other community events, as well, she had accompanied the Minister of Justice to our proclamation signings.

Amy asked for details about my personal childhood experiences. She then told me about a pilot project between the federal and provincial Departments of Justice, as well as Victim Services to support victims of sexual assault and help them on their healing journey. This was completely in line with what I wanted to do.

Amy then asked if I would consider being the spokesperson for victims. That was timely - after all, it was Child Abuse Prevention Month.

She elaborated, "You're a good speaker and you speak openly about your past sexual abuse. You represent positive outcomes for victims, and you demonstrate there is life after abuse."

She told me a little more about an upcoming presentation where I would be expected to speak. I was honoured and eagerly accepted the invitation for which I had two weeks to prepare.

Momentum was building with Miles for Smiles and I was encouraged by the government's commitment to change. That year our annual walk grew significantly, and it was now taking place in five locations throughout North America. I was thrilled with the growth and excited to continue to advocate for other victims.

It was a Tuesday morning when I met with government officials to launch the new program. On April 25 , I joined the Honourable Jody-Wilson Raybould, who was the Federal Justice Minister and Attorney General at the time, as well as the Honourable Andrew Parsons, Provincial Minister of Justice and Attorney General, as well as other elected officials and members of the community.

In the community room at Rocket Bakery on Water Street, the pilot project Amy had described was officially launched. Tom and I arrived early, which allowed time to relax and mentally prepare for the presentation. The large open room had rows of chairs set up facing a focal point; an open area flanked by the provincial and Canadian flags, plus a provincial banner. Journalists from every local radio and television station were in the room and were busy setting up equipment. As I scanned the room, I noticed there was no podium in the designated area. Immediately, I looked for Kelly, the bakery owner, and asked if she had one. "I am more comfortable behind a platform than free-standing," I told her.

Kelly left the room and returned with a stand. I noticed it was short in height, and before I had time to comment, one of her staff entered the room carrying a large wooden base. He placed it down in front of the flags and moved the podium on top of it.

"Perfect," I told Kelly and thanked her for going that extra mile. What may seem like a small detail to one can be a large concern for another. For me, it made all the difference.

Anita, a soft-spoken lady from Victim Services, introduced herself and told me she would be the emcee for the presentation. Seeing groups of politicians, government staff, and others entering the room added to my nervousness. Tom and I took seats behind Anita. A couple of minutes later, she was standing at the podium to welcome everyone. Then she introduced me.

I started by telling the group that I was born to a single mom in Central Newfoundland. "I like to believe she thought she was giving me a better life when she gave me up for adoption just weeks after my birth."

I knew my story, like many other suvivors' stories would be difficult for some to hear. However, I believe, if we want to make a difference, these stories *must* be told. Although nervous, I went on to describe my life, post-adoption, in Georgetown.

"I was treated differently and grew up in an environment that could only compare to a Hollywood horror film. While most children are raised in love and nurturing, I was raised in an atmosphere of hate, sexual exploitation, and violence."

The speech was from the heart and I ended by encouraging other survivors to avail themselves of the services being offered through the pilot program. "Sexual abuse and rape are monstrous crimes. Whether you are a child or an adult, and whether the abuser is a parent, relative, a partner, or a complete stranger, the violation seeps to your very core. Many victims withdraw and never recover. Proper programs and support systems, including legal counsel, help survivors move on and heal."

Before giving their own speeches, the Ministers of Justice, provincial and federal, both publicly thanked me for my bravery and for sharing my story.

The Ministers announced funding for a new program to help survivors of sexual assault. The Sexual Assault Response Pilot Program would provide free independent legal advice on criminal matters to help victims make informed decisions about the court process. This valuable initiative complemented existing support provided by the government's Victim Services Program.

When the announcement concluded, the federal Minister of Justice, Jody Wilson-Rayboult, walked directly to me and asked for a hug. She asked questions about my past and listened attentively to my responses. I was humbled by her obvious compassion. Members of the media snapped photos of our interactions as they waited to interview the Minister.

The provincial Minister of Justice and I had a similar conversation and he talked to me about his two small children and the importance of child protection.

Cathy Bennett, the provincial Minister of Finance, also waited patiently for the chance to speak with me; she then offered a supportive hug. We had met at other events and although we knew each other from our respective work, this was the first opportunity to actually have a conversation. She told me to reach out if there was anything she could do to help me with my work. I appreciated the offer.

All local radio and television stations reported this news and CBC's *Here and Now* aired a two-part segment that featured most of my speech. The speech was also shared on social media and I soon started receiving messages.

The messages were from friends, some of whom I hadn't spoken to since high school. There were also notes from strangers. All of these messages included kind and supportive words from people that had seen or read the news story.

"Your speech has impacted a lot of people," I was told in a surprise follow-up email from Anita, the emcee.

Anita told me she was deeply moved and would like permission to nominate me for an award; namely, the Justice Canada Excellence in Victim Services Award. It was the first year for the prestigious award and only one candidate would be nominated from each province or territory. I had been selected to represent Newfoundland and Labrador; however, without my permission, the nomination process could not proceed.

I was quite surprised and reread the email several times before calling Tom into my office. "Is this for real?" I asked as he leaned over my shoulder to read the screen.

"Looks real to me. Congratulations, babe, this is a big deal," he said.

As Anita and I exchanged emails, I learned more about the award. I needed letters of reference and the selected winner would be flown to Calgary to accept the award on May 29, 2017. It was an incredible honour and I couldn't believe I had been selected. On accepting the nomination, I reached out to suitable people who might be able to offer a reference and requested their help. It took a full week to collect reference letters and I helped Anita gather information about my life for the official nomination forms.

As the date approached, I received notice that I had not won the national award. It wasn't a surprise. There were survivors with similar stories all over the country and like me, many were using their experiences to help others. Obviously, I was somewhat disappointed, but not deeply. The nomination itself had been an unexpected surprise and an absolute honour.

A second surprise was delivered by mail in the form of a letter from the federal Minister of Justice who acknowledged and congratulated me on the nomination. The entire experience had been surreal.

July brought warmer temperatures and bright, sunny days. It also delivered four migraines in twelve days. When I admitted to feeling miserable, a discussion ensued and Tom implied that I hadn't been taking good care of myself - again. I admitted to working too much and maybe I wasn't getting enough sleep. However, in my defence, I reminded him that I ate super clean 90 per cent of the time.

Tom emphatically stated, "If I suffered as much as you did, I would be hypervigilant about everything. I would be eating dandelions three times a day and adding turmeric to all my food."

I dismissed the food criticisms, although I knew he was right about one thing. I needed to take my health more seriously. Back surgery at age 19 had altered my life with limitations and regular flare-ups. I had lived with it for over 20 years and for the most part, I pushed through the pain. Migraines started at age 23 and were triggered by bright lights, and especially the sun. Being overtired, or stressed made me even more susceptible, which meant I suffered more than my fair share of migraines.

My overall health continued to be monitored by an internist and although I tested positive for ANA (Antinuclear Antibodies – a marker for autoimmune conditions), she had been unable to positively identify the exact type. I continued to experience periods of extreme fatigue, inflamed joints, regular headaches, aches, and pains, and my body had produced several benign growths. The most recent was a 4.5 cm growth on my liver.

Tom's concern motivated me to investigate why I had been experiencing these health issues. I was reminded of articles that I had read about childhood trauma. According to research, suppressed childhood trauma was toxic to the body and could manifest as pain. In time, it could also turn to cancer and other life-threatening diseases.

I had been in therapy for a long time and that had helped considerably. However, even with years of therapy, I was still unable to talk about the sexual abuse. Maybe it was time to find a way to release the pressure and the heavy burden from my body. Maybe it was time to face my demons, I thought.

It had been two years since I visited Mother at the Carbonear Hospital. Back then, I thought I had been ready for the visit, but like a frightened child, I was unable to enter her room. Instead, I had remained in the hallway desperately trying to stay out of her field of vision. After all those years, I was *still* afraid of her.

She had been sick for several years, and I knew the window of opportunity to speak to her was closing. I realized I should try and see her, otherwise, I might spend the rest of my life regretting it.

I mentally prepared for a visit by continually reminded myself that I was now an adult and she couldn't hurt me.

Unlike Father, Mother was quick and unpredictable, she attacked without warning. I spent my entire childhood and adolescence walking on eggshells. As an adult, I was just as jumpy as when I was a child. If I walked into what I assumed would be an empty room, I'd be startled every time someone appeared. This reaction happened in public places as well as in my own house. Without totally understanding, Jacob was amused each time he quietly walked into a room and I screamed. I was embarrassed by my screams anytime they happened in front of anyone outside my family.

Weeks later, when April casually called to check-in, I asked for an update on Mother's health. She told me Mother was a patient at the Health Sciences Center and her health was deteriorating. I immediately called Tom. "I want to visit her at the hospital," I said, "and I want you to come with me."

Tom was surprised, but he agreed, and we planned an evening visit.

When we arrived at the hospital, I was visibly shaking and consciously attempted to calm myself with deep breaths before stepping into the elevator. Tom squeezed my hand, "Bev, she's on her deathbed, what's the worst she can do?"

From outside her room, Tom hugged me, "I'll be waiting just outside this door. Speak up if you need me to come in, I will hear you."

With another deep breath, I turned and slowly walked into the room. It was a private room with a single hospital bed and one chair. The curtains were wide open and the evening light illuminated the entire space. Mother was sleeping on her back with one hand across her stomach and the other resting up over her head. The top half of the bed was slightly raised, and she was covered with extra blankets.

Although sleeping, she was wearing a modern style pair of eyeglasses and her long gray hair was curled around her shoulders. As I moved closer, I was careful not to make a sound. I noticed her face was sunken and she had aged considerably since the last time I had been this close to her.

While standing away from the side of her bed, I spoke. "Hello!"

Her eyes flicked open and were instantly fixed on me. With a hoarse voice, she said, "My arm hurts."

"Are you okay? Are you having much pain?" I asked.

She responded, "Yes. If anyone wants to know about pain, I can tell them."

"Do you know who I am?"

"Yes. Beverly."

There it was, the sound of my name, as she pronounced all three syllables. I hadn't heard her voice for a long time, yet I instantly remembered why I so strongly disliked the sound of my name. I swallowed and cleared my throat before asking how long she had been in the hospital. Nervously, I forced conversation with small talk about the room's view and other unimportant topics.

Mother abruptly changed the subject.

"Did you know April and her man split up? Did you know this was coming? How much is she paying in rent?"

As much as Mother liked to gossip, I disliked it. I declined to provide information to any of her questions about April's personal life. I interrupted her train of thought by stating, "I have a question to ask."

Mother appeared ready as if she knew the day would come when this question would be posed.

My voice quivered.

"Did you know what Father was doing to me as a child?"

She was direct in her reply. "Explain."

"I can't verbalize it. It was bad... as a little girl - with me."

In a softer, more gentle tone, she encouraged me to share with her.

"You can tell me. You know you can tell me anything."

The tone was unfamiliar and not at all comforting.

"It was sexual. And, I have wondered if you knew it was

happening."

Mother's voice changed as she switched to defence mode. "No, I didn't know. I swear to God that I didn't know. How could that happen with so many people in the house?"

"It did happen, and I worried that it also happened to Katie," I replied.

"Well, It didn't happen to Katie and I know because Katie slept in the bed with us."

"If, while drinking, he managed to come out into my bedroom at night, I wouldn't be so sure." I paused and then continued, "Are you saying you don't believe me?"

"I am not saying I believe you, and I am not saying I don't."

In a stern voice, she asked, "how old were you?"

"My earliest memory of it was around age five."

Mother asked questions about an incident from my past. An older male from the community had made an advance towards me when I was in my early teens. When I confessed to not remembering *all* the details, she sarcastically remarked, "You can't remember all the details, yet you remember when you were five?"

With a coldness in her voice, she inquired, "Why was everyone drawn to you sexually?"

Hearing sarcasm in her voice, I refused to allow it to upset me. I explained that I had studied this particular topic in psychology. I told her pedophiles are very good at targeting victims. They prey on shy children who are withdrawn, and can be pressured into silence. Mother snorted a comment under her breath and I only heard the word, *studying*.

"How is it that no one else in the house knew about it?"

"Some did. One of the older kids witnessed an incident when he was exposing himself to Christine and me."

"Why was I not told by the others? Why did you not tell?"

"I can only speak for myself. I never felt as though I could. Remember, you hated me?"

"Where did that come from?"

With more confidence than before, I replied. "Remember you would tell Louise while talking on the telephone. You usually followed up with, 'Yes Louise, I *really* hates her.'"

"Why did you not bring this up when Louise was alive?"

"I didn't see the benefit."

"And, what's the benefit now?"

Intimidation seeped in. "When a little girl is hurt in that way... it violates on a deep level. It eats away at your soul. I wanted to know if you knew it was happening."

"Well, I didn't know and now it's in the past," she grunted.

226

I surprised her when I announced, "I went to see Father at the Waterford Hospital and I asked if he remembered. He did remember and admitted to doing it."

Mother became aggressive. "You had no business going there (to see him) and don't go back!"

"I have no desire to go back."

There was an awkward silence and I asked if she had seen Clarence or Leonard since they left many years prior. She bluntly said, "No, and I don't want to see them. I would like to know who was behind them being taken and costing me $43,000 in legal fees."

Another awkward silence and I saw Mother was irritated. I was too. I wouldn't dare mention the physical and mental abuse. There was no point. I knew she would deny it. I truly believe she knew I was being sexually abused by her husband. Why else would I be singled out and treated so differently from everyone else?

She was mean to the children in our care. Many were physically or emotionally abused, yet she didn't profess to *hating* any of them. Mother's contempt for me came from a different place as she tortured me on a deeper, much more sadistic level.

Why was I the only girl with my hair chopped short, dressed in unflattering clothes, and my every waking moment controlled like a prisoner?

Father was a long-term patient at the Waterford Hospital and Mother had been living with her boyfriend for approximately 20 years. She was on her deathbed and had nothing to lose. A part of me hoped she might confess to knowing about the sexual abuse and maybe confess to not knowing what to do about it. The sad reality was that I would have accepted that. I was looking for remorse, and the smallest shred of it would have been sufficient. In the end, there was no remorse. Mother hadn't changed.

"Are you in pain?" I asked.

"Yes."

"I will go ask the nurses if they can give you something for it."

Mother grunted again. Tom was sat on the other side of the door with an elderly lady in a wheelchair. They had a small table between them and were playing cards. Tom stood up when he saw me.

"Are you okay?"

I nodded my head, "Yeah, just give me a minute."

I walked to the nursing station to let them know Mother, calling her by name, was in pain and requesting medication. Upon my return, Mother complained that she waited until 10:30 pm last night for her medication.

"Visiting hours are almost over, I said, "I'll go back and see if they can come sooner."

I walked out of the room and as Tom stood to join me, we quietly walked away. Once we were outside the unit, Tom looked at me, "Babe, are you okay? You look like crap."

"That pretty much sums it up," I replied.

Not surprisingly, the visit with Mother triggered nightmares. I was bothered by her comments, though I realized I was mentally stronger and consciously blocked her negativity from penetrating my brain. In earlier years, those comments would have forced me back into a shell, leaving me to believe I was somehow responsible for the actions of the adults in my life. The visit was painfully stressful. I would not be returning.

***

Family life kept me grounded. We learned that Jess's boyfriend loved to cook exotic meals. When I saw him bringing a wooden block with his own sharp knives, to prepare food in my kitchen, I was embarrassed. My fear of sharp objects, especially knives, razors, and box cutters, had prevented me from bringing some of those objects into my home. That's not to say we didn't have knives; we did, just not overly sharp ones.

At some point, Jake (Jacob) noticed the lack of sharp knives in the house and questioned me on it. I explained my life-long fear as he tried to sway me with reason, "We can have sharp knives, Bev, you just have to be extra careful using them."

I realized that Jake was right... it was time for me to get over my fear. I made an honest effort which began with the purchase of two sharp knives. About a month later, I further challenged my fear by purchasing a mandoline - a razor-sharp kitchen utensil used for slicing fruits and vegetables. A video had been repeatedly playing in the kitchen gadget section of Bed, Bath and Beyond to demonstrate its efficiency, and I was sold on the concept of saving time with meal prep.

About two weeks later, as I rushed to prepare dinner before an appointment, I dragged out the mandoline to give it a try. Jake watched as I sliced the first few pieces of a large onion - without using the protective handle. When Jake challenged me on it, I explained the onion was round and I wanted to flatten one side before continuing with the hand protector. The onion was firm, and I was being careful; there was no need for concern, I told him.

The first batch of ingredients was added to the slow cooker and I moved on to slicing peppers. Once again, I continued to cut the first few slices from the rounded bottom without protection. It seemed that the peppers were not quite firm enough to be held securely in place by the holder. I continued slicing while being mindful of the blade as the pepper and my hand glided over the base.

Suddenly, I felt a foreign sensation in my thumb and I immediately knew I had been cut. Blood covered my thumb and I rushed to the kitchen sink to run cold water over it. As the water cleared the area, I noticed the entire side of my thumb had been sliced off and I was quickly losing blood. Realizing the severity of my wound and the fact that I am considered a bleeder, I began to worry.

I enveloped my thumb in a large bundle of paper towels and called out to Jake. He was in the basement playing video games and didn't hear me right away. I moved to the top of the stairs and screamed, "Jake, I'm in trouble! I need your help!"

Jake came running and immediately knew what had happened. The paper towel was drenched with blood and I directed him to the first aid kit. After removing the towels, we saw the blood was still gushing and I told Jake to call his dad. "He's in a meeting at work, but tell them it's an emergency."

Within minutes, Tom was at the house and in control. He instructed me to increase the direct pressure on the wound as he called the Emergency Health Line. As I cradled my wrapped hand into my chest, I began pacing and anxiously tried to clean up the accident site with my other hand.

Tom, clearly frustrated, told me to sit down and keep more pressure on my thumb. Unbeknownst to him, I was anxiously looking for distractions as images of my thumb being sliced by the blade continued to replay in my mind. At the same time, I felt immobilized with fear.

The health line nurse advised that we should immediately go to the Emergency Department. They may not be able to stitch it up, but the size of the gash causing such a loss of blood was a concern. Jake grabbed my car keys and offered to drive.

At the ER, a triage nurse inspected the wound and said, "You really did the job on yourself."

I held my bleeding hand over a large bucket, and she poured a full bottle of solution over my thumb to clot the bleeding. The nurse then bandaged my hand and sent me to the waiting room.

I patiently waited three hours to hear my name called. The attending doctor told me I had lost a lot of tissue and confirmed there was nothing they could do. The large open wound could not be sewn, and it would take a considerable amount of time to heal. As for the severe pain, she said it would have been no greater had I lost the entire thumb, a direct result of the severed tissue and nerves.

An ER nurse gently cleaned the injury as I squirmed in pain. She applied a brown gauze-like fabric to stop the bleeding. Next, my thumb was wrapped and a tight finger bandage, similar to a deflated balloon, was forced down over my thumb.

My thumb was no sooner wrapped when she noticed a piece of the gauze had twisted and blood was seeping through. The pain was excruciating. I stood up and insisted I remain standing as she restarted the process. Extra pieces of the blood-clotting agent were applied before new bandages. Forcing the balloon-like bandage down over my thumb for the second time was almost unbearable. Once finished, I was given pain medication and sent home.

The medication reduced the pain and initially helped me sleep. Hours later, I woke and had difficulty getting back to sleep. Once again, I was being tormented with graphic images and painful memories of my thumb being sliced as my body flinched with every visual.

As a teenager, I remembered Mother holding a sharp knife next to my throat or face as she threatened to, "Just get it over with." With time, I had developed coping mechanisms by stiffening my entire body and forcing myself to be stronger as I mentally challenged her to 'go for it.'

Maybe I realized it was only a threat and she would never follow through, or maybe I just wanted the misery to end. Either way, I was traumatized by the knife. I have lived a lifetime of coping with unwanted, disturbing visuals of knives and other sharp objects slicing through my skin.

I have spoken to countless people, including many government representatives, about child abuse prevention. Although they acknowledged the need and were sympathetic to the cause, there was no real drive to take action. In a subsequent conversation with an employee from the Department of Justice, I had become somewhat discouraged as I once again explained the situation and the need for action. "Maybe you should call Chief Boland," she suggested.

Joe Boland was the Royal Newfoundland Constabulary's (RNC) Chief of Police. I wanted to go ahead and make the call but the thought of disclosing to yet another professional man, and someone as powerful as the chief of police, was unsettling. So much, that it took me over three months to pick up the phone and actually call.

When I did, I spoke with the Chief's assistant and gave a brief summary of why I wanted to schedule a face-to-face meeting with him. To my surprise, it was not a difficult process and the appointment was scheduled before I even hung up the phone.

Upon my arrival at the scheduled time, there were three other members of the RNC - two female and one male - all wearing regular dress clothes and seated at a boardroom table with Chief Boland.

The Chief introduced himself before inviting the others to do the same.

He also requested they take a moment to explain their respective roles within the organization. All three worked in departments that oversaw crimes against children. I immediately felt the assurance that my request had been taken seriously.

When it was my turn to speak, I gave a brief version of my abusive childhood and talked about my primary reason for the meeting: to prevent other children from enduring similar abuse. I explained that I had visited a Child Advocacy Center in Arizona and had learned how we could develop such a Center for Newfoundland and Labrador. Since we did not already have one in the province, I thought that would be a great place to start.

When I had finished speaking, the male officer spoke in a calm, quiet voice while explaining that construction for an Advocacy Center for Newfoundland and Labrador had already begun. "The site is due to open in St. John's in 2021," he added.

Like me, I could see some of the others were surprised to hear about this federally-funded project. We knew nothing about the project's existence and here it was just two years away from opening.

Without commenting or expressing any form of emotion, I nonchalantly opened a file folder and slipped my notes inside before moving it to the bottom of a pile in front of me. With both hands resting on the stack of files, I turned my attention back to the head of the table.

"Chief Boland, there are other ways we can work together on child abuse prevention." I paused, shifted in my chair, and took a deep breath.

"As a child, I was sexually abused for over twelve years. I went through the entirety of my school years - Kindergarten to Grade Twelve - without confiding in one single person. There was nothing in my school curriculum educating me on sexual abuse. And how could I stop the abuse if I didn't know it was wrong?"

Without saying a word, Chief Boland simply nodded his head. I continued, "School was my safe haven. It was the only place I felt safe. And it was the only place where there would have been an opportunity for me to receive such information."

We scheduled a follow-up meeting and I left feeling more optimistic than I had in a long time. Over the next few months, we met regularly to strategize how best to achieve the goal of having some form of sexual abuse education introduced into the provincial school curriculum.

In a follow-up meeting, Chief Boland had invited two pediatricians to sit in on the conversation and offer feedback. These doctors were immediately drawn to the cause and, medically speaking, they were able to validate the critical need for such an education program.

Collectively, we developed a presentation designed for various groups and levels of government. It was not a lengthy process as everyone involved knew what needed to be said as well as the limited time to present this information. We fine-tuned a proposal that was compelling, informative, and could be delivered in as little as 40 minutes.

Chief Boland began the meetings with introductions and an explanation of our objective. I gave a brief description of my childhood and was followed up by the police officers as they described an educational program that they had personally researched.

It had been created by the Canadian Center for Child Protection and was currently being taught in schools worldwide, including New Brunswick, Nova Scotia, the Yukon, Ontario, and other provinces throughout the country. The program was affordable and offered training for teachers and support people.

Next, the doctors would educate the group on the phenomenon of Adverse Childhood Experiences (ACEs). ACEs are the negative, stressful and traumatizing events that occur before the age of 18 and the subsequent health risks across a victim's life span that are a direct result of this trauma. These risks include all types of abuse and neglect, as well as parental mental illness, substance use, divorce, incarceration, and domestic violence.

A landmark study in the 1990s found a significant relationship between the number of ACEs a person experiences and the possible outcomes in adulthood, including poor physical and mental health, substance abuse, and risky behaviour. The more ACEs experienced, the greater the risk for these outcomes.

This portion of our presentation had a high level of impact. The doctors were able to present real facts based on their personal experiences with children from this province. As well, they took time to elaborate on the financial burden of ACEs on society. The numbers are staggering.

In January 2020, we presented one last time to a group that included the Minister of Education, Brian Warr, and the CEO of the English School District (NLESD), Tony Stack. I was more nervous than usual while presenting to 13 people, most of whom were predominantly influential men. Having Chief Boland, the two additional police officers, and Tom with me did help considerably.

Minister Warr started the meeting by apologizing for my childhood suffering and saluted me for the courage to speak out.

Following the usual format of the presentation, Mr. Stack announced that the decision had been made to implement the recommended program into the Kindergarten to Grade Three curriculum, in all schools in Newfoundland and Labrador. He also noted that modifications would have to be made to the Grades four to nine program before they could be introduced into our schools.

The program would engage students with interactive activities. These would help build skills designed for increasing their personal safety and reducing the risk of victimization both online and offline. It was suggested that I could help introduce the program by speaking to school principals across the province. I was anxious to help in any way possible.

If ever there was a moment when I felt like I needed to pinch myself to confirm reality, this was one of them. As we left the Minister's boardroom, Chief Boland, the officers, along with Tom and I, all headed to the cafeteria to grab a coffee and deliberate. For this particular presentation, I had been more nervous than usual and was only now starting to unwind. As we talked about the magnitude of our accomplishment, I looked around the table and felt an incredible sense of pride. I could see that every person from our team was just as excited and gratified as I was.

This program would offer education - the first line of defence - in protecting children of Newfoundland and Labrador from child abuse. If a child is being abused and has been trained to know that it is wrong, they have an exponentially greater chance of stopping the abuse (by telling someone), or, preventing the abuse from happening in the first place.

It was a most satisfying feeling as we acknowledged that the proposed education program, the first of its kind for the province, would potentially protect children for generations to come.

***

Mother had been on her 'deathbed' for several years. She passed 13 months after my final visit. I was glad I had found the courage to visit her when I did. Although she never confessed to knowing about the sexual abuse, I believed she did know and had made a conscious decision to take that information with her to the grave.

The news of her death felt surreal, and I was left feeling empty. I couldn't feel sadness or mourn the loss of her as my mother. I never knew her as a mother. As a young child, I had often cried myself to sleep while praying for a rescue from her cruel behaviour... any rescue, even cancer. I didn't know what cancer was but knew it resulted in death and for me, a way out.

When Mother told me she hated me, I called it the *h-word* and refused to allow myself to feel or say that word about anyone, including her. Even after a lifetime of the most horrendous abuse, I never used that word about her or anyone else.

When I became a mother, I was dealt a whole new set of challenges. Raising a child without a proper role model was difficult and I often found myself in situations where I didn't know what to do. Fortunately, I always knew what *NOT* to do. That fact governed my parenting; and thankfully, I was nothing like the monsters who adopted me.

Despite the pain she caused, and the damage she inflicted, her death did not deliver any sense of pleasure. I thought if I allowed myself to feel any form of joy in her pain, I would be no better than her.

If any emotion did register, it was sympathy for her children - my siblings. No matter what the rest of the world thought about her passing, they had still lost their mother and I remained respectful.

With the news of her death, I chose to spend time alone and reflect upon my past.

I thought about the day I was brought to the Moore household as a foster child. It was on my first birthday and I was the first child they would foster. I couldn't help but wonder if social workers thought they had been giving me some kind of gift that day as I was placed in Mother's and Father's care!

Nothing could have been further from the truth!

Bev is the guest speaker for a Federally Funded Pilot Project for survivors of sexual abuse

Acknowledgments

I have many people to thank but couldn't possibly mention all of them here. Please don't take any omissions personally, I am incredibly grateful for each and every one of you and for the part that you have played in my journey.

To Geoff Meeker, thank you for helping me get the story out of my head and onto paper. It's been quite a process and I am thankful for your constant support and advice. Joshua Jamieson, thank you for the time and effort you put into the first round of edits on this book and for your patience during that time. Tony Burke, I am forever in your debt for believing in the Miles for Smiles Foundation and for helping us every step of the way. I told you we would make a difference. Do you believe me now?

For my beautiful friend, Linda Dunn, I am grateful. Thank you for accepting me - a shy, nervous, awkward girl with no experience in fashion or makeup - as a Classique Model. You helped build my confidence while teaching me to smile for a camera and walk on the runway. I don't think you knew at the time, but you quite literally changed my life.

Berdina, you are one of the most gentle and compassionate souls I have ever met. Thank you for loving me like a daughter, and Jess, a granddaughter.

To my friend, Doreen Samways, you were more than a manager or supervisor, you were a mentor. I had great respect for your work ethic and approach to everyday life. "Anything worth doing was worth doing 100%". You set the standards pretty high and while most were intimidated by you, I admired and adapted many of your habits - including your signature happy face. Decades later, I still include a hand-drawn happy face along with my signature on everything from greeting cards to staff pay-cheques.

As a frightened seventeen-year-old runaway, I had very few options. I am grateful to my aunt and uncle (names changed in the book) for inviting me to live with them and their family as I completed the remainder of my senior year of high school.

To Jessica's father (name changed), it has been a difficult road and although we did not always see eye to eye, you have saved my life more than once. When I was beaten to what felt like inches of my life, you not only encouraged me to run away but you were waiting on the other side when I finally escaped. With only four months of school remaining, you ensured I got a ride to and from school every day until I completed my last semester of high school. I moved back home with my parents four years later and once again found myself needing help to escape. When my mother threatened to keep Jessica if I left her house, it was you who came to my rescue. You physically held her back as she threatened to burn me with a boiling kettle of water as I fearfully ran out of the house with Jessica. I am incredibly thankful for all that you have done.

To my special friend, Connie Pike, where do I begin? We met at the first Miles for Smiles walk when you agreed to be a guest speaker. Little did I know that the guest speaker would become such a dear and trusted friend. Connie, I adore you. I admire your passion and determination to make a difference in all forms and levels of violence prevention. I wish we had met a couple of decades earlier. Thank you for being my friend and supporter throughout the years. And, for the months of editing that you put into helping me complete this book. Oh my gosh, I am sure you had no idea what you were getting yourself into, but I am grateful that you stuck around.

RNC Chief Joe Boland, Constable Lindsay Dillon, Sgt. Bill Rossiter, Malin Enstrom (RNC), Dr. Vicki Crosbie and Dr. Sandra Luscombe - it has been a pleasure working with you on the mission of delivering a child safety educational program to the province. Thank you for helping me recognize the importance of my voice, my story, and for believing in this project as much as I did.

As a child, I may have been unfortunate when it came to a loving family, however, as an adult, my luck has completely turned around. Thank you to my Colliers family - Rose, Bill, Cathy, Art, and the rest of the Mill Road crew. They say it takes a village to raise a child; Jess and I are incredibly grateful for our time in your village.

A heartfelt thank you to my biological father, Rex, and his family. I will be forever grateful for your complete acceptance of me. At 23 years of age, I was a stranger (and a surprise); yet you all welcomed me into your home and family as though you had known me forever. I wish every adoptee was greeted with as much love and support when meeting biological relatives for the first time.

To the Davis family, you have truly become my own. You are an intuitive bunch and it didn't take you long to figure me out. That's not a bad thing as you seem to know when I need comforting as well as when I need my space. Thank you for your unconditional love. I am proud to have found my place with the family.

For my stepchildren, Sarah and Jacob, I am thankful for you

both. Being a stepparent is not an easy job and it comes with no guarantees of a mutually respectful relationship. Thank you for accepting me as the 'other mom' and never using the: "You're not my mom," line on me. I feel blessed to have met you early in life and to share in the responsibility of raising you. I am especially proud of the productive young adults that you have both become. Where did those years go? I love you both.

To my siblings, including my adopted, foster and biological family members, I am extremely thankful for each and every one of you. For those that spent time in the same dysfunctional house as me, you too have a story within. In writing this book, I purposely choose to focus on telling my story and not to infringe too much on yours. To my older sister (name changed in the book), I will never forget your courage in acknowledging the abuse and agreeing to a police interview. I realize how difficult that was for you. I am grateful for you and love you.

Clarence, my little brother, I am so sorry for the pain you endured at the hands of our adopted/foster mother. My heart remembers your pain and I wish I could have made things different for you. Adam, I am eternally thankful you took the time to find me and agree to a coffee date while hoping to catch up all those years later. It was while listening to you talk about how the abuse had affected you in childhood that I realized what it was doing to you as an adult - and to all of us. I had an epiphany that day! We, as survivors, were silently protecting our abusers while dealing with the unpleasant consequences of childhood abuse. It was this very conversation that influenced me to speak up and not just for me but for all of us that had been abused as children. Thank you, Adam, you gave me the motivation I needed to speak out. Leonard, Christine, Guyliane, Lorraine, you all hold a special place in my heart.

For my quick-witted, MacGyver-type friend, Eddie Pardy, I don't think I can ever repay you for the love and generosity you and your family have given us over the years. You are not only an incredible friend, but you have also been like a brother to me, and your parents have been incredible grandparents to Jess. We have all heard the expression, "Salt of the Earth" when referring to good people, this perfectly describes your family. Eddie, you are one of the most reliable, supportive and selfless people I know, and I am beyond thankful for your friendship.

Tracey Moore Gurney, you are a pillar of strength, and so much more. I am grateful for you as my sister, friend, and confidante. As a child, I adored you and took great pleasure in helping my little sister. As adults, we have shared in the good times and the bad, while helping raise each other's children. I have enjoyed my annual trips to Maine and especially the get-togethers that would evoke laughter lasting until my belly hurt. Poor Jess was so embarrassed when the laughter happened in public places. Thank you for being my friend and a constant source of encouragement.

To Jessica, my beautiful daughter, you came early in my life, at a time when I needed you the most. At 17 years of age, I was ill-equipped to know what to do with a child; however, my determination to be a good mom kept me on a good path and forced me to make good choices. You immediately became my reason for everything. I was a mom first, and proud of it. We have been through a lot together and I am proud of you and your strength in overcoming adversities. My heart is incredibly full with love and pride for you and the beautiful person you are. Watching you become a Registered Nurse has been a bonus. Thank you for your unconditional love and support. I love you with all my heart and cannot imagine this journey without you.

For my husband, friend, travel companion and business partner, Tom Davis, you can argue with me until the cows come home but I still believe I am the 'luckier' one in this relationship. In almost twenty years together you have taught me so much about life, the world, and myself. You've not only supported but encouraged me to step out of my comfort zone. You have allowed me to let my shield down and truly be myself, and in doing so become more accepting of myself. Tom, you believed in me when I didn't. You are by far one of the most patient people that I have ever met, and I am thankful that I get to wake up and go to sleep next to you every day. I love you babe!

The Last Word

I am a private-person, quite content to live my life away from the spotlight. I became accustomed to public speaking not for personal publicity, but to push for greater awareness and prevention of child abuse. It has taken an enormous amount of strength to release such intimate details of my life as evident by the number of years it has taken for me to write and release this dang thing!

In this book, I have spoken about the need for caregivers to speak up when they suspect something is not quite right. I cannot over emphasize the importance of this. Please don't ever turn a blind eye on a child - you may be the only chance they have.

To the victims of abuse, if you have not already done so, please tell someone. If that person doesn't believe you or offers no support, tell someone else. Keep talking until you find someone who is willing to help you. This is not your fault, and you have nothing to be ashamed of. A child can never take the responsibility for the actions of an adult. Never! If that abuser is still active, it may save another child from being abused right now or prevent it in the future. Next, you need to deal with your trauma. Please get help. Take care of yourself and nurture the child within. If you are not quite ready to talk about it, try capturing your experiences in a journal. For survivors that have not yet disclosed, I want you to know that having just one supportive person in your life will make an incredible difference. Please find that person.

To abusers, bear in mind that we, your victims, are younger than you, sometimes by decades. We may be innocent children when you abuse us, but we will grow up. We will never forget. We will outlive you most of the time.

We will find our voices.
We will tell our stories.
And in the end, we will have the last word.

Bev at age 8

Made in the USA
Monee, IL
19 May 2021

69042598R00146